Sir Thomas Browne

A Biographical and Critical Study

Sir Thomas Browne

A Biographical and Critical Study

BY FRANK LIVINGSTONE HUNTLEY 1902-

Ann Arbor Paperbacks

The University of Michigan Press

In loving memory of my father,
GEORGE ARTHUR HUNTLEY, M.D.,
physician, scholar, and man of God

PREFACE

In Sir Thomas Browne one finds three great nourishers of the mind and heart of man: religion, poetry, and science. They met in the seventeenth century and may be coming together again in this mid-term of the twentieth. Hence my book is addressed to the general audience as well as to students and scholars in literature.

The biographical parts emphasize Browne's earlier life. For an understanding of his achievement, the crowning years of his fame are less important than the education that prepared him to be what he was. As part of his biography in a generally chronological pattern, certain chapters serve to place him in the seventeenth century.

The final chapters are devoted to the occasions and characters of Browne's five main works. Given the historical and biographical facts and the texts of particular works which all can read, criticism is or hopes to be a kind of intellectual and emotional reassessment of the meaning that Sir Thomas Browne may still have three hundred years after he lived and wrote. There is no chapter entitled "Browne's Style." Rather, his words have been examined as they convey his meaning within the structure of separate works.

The text I have used throughout is the six-volume

edition of Browne's works edited by Sir Geoffrey Keynes (London: Faber and Faber, 1928-31), with one exception: for *Religio Medici*, the text by Jean-Jacques Denonain (Cambridge University Press, 1953).

I could not have written this book if The University of Michigan had not granted me leaves of absence from teaching and generous support from its Rackham Research Fund. The staffs of the libraries of Michigan, Harvard, Yale, Huntington, the Bodleian, Cambridge University, and the British Museum have gone out of their ways to help me. And thanks to a Fulbright lectureship in Japan, for a whole year I wrote in a dreamy house overlooking the Imperial Gardens of Kyoto, one of the ancient and beautiful cities of the world.

I have benefited by the universal freemasonry of scholarship in the form of articles and books and of encouraging and blasting correspondence. More particularly, for expert advice I am grateful to Sir Geoffrey Keynes of England and to my colleagues at home, Austin Warren and Clifford Stewart. Douglas Bush read the book in one of its embryological stages with his usual brilliance, patience, and generosity; my debt to him is large.

Funds for publication were provided by the Horace H. Rackham School of Graduate Studies, The University of Michigan.

Frank L. Huntley

Ann Arbor, Michigan

CONTENTS

Chapter I

BROWNE'S BOYHOOD
AND
EARLY SCHOOLING

Sir Thomas Browne, famed physician and scholar of Norwich, was born on October 19, 1605, the son of Thomas Browne, mercer, in Cheapside, London. He was probably baptized in the family parish church of St. Michael le Querne by Paul's Gate, in the heart of the mercers' guild. From Blackfriars (an old history tells us) one turned through Ave Maria Lane and Paternoster Row ". . . to the church of Saint Michael ad Bladum, or at the corne (corruptly at the Querne) so called, because in place thereof, was some time a corne market stretching up west to the Shambles."[1] This church, one of nine in Faringdon Ward in addition to the pre-Wren St. Paul's Cathedral, was destroyed with all its records in the Great Fire, and today the Peel monument stands near its site.

The Browne home was surely one of Christian harmony. There is a family legend that the father, a pious and prosperous cloth merchant who had three daughters and only one son, would sometimes kiss the sleeping infant on the breast and pray that the Holy Ghost might inhabit there[2]—a story also told of Origen's father. Basking all his life in "the mercifull disposition, and humane inclination I borrowed from my Parents. . . ,"[3] Thomas Browne the son was grateful for an "inbred loyalty unto vertue."[4]

For a man of science Sir Thomas Browne was surprisingly inaccurate in the details of his family history. In 1664 he confused his great-grandfather Richard with his grandfather Thomas; he placed his younger son Thomas before his older son Edward, in whose age he was off by a year; and he omitted the married name (Cottrell) of his eldest daughter. He also forgot to mention the seat of his mother's father in Sussex.[5] Only from a letter to Edward do we know that his maternal grandfather Paul Garroway of Acton, Middlesex, had a house in Lewes, Sussex: "I remember," he wrote, "when I was very yong & I thinck butt in coates, my mother carryed mee to my Grandfather Garrawayes howse in Lewys. I retaine only in my mind the idea of some roomes of the howse and of the church."[6]

His genealogy has since, however, been accurately compiled. Begun by Bysshe in 1664, added to by Le Neve in 1708 and by Blomefield in 1745, it was first put into full order by Wilkin in 1836.[7] Even Wilkin made errors, and these were corrected in 1899 by a Cheshire antiquary named William Irvine.[8] The final pedigree was made by Charles Williams of Norwich in 1902[9] and has been adequately commented upon by Miss Tildesley.[10]

Browne seemed far less certain of his earthly descent than he was of his heavenly one. Throughout his entire life he was concerned, more or less seriously, with the stars that presided over his birth. Of the twelve signs of the Zodiac, Scorpio, the eighth, was rising over the eastern horizon when he was born in the month of October. Each zodiacal house, before it is modified by conjunction within that house of a planet, has its particular associations: Capricornus implies health; Taurus, riches; Virgo, honor. Scorpio, signed by the scythe, 3, means malignancy, horror, and death.

As Scorpio was his month, so Saturn was his "planetary hour." Browne confessed to being "saturnine"—of a morose and melancholy humor. Because of its rings Saturn was known as the "circle planet" and very early became the god of the wheel,[11] sometimes depicted as a serpent biting its own tail. This emblem of Saturn was used to symbolize time, the year, the universe, and the completion of the alchemical process.[12] It was the farthest reaching of all the planets. There was perhaps some comfort, too, in the "attendants of Saturn" which showed up in Galileo's telescope in 1610; Browne would feel that the satellites had been placed around his planet by God and kept there as two attendant angels. Nevertheless, "At my Nativity," he tells us in *Religio Medici*, "my ascendant was the watery signe of *Scorpius*; I was borne in the Planetary hour of *Saturne*, and I think I have a peece of that Leaden Planet in me."[13] Saturn's minerals were lead and loadstone; its color was black; its plants, anodynes and all poisons. Browne affirmed that if astrology has any truth it is not contrary to religion: ". . . if to be born under *Mercury* disposeth us to be witty, under *Jupiter* to be wealthy, I doe not owe a knee unto these, but unto that mercifull hand that hath disposed and ordered my indifferent and uncertaine nativity unto such benevolous aspects."[14] But the conjunction of Scorpio and Saturn was hardly a happy one. Born with so unlucky a horoscope, Browne looked upon each day of his life as a special gift of Providence that stayed his natural destiny.

The Reverend John Whitefoot, Browne's earliest biographer, speaks of his stochastic talent, that is, his ability to foretell events.[15] His was the type of mind that could be impressed by the death on April 10, 1630, of his college's benefactor at Oxford, the Earl of Pembroke, according to the calculations of the Earl's horoscope made several years before by Thomas Allen of

Gloucester Hall.[16] The "humor" Browne was born with led him into one of his early heresies, Origen's—that God's mercy would call a halt to His vengeance—because he found in it ". . . a ready weight to sway me from that other extream of despaire, whereunto melancholy and contemplative natures are too easily disposed."[17] And no one who has ever read Browne can forget his premonitory wonder about people who die on their birthdays: ". . . that the first day should make the last, that the Tail of the Snake should return into its Mouth precisely at that time, and they should wind up upon the day of their Nativity. . . ."[18] Browne died on his own birthday, October 19, 1682.

The good mercer of Cheapside died when his son was eight years old and left ample means for young Thomas' education. Though he did have one of the best educations available in his day, however, there is no indication that he was ever wealthy. "I was not borne unto riches, nor is it, I thinke, my Starre to be wealthy. . . ," Dr. Browne wrote.[19] His later letters to his sons repeatedly stress the need to economize. The amount of money left by his father in 1613 is not mentioned in the will, but only the disposal of it, as the law demanded, into thirds: one-third for taxes, legacies, debts; one-third "I give and bequeathe unto Anne my loving wife"; and one-third "unto Thomas Browne, Anne Browne, Jane Browne, and Mary Browne, the children of me the said Thomas Browne and Anne Browne my wife, and unto such child or children as Anne my now wife is great withal, equally amongst them to be divided."[20] Ellen, a fourth sister to young Thomas, was born after their father died.

Mrs. Browne married, within a year of her husband's death, Sir Thomas Dutton, a man who was not very careful about the money set aside for his five stepchildren. In those days the children of a deceased father, despite the mother's survival, were declared "orphans."[21] A document dated July 5, 1614, in the Orphans' Court Records describes the appointment of three men to examine the estate of Thomas Browne, mercer, deceased, ". . . and shall conferre and deale with Sir Thomas Dutton knight who hath lately married the late wief and executrix of the said Thomas Browne. . . ."[22] More significantly, the appointment refers to the possible "loss" of the estate to the five orphans, as though (which is very probable) Sir Thomas Dutton had already begun to squander it. The orphans' third of the estate was computed at about £3222, and Browne's mother and stepfather were bound over by the Court to give security for that amount. Young Thomas' share, then, should have been one-fifth of this or over £600, an amount which probably supported his long and expensive training at home and abroad. These figures square with the report of Mrs. Elizabeth Lyttleton, Browne's daughter, to Bishop Kennett, that the ". . . mother took her thirds, which was three thousand pounds. . . ."

Whitefoot mentions neither the money nor the death of the father. The anonymous biographer of the 1712 *Posthumous Works*, published thirty years after Sir Thomas Browne's death, states:

Browne's father, dying when he was very young, left him a plentiful fortune, his mother took her third, which was three thousand pounds, and some time after married Sir Thomas Dutton, a worthy person, who held several considerable places in the kingdom of Ireland, by which means he was left to the care of his guardians, who sent him to be educated in grammar learning to Wykeham's School, near Winchester.[23]

Had the author consulted Mrs. Lyttleton? The letter supposed to have been written by her to Bishop Kennett uses strikingly parallel phraseology, but whether the anonymous biographer got the information from her or she (or the Bishop) was using the anonymous life is impossible to determine. In the 1730 *Biographia Britannica*, Andrew Kippis wrote: "His father left him a considerable fortune, of which he was not a little injured by one of his guardians."[24] The story received some embellishment in the 1736 short "Life" prefixed to J. Torbuck's edition of *Religio Medici*: young Thomas ". . . was entirely left to the care of his guardians, one of whom had the villainy to defraud him of a great part of his fortune."[25]

By 1756 Dr. Samuel Johnson magnified the malignity of the stepfather by multiplying the amount of young Browne's lawful inheritance by ten:

. . . his mother having taken three thousand pounds as the third part of her husband's property, left her son by consequence six thousand. . . . But it happened to him, as to many others, to be made poorer by opulence, for his mother soon married Sir Thomas Dutton, probably by the inducements of her fortune, and he was left to the rapacity of his guardians, deprived now of both parents, and therefore helpless and unprotected.[26]

Mr. Endicott's researches in the records of the Orphans' Court show that there was indeed a basis for the suspicion,[27] but Johnson's sympathy for the poor boy is surely exaggerated.

At the age of ten, two years after his father's death, Thomas Browne was enrolled at Winchester College, founded in 1387 by William of Wykeham; the entry in the register there reads: "Thomas Browne de parochia Sancti Michaelis praeteritum admissus—20 Augusti 1616."[28] Why, in view of his stepfather's rapacity, young Thomas was not sent to St. Paul's is a question. It was next door, free to all members of the mercers' guild and famous for its curriculum under the eight-year-old headship of Alexander Gill. Milton became a student there. Perhaps the answer is political. Gill was educated at Puritan-minded Cambridge; he was anti-Laudian and anti-Royalist. Among Browne's scant references to his school in later years is a rather shocked memory of the Puritan son of Dr. Love, warden of Winchester, fighting against his king.[29]

Winchester, like Eton, was Anglican and Royalist. William Waynflete, Eton's first provost, was a "Wyke-hamist," as later Arnold of Rugby was. Winchester's supremacy has been due to its intellectual leadership in the fields of religion, education, and scholarship. Izaac Walton wrote of Sir Henry Wotton's being ". . . sent to *Winchester School*: a place of strict Discipline and Order: that so, he might in his youth be moulded into a Method of living by Rule. . . ."[30] Winchester has not produced (until quite recently) the prime ministers and cabinet members that Eton has. In the words of John Rodgers, ". . . to be a Wykehamist, success is a sign of failure, since success would seem to demand qualities which are contrary to Winchester tradition."[31]

To be admitted to Winchester, Browne probably construed some Latin before examiners on a Monday early in August 1616.[32] Beginning in the Michaelmas term in late September, then, he attended every year until he was eighteen, four terms a year of approximately nine weeks each, with the customary vacations at Easter, Whitsuntide, summer, and Christmas. In Browne's day there were seventy students, of whom eighteen were senior prefects. Their slang had already had a long history: "Jubilee" was merely a pleasant time, as in "What a jubilee we'll have next Wednesday" (echoed perhaps in Browne's "great Jubilee"[33]); "pitch-up" referred to one's parents; the boys' top hats were "cathedrals"; to go to the "continent" was to be sent to the school infirmary; and a holiday was invariably a "thoke."[34]

The boys slept eleven or twelve to a room, with three prefects to keep order. At five each morning they were awakened by a bell and the prefects' cries of "Surgite!" They sang a Latin Psalm while dressing and cleaning their room. A second bell at 5:30 called them to chapel. Hugh Robinson, the headmaster, had included an English "morning prayer for a Child" in his *Preces*:

O most gracious and merciful Father, which hast ordained that the mouthes of children should praise thee, heare my prayer, my Lord and Saviour, Iesus Christ. Almighty God and heavenly Father, which hast given unto mee my soule, my body and breath, and blessed me from infancie untill this time, sanctifie my childhood, I humbly beseech thee, through my Lord and Saviour Iesus Christ. Pardon, O Lord, the infirmities of my youth, and beget my soule anew by thy holy Spirit: that as a new born babe I may desire the milke of thy word, and grow to be a perfect man in thy truth. Teach me, O Lord, the Scriptures of thy Childe; enlighten my understanding that I may readily conceive; confirme my memory, that I may faithfully retaine the knowledge and learning wherein I shall be instructed; that as young *Samuel*, I may profit both in virtue, and stature and favour, both with thee and Man. Give me grace to imitate the sacred childhood of my Saviour; and that I may avoid the riotous company of youth, that I may grow up in vertue and knowledge, to my parents joy and thy glory. And whenas thou hast refreshed my body with sweete sleepe, so I most humbly ask thee to keepe my soule from sinne this day, defend my bodie from all dangers that may befall mee, and guide me with thy Holy Spirit in all my waies, through Iesus Christ our Lord and Saviour. Amen.[35]

Though school was mostly prayers and Latin and Greek exercises, a master could dismiss the boys any time with the cry of "Remedies!" and off they would walk two by two to the hills outside Winchester town, there to disport themselves in running and wrestling, or on rainy days to enjoy a "jubilee" before the fireplace in the great hall.

The fact that Browne went through all six forms in the eight years of his attendance at Winchester calls for an appraisal of the books he probably studied.[36] Religion, arithmetic, drawing, and penmanship were practically diversions from the rigorous construing of texts. Rhetoric did not rest even on Sunday: "In the highest forms, cause them to set down the Sermons. As text, division, exposition, or meaning; doctrines, and how the several doctrines were gathered, all the proofs, reasons, uses, applications."[37] Brinsley, whose advice to schoolmasters this is, adds: "You may (if you think good) cause them the next morning to translate it into a good Latin style, instead of their exercise." For numbers, the boys probably studied Robert Recorde's text, which, first published in 1540, held its own for over a hundred years. Browne owned a copy.[38] Drawing as a school subject had been urged by Sir Thomas Elyot, Richard Mulcaster, and Henry Peacham. The last named was so enthusiastic about it that when he was master of the Free School at Wymondham, Norfolk, he published in 1605 *The Art of Drawing* and *Pen and Limning in Water Colours,* reissued in 1612 in one volume entitled *Graphice.* As Milton took most naturally to the exercises in verse, so it is likely that young Browne excelled in sketching, an exercise which aided him later in anatomy and microscopy. Penmanship was often taught by a master penman, and popular texts were Peter Bales's *The Writing Schoolmaster* (1590) and Martin Billingsley's *The Pen's Excellency or the Secretary's Delight* (1618).

It was Lily for Latin grammar, Camden for Greek, and in the higher forms Buxtorf for beginning Hebrew, though there is no evidence for Hebrew at Winchester.[39] Each day from Monday to Thursday in the first form the boys took a lesson in Lily's accidence, translated it, and copied the exercises into their notebooks after they had been corrected by the usher. They added four words a day from a book like Stanbridge's *Vocabula*, the whole week's work reviewed each Friday. Before breakfast on Fridays they had to memorize four verses from Cato's distichs. In spite of Ascham's advice not to teach Latin conversation until Ciceronian purity had been achieved, boys everywhere were encouraged to converse in Latin.[40] The second form was similar to this, with Aesop's *Fables* for variety. In third form they advanced to Lily's *Brevissima Institutio* in four divisions: *orthographia, etymologia, syntaxis,* and *prosodia*. Here the rules were committed to mnemonic rhymes; thus the section on nouns begins "Propia quae maribus tribuuntur, mascula dicas," which Browne refers to in "How many Synods have been assembled and angerly broke up again about a line in *Propria quae Maribus*."[41] On Saturday mornings the boys in third form wrote Latin themes, sometimes based on Erasmus' *Colloquia*.

The fourth form introduced them to poetry with Ovid's *Metamorphoses* and to Greek in the New Testament. The main Latin fare was Terence, which appealed to the boys' dramatic sense as they often acted out scenes. This taught them an easy colloquial style, and their exercises often called for epistles in familiar rhetoric, for example: "Write a Latin letter to your father (uncle, friend) exhorting (chiding, begging) him to refrain from war (hunting, gambling, seeing plays)." During the first half of each week the fourth form boys were taught four lines from Ovid by the fifth form boys, so that during the course of this year they memorized about four hundred lines from "Shakespeare's poet."[42]

In the upper two forms a thorough reading in most of the Latin and Greek classics furnished a content in ancient history, biography, and morality, as well as *exempla* in different styles. In Latin the most popular authors were Cicero, in his *Tusculanae Disputationes*; Lactantius ("the Christian Cicero"), especially Book ii of his *Institutes, De Origine Erroris,* which gave Browne the end quotation for his *Vulgar Errors*; Prudentius ("the Christian Pindar"), for his *Psychomachia,* which describes the battle of the soul between virtues and vices—Browne owned a Basle 1562 octavo copy;[43] and Lucan—Browne knew this poet well and recommended him to his younger sailor son.[44] And there was always Vergil, "the Prince and preest of all Latin poets," in Hoole's phrase. Hoole recommended for the fifth form boys on Monday and Tuesday afternoons ten or twelve verses in the *Eclogues* to be memorized, construed, parsed, scanned, the tropes identified, "the phrases and epithets and other elegancies noted out," and the proper names furnished with their histories.[45] In Greek the boys concentrated on Isocrates, the New Testament, and Homer.[46]

Throughout the years at Winchester the single most important training for Browne's future was that in rhetoric. T. W. Baldwin has shown that Shakespeare's school was in the Erasmian tradition; Clark, that Milton's rhetoric under Alexander Gill was Ramist. Browne under Hugh Robinson at Winchester was raised in a non-Ramist modified Erasmian rhetoric peculiar to Winchester because of Robinson's own school texts. This headmaster strove to bring rhetoric away from Ramist principles back to the classical tradition.[47] Ramus (1515-72) had split *elocutio* off from *inventio* and *dispositio,* and thus had unintentionally taught "stylish" writing. The classical Erasmian rhetoric, on the other hand, had insisted upon *elocutio's* growing out of the two preceding divisions of rhetoric on the principle that the style must seem an echo of the sense.

So Hugh Robinson justified *amplificatio,* for example, only if the subject matter warranted it.[48] He emphasized Ciceronian "aptness" of words to the subject matter, a lesson Dryden was to learn well. Robinson himself furnished the whole matter for rhetoric at Winchester, with his *Rhetorica Brevis* (1616) for method, his *Phrases* (1658) for vocabulary and illustration, and his *Antiquae historia synopsis* for content: in history, geography, and astronomy.

Thus what Browne finally learned from his eight years at Winchester, then, was rhetoric for persuasion and wisdom for piety. In Erasmus' words: "For this are learned the disciplines, for this philosophy, for this eloquence: that we understand Christ, that we celebrate the glory of Christ. Of all erudition and eloquence this is the goal."[49] Many of Browne's quotations, examples, emblems, and very phrases were the result.

Such an education left little room for natural science. Browne remembered seeing an ostrich at Greenwich when he was a boy[50] and in a letter to Evelyn in 1663 about large trees he said: "You may please to take notice of the very great yewe tree in Sutton church yard by Winchester."[51] It was probably during his long and frequent vacations spent with his mother and sisters that the boy learned how to "simple" for herbs in the market.[52] When he was thirteen years old he carefully traced the path of a comet: "That wch I sawe [in] 1618 began in Libra & moved northward, ending about the tayle of ursa major. It was farre brighter than this & the tayle extended 40 degrees, lasted little above a moneth."[53]

Browne matured slowly and entered Oxford at eighteen, older than was customary in the seventeenth century. He had to wait until he got to Oxford to continue his interest in natural science, as he had to postpone his real study of medicine until he arrived at Padua.

Chapter II

THE
RELIGIOUS
MILIEU

The boy who left Winchester School faced an adult world in which religion seemed to dominate every part of life—personal safety, economic security, science, politics, peace, and even war. To make this clear will require a few basic distinctions, for Browne starts out by being a Christian in the seventeenth century, when the various kinds of Christians held little charity for one another.

If the central problem in theology is the relationship between God and man, then the major differences in the Christian solution of this problem can be shown, at least for our purposes, quite simply. Christianity holds that the law of God of the Old Testament is fulfilled by the love of Christ in the New; that God and man became one in the Incarnation. This means that it is not the ethics of Jesus that distinguish Christianity from Judaism. In fact, St. Paul hardly mentions the sayings of Christ. Rather, it is the belief that the Word became flesh. In Jesus' view this was a process of God's getting inside man instead of remaining above or outside of man; Jesus psychologized the Jewish religion of his time. A fair example of this would be the story of the woman taken in adultery. The law said that such a woman should be stoned, and the people were ready to carry out this command. But when Jesus calmly said that he who is without sin may cast the first stone, the "law" was changed from an outer one to an inner one.

The split in western Christianity between the Roman Catholic and the Protestant churches arose over the guardianship of that "inner light" which God through "His Son" placed in man. The Roman Catholics believe the Church to be the institution commissioned by God as the main mediation between man and God. Its history is the history of the Church's canonizing the Bible, formulating the creeds, and prescribing the forms of worship. That the clergy have been divinely commissioned for this redemptive work appears in the Apostolic Succession from St. Peter to the present, and in the distinction between priesthood and laity. The divine commission operates through the priests and the sacraments. The Roman Catholic traditionally emphasizes the institution more than the Bible, the priest more than the layman, the authoritative interpretation of the Church in matters of faith more than the individual's judgment. The Protestants, on the other hand, rallying to Luther's great translation of the Bible into simple German which "the community of all believers" could read, find God speaking directly in His revealed "Word" (1 Cor. 12:27-30; Eph. 3:14-19; 1 Peter 2:9, etc.). The individual's conscience, not the Church, becomes the guardian.

England was anti-Catholic not merely out of perversity but because of real and imagined danger from Spain. Only after the defeat of the Spanish Armada and the discovery of the Gunpowder Plot—both regarded as providential rescues—could she feel free. But released from outside pressure, England was free to fight out the problems of religious settlement within her own shores. Three Protestant groups helped to create the crisis—the Calvinists, the Anglicans, and the sects.

A better theologian and organizer than Luther, John Calvin (1509-64) formed a church-state at Geneva which spread throughout northern and western Europe. Partaking more of the Old Testament structure than of the New, Calvinism holds that, contrary to what is called synergism in Christian doctrine—that there are two efficient agents in regeneration, the human will and the divine Spirit—the one primary initial force is God. The will of God elects or damns even before birth those whom He chooses for eternal life or death. Asked how one can tell whether he is elected or damned, the real Calvinist (not the modern Presbyterian) will answer that that is your problem. Asked again why God should be so arbitrarily unfair, he will answer that no man can know how the Divine Will works or why it works that way: some people God simply passes by. Election and reprobation are no more symmetrical than nature, for God works through nature asymmetrically in choosing, for example, a single sperm out of millions to create you. Why? And where are the rest?

In Holland, Jacobus Arminius (1560-1609) continued the opposition to such a theory, pleading for the place of reason, both human and divine. After Arminius died, the action was led by a professor at the University of Leiden, Episcopius, until the Remonstrants, as they were called, became strong enough to be heard. The hearing was the Synod of Dort, held from November 1618 to May 1619 at Dortrecht, Holland. Sitting in the balcony taking notes was the secretary of the English ambassador to the Hague, "the ever-memorable Mr. John Hales of Eton." Though when Hales said "Goodnight" to John Calvin, he did not quite say "Goodmorrow" to Arminius, nevertheless he brought back to strengthen the Anglican church at home some very strong grounds for the place of reason in the Protestant lay-mind. The Synod of Dort was a victory for the Calvinists: Episcopius was banished, and Hugo Grotius, the founder of international law, put into prison. Their doctrines were declared a heresy under Calvinistic Protestantism.

Ever since the views of Calvin's *Institutes* (1535) officially won the day in the Dutch city of Dort, its five main doctrines have been associated for easy remembrance with T-U-L-I-P, the national flower of Holland:

Total depravity	the inability of the sinner to initiate his own redemption. We derive from the original sin of Adam "not only the punishment but also the pollution to which that punishment is due."
Unconditional election	man "in his present state is despoiled of freedom of will and is subject to a miserable slavery."
Limited atonement	by God's grace alone can any atonement be effectual; "The Lord both begins and completes His good work in us."
Irresistible grace	nothing can deflect God's will; this is predestination, "the eternal degree of God by which He has determined in Himself what He would have become of every individual of mankind."

| Perseverance of the saints | all the elect will certainly be saved, for once a Christian always a Christian. |

John Knox converted Scotland to this faith, but Milton modified it to make freedom of will central in *Paradise Lost*. Froude said: "If Arminianism most commends itself to our feelings, Calvinism is nearer to the facts, however harsh and forbidding those facts may seem."[1] Many Christian theologians from Kierkegaard to Paul Tillich start as Calvin did, with the existentialist "fact" of the sinner's initial consciousness of alienation. And the Bible does not gloss over it.

ANGLICANS

The Anglicans are Protestants whose creed specifies "the holy Catholic church." Browne confesses that he is of "that reformed new-cast religion, wherein I dislike nothing but the name." A commonplace distinction in the seventeenth century was a metaphor of two women: the one in Rome too gaudily dressed (a Puritan epithet was "whore of Babylon"), and the other, in Geneva, too bare. Thus George Herbert hails his middle way in "The British Church":

> A fine aspect in fit array,
> Neither too mean, nor yet too gay,
>   Shows who is best;
> Outlandish looks may not compare,
> For all they either painted are
>   Or else undrest.

In addition to the mean between too much and too little, Herbert praises the British center between the two "foreign" extremes.

No great force molded it into shape, such as a

Luther or a Calvin; rather it grew, twisting, turning, compromising with political events, receiving influences from both sides of the great split, fitting itself to life rather than to logic:

The Elizabethan church, maintaining a balance between powers never perhaps completely harmonized, was a Reformed Church, but it preserved continuity with the past; . . . it asserted the right of private judgment, but it also recognized the living voice of the Church; it possessed a strong element of individualism, but it restrained individual caprice and the extravagance of private inspiration. In a word, it has not the unity of a logical system, it has the comprehensiveness of a rich and varied life.[2]

An Anglican does not like to be told that his church began with Henry VIII's divorce from Katharine of Aragon. He will insist rather on the historical difficulty of Rome's ever being able to control the church in England. For him the Council of Whitby is evidence in 644 A.D. of vigorous British opposition, though a victory for Rome. He will cite the Wycliffites, those staunch "Bible men" opprobriously called Lollards, who anticipated Luther by two hundred years, so that even the Roman Catholic Chaucer's host, rising in his stirrups, pinched his nose and said, "I smelle a Lollere in the wynd." All this and more, the Anglican argues, bespeaks a British church with its own traditions protesting against those of Rome long before the quarrel between the Pope and Henry the Eighth. Early in his *confessio* Browne inveighs against the "unjust scandall of our adversaries . . ." which is "to compute the Nativity of our Religion" from this much married king.

The emphasis the Anglican church places on the Bible makes it Protestant. In Archbishop Cranmer's Preface to his *Book of Common Prayer* (1549)—based on Tyndale's vernacular Bible, as well as on a Latin missal and a tradition kept by the clergy—occur these words:

Here you have an order for prayer . . . much agreeable to the mind and purpose of the old fathers, and a great deal more profitable and commodious than that which of late was used. It is more profitable because here are left out many things whereof some be untrue, some uncertain, some vain and superstitious: and is ordained nothing to be read but the very pure word of God, the holy scriptures, or that which is evidently grounded upon the same; and that in such a language and order as is most easy and plain for the understanding both of the readers and the hearers.[3]

If a rector actually follows the Anglican lectionary for morning and evening worship together, his congregation will hear read the Psalms through once a month, the rest of the Old Testament once a year, and the whole of the New Testament every four months. The King James Bible itself was a Protestant enterprise, carried out by scholars like Bishop Launcelot Andrewes. Whereas the Roman church from time to time adds official requirements for salvation (the latest being the dogma of the bodily assumption of the Holy Virgin Mary), the Anglican church repudiates purgatory as non-Biblical and insists that everything necessary for salvation is to be found in the Bible. The seven sacraments of Rome are reduced to the two Biblical ones— baptism and Holy Communion, "ordained by Christ himself" (*Book of Common Prayer*, Catechism). This Protestant mode was given official sanction in the Thirty-nine Articles to make peace with Calvinism. Browne with the other Protestants makes the Bible one of his two main manuscripts from which to read about God. The other is not the church tradition but nature.

The Anglican finds validity not only in history and in the Bible but also in reason, which is given by God to the community of all believers for interpreting both the tradition and the Bible. Inseparable from Anglican thinking about the Bible, therefore, is the distinction between fundamental and nonfundamental points: those things from the Bible set down in the Apostles' or Nicene creed are necessary to believe, but the apple Eve ate or the exact dimensions of Noah's ark are points hardly necessary to salvation. So Browne in the opening section of *Religio Medici* describes his double validity: " . . . I find my selfe obliged by the principles of Grace, and the law of mine owne reason. . . ."[4] The Anglican apologetic against the Roman Catholic stressed reason and the Bible; against the Calvinist and sectaries, reason and the validity of historical development.

This was the church whose rationale was set down in Elizabethan prose of a high order by Richard Hooker in *Of the Laws of Ecclesiastical Polity*. In 1584 Richard Alvey, Master of the Temple in London, died; and Walter Travers, the learned and eloquent afternoon preacher, was due to succeed him. But Travers was Calvinist. Archbishop Whitgift, himself in controversy with the Calvinist Cartwright, appointed Hooker as the morning preacher and kept the Calvinist on for the afternoon. Each preacher was more intent on rebutting his predecessor than on enlightening the flock, so that, in Thomas Fuller's often quoted words, "Here the pulpit spoke pure Canterbury in the morning and Geneva in the afternoon. . . . "[5] When the archbishop peremptorily silenced Travers, Hooker retired from the Temple to a living in Wiltshire, where he meditated upon the authority and laws of ecclesiastical polity.

Not the sole and exclusive authority of Scripture, Hooker began, can be the mainstay of the church, but the concurrence and co-operation of all possible means of knowledge, including history and reason. God's law, which becomes operative as "natural law," is not that of an arbitrary tyrant, but that of a Will which accepts reason as its rule. Reason and revealed religion do not conflict, since revelation is God's manifest Reason. To degrade human reason and set Scripture as the sole authority is disguised arrogance, for God gave man reason before He gave him the Scripture to be interpreted by it. Nor, on the other hand, is mere tradition enough, since ten thousand church councils, all voting in majority, cannot resist a plain demonstration that two and two are four. How the human institution of the church should be governed, Hooker continued, is not told us in great detail in the Bible: a government by bishops seems rational for the time being, but no one is bound to it forever. Reason can adapt government to broad principles of expediency as it can adapt our minds to goodness and to God.

"In his religion," Whitefoot wrote, ". . . [Browne] continued in the same mind which he declared in his first book . . . *Religio Medici*, wherein he fully assented to that of the church of England, preferring it before any in the world, as did the learned Grotius." The use of human reason humbled before the facts of creation strengthened Browne's attachment to the Anglican church. He particularly recommended two works on reason in religion by fellow laymen, Grotius and Sébonde:

Whereas notwithstanding the solid reason or confirmed experience of any man, is very approvable in what profession soever. So Raymund Sebund, a Physitian of Tholouze, besides his learned Dialogues *De Natura humana*, hath written a natural theologie, demonstrating therein the Attributes of God, and attempting the like in most points of Religion. So Hugo Grotius, a Civilian, did write an excellent Tract of the verity of Christian Religion. Wherein most rationally delivering themselves, their works will be embraced by most that understand them, and their reasons enforce belief even from prejudicate Readers.[6]

Hugo Grotius, a product of two of Browne's universities, Padua and Leiden, wrote his *De Veritate Religionis Christianae* in order to help Dutch seamen convert Hindus. His book, like Browne's, is divided into two parts: Part I, "Of God and His Providence," and Part II, "Of Christ, His Miracles, and Doctrine." That God exists is proven by the *consensus gentium*: "If any one oppose, I say seeing they were but few, and their opinion was generally rejected, so soon as their Arguments were heard, it is manifest, it was not the issue of right Reason (which is common to men) but of an innovating Spirit."[7] Grotius, like Browne, emphasizes wisdom among God's attributes:

Nor is this evinced by Reason only, but after a sort of Sense. For, if we behold the admirable structure of man's Body . . . and how all parts there . . . have their use . . . with so much art, that the most skillful Philosophers and Physicians could never enough admire it: This speaks the Maker to be a most excellent Intelligence: Whereof, Galen may be seen, where especially he examines the use of the Eye, and of the Hand.[8]

There is little new here; Grotius confesses that he bases his apology on Vives, de Mornay, and Raymond de Sébonde. Indeed, Montaigne's famous "Apology" for Sébonde is a two-edged sword: one edge for those who think reason should not be mixed with faith, the other for those who put too much faith in their reason. Throughout Grotius' book there is the quiet conviction that reason and faith are not at war; that no religious controversy is worth the temper and paper it uses up; that all sensible men can see the reasonableness of Christ's teaching. Browne "condemne[s] not all things in the councell of *Trent* nor approve[s] all in the Synod of *Dort*."

But the dangers in the emphasis upon reason in religion were real as well as suspected. While the strict Calvinists called anyone who used reason first an "Arminian" and then a "Socinian," actually reason in some quarters began to oust religion entirely. Lord Herbert of Cherbury, the elder brother of the poet, while boasting and dueling his way across the continent of Europe, worked out in *De Veritate* (1624) the beginnings of a rational, almost anthropological view. He found five main points to all religions: that God exists, that man's duty is to worship Him, that virtue and piety are the essentials of worship, that repentance and retribution are divinely called for from us, and that there must be a future life of rewards and punishments. As extended by John Toland's *Christianity Not Mysterious* (1696), this grew into eighteenth-century Deism, which succeeded in pushing God out of the universe as a kind of absentee landlord.

SECTS

With neither reason as a norm nor an official clerical umpire, two interpretations of the same Biblical text held with equal vehemence by two individuals always conflict. The only course would be for each to enlist supporters for his side and begin a new "sect" of Christianity. Often when such a crisis in "prophesying" was reached, one group would stick by its founder as "orthodox," the other calling themselves "new" or "reformed." As sects multiplied in the new-modeled Parliamentary Army, it was first pleaded that a gifted brother had better preach than nobody, but by 1646 all learning, good sense, and a rational interpretation of Scripture seemed to have disappeared:

. . . every bold pretender to inspiration was preferred to the most grave and sober divines of the age; some advanced themselves into the ranks of prophets, and others uttered such crude and undigested absurdities as came first into their minds, calling them the dictates of the Spirit within them: . . .[9]

How many sects there were in Sir Thomas Browne's day we do not know, though a rough estimate would place their number between seventy-five and one hundred. A few of the best known books describing them are an anonymous work of 1646 entitled A *Relation of Several Heresies,* Thomas Edwards' *Gangraena* (1646), D'Espagne's *Popular Errors in Religion* (1648), and Alexander Ross's A *View of All Religions in the World* (1653). Some of the invectives against the sects were written by Anglicans, some by Presbyterians—equally scabrous; and every pamphlet had to be answered. Most of the criticisms were compiled from well-known sources on the continent, from St. Augustine, through Bullinger, to Pagitt's *Heresiography,* with each English book adding the peculiarly English sects. Thus Ross ends his book: "But this age, which is much more fruitful of Religions, then of good works, of Scripture Phrases, then of Scripture practises, of opinions then of piety, hath spawned more Religions, then that lady of Holland did infants; . . . ."[10] Browne almost despairs for any Christian: ". . . for first the Church of *Rome* condemneth us, wee likewise them, the Sub-reformists and Sectaries sentence the Doctrines of our Church as damnable, the Atomist, or Familist reprobates all these, and all these them againe."[11] To him it seemed that no one could hold an opinion without creating followers to support it: ". . . the villainy of the first Schisme of *Lucifer,* who was not content to erre alone, but drew into his faction many Legions of Spirits. . . ,"[12] a process of "sub-dividing" and "mincing" themselves "almost into Atomes."[13]

There were Adamites, Anabaptists (eighteen varieties of them according to Ross), Antinomians, Antisabbatarians, and Antitrinitarians; Apollonarists, Apostolics, Arminians, Arians, and Atomists (from Mrs. Atomy); Barrowists, Behemists, Brownists, Cerdonians, Divorcers, Enthusiasts, Expectants, and Familists; Independents, Johnsonists, Marcionites, Millenaries, Pellagians, and Perfectionists; Ranters, Sabellians, Sabbatarians, Schwenkefeldians, Seekers, Servetians, and Socinians; Soul-sleepers, Tertulliants, Traskists, Valentinians, and Vanists—and others.[14] How many names one comes across were actually congregations or mixed groups of individuals against whom the author is venting his theological pique is difficult to say.

The Adamites, however, were real. They were religious nudists: "They pray, heare, and celebrate the communion naked according to the similitude of Adam before his fall."[15] On the continent the paintings of Hieronymous Bosch, particularly the nude forms of his "Garden of Earthly Delights" (more accurately known as "The Millennium"), are thought by one critic to have been inspired by the religious eroticism of the Adamites.[16]

The Antiscriptarians and Familists caused a lot of trouble. They held in common that the Bible could not be the word of God because God speaks to the spirit of man. Scripture, they said, was written by mere men in the same way that men write today—insufficient, uncertain, and fallible.[17] Founded by Henry Nicolaus, who was born in Münster in 1502, the Familists became so strong in England that Elizabeth banned them in a proclamation of 1580. Their fourth article declared: "That those that be doctors or learned cannot preach the word truly because Christ sayeth it is hidden from the wise and prudent." They took the Bible not literally as so many of their brethren did but figuratively: "The Bible is not the Word of God, but a signification thereof, and the Bible is but ink and paper, but the word of God is spirit and life."[18]

The Brownists, finally, were early Congregationalists, led by Robert Browne (1580-1633), who did a lot of preaching in Norfolk and Suffolk. Books like George Gifford's A Short Treatise against the Donatists of England, whom we call Brownists (1590) and Joseph Hall's A Common Apology against the Brownists (1610) denounced the Brownists for dissenting from all ecclesiastical control. As English Erastians, they drew the ire of Anglicans and Presbyterians alike for their "independence." Shakespeare made Sir Andrew Aguecheek say in Twelfth Night: "I had as lief be a Brownist as a politician" (III, ii, 34). The Anglican James Howell wrote: "If I hate any, 'tis those Schismatics that puzzle the sweet peace of our Church, so that I could be content to see an Anabaptist go to Hell on a Brownist's back."[19]

Archbishop Laud's Anglican church and the Presbyterians who wished to "establish" themselves in its place had one thing in common: both were disturbed by these separatist sects which were rapidly increasing in number, variety, and enthusiasm, particularly up in Thomas Browne's part of England. As the sects were persecuted in Holland, it was to the bulge of East Anglia in England that.they came for refuge, prophesying in all the tongues of the Reformation. And not only propinquity accounted for this emigration: Norfolk reminded the Dutchmen of home. It is a lowland, surrounded by water and often under sea level. The terrain even today is crisscrossed with waterways, so that a traveler is often surprised by a sailboat gliding across what from eye level looks like a meadow; and Dutch windmills still dot the landscape.

Back in Bishop Parker's time, Norwich was infamous for nonconformity, and Strype in his *Annals* (1709-31) gives a fine character of this Anglican bishop who in the 1560's and 1570's proclaimed his desire to see all England follow the church of Zurich. Naturally Queen Elizabeth ordered that her campaign to suppress the "hereticks" and "schismaticks" should begin in Norfolk.

IN NORWICH

As an Anglican Browne was wary of the Roman concept of the Church and its clergy which had gained favor in segments of his own Royalist party. But he had no sympathy with those Puritans who destroyed any piece of ecclesiastical art—statuary, stained glass, or organ—on the grounds that it was "Popish." A peace-loving Englishman loyal to his king, he took sides when the Puritan party went to extremes.

On February 22, 1641, the beautiful structure of his own Anglican cathedral of Norwich was threatened, as we are told in the title of this pamphlet:

True News from Norwich: Being a certain Relation how that the Cathedral Blades of Norwich . . . did put themselves into a posture of defense, because that the Apprentices of Norwich (as they imagined) would have pulled down their Organs. In which Relation the foolishness of these Cathedrall men are to be understood, and deserve to be laughed at for this silly enterprise; there being no such cause to move them thereunto. 1641.

The work that follows is a scurrilous but fairly witty Presbyterian attack on the practices of Anglicanism: "There being a rumour that the Apprentices of

Norwich would pull down the Rayles of the great Church, (Christs-Church they call it but there is but little of Christ taught, and less practised)."[20] The organ in the cathedral, it is argued, was threatened "only to skarre the fools." But the cathedral blades, numbering about five hundred, resolved to protect the church against "the rebellious Puritans, as they term'd them." The author says of the Anglicans: "Oh how they loathe to part with their Diana's, their Altars, Images, Crucifixes, Coapes, Surplices, and Romish vestments; no (as some of them said), they would rather lose their lives than their organs, so fast they glewed to their Pipes and Popish trinkets."[21] Within three years the organ was destroyed by a Puritan mob.

Though sharp lines were drawn in battle, both creed and worship often overlapped. Calvinism made its inroads upon the Roman Catholics of Pascal's Port Royal; and most Anglicans, from the period of the Marian exiles forward, were Calvinists in their theology. Such was Joseph Hall, who as dean of Worcester had been sympathetic with the majority when he was at Dort, who became Anglican bishop of Norwich, who was attended in his final illness by Dr. Thomas Browne, and whose funeral sermon was preached by the Reverend John Whitefoot, Browne's earliest biographer. But Bishop Hall, though a Calvinistically inclined Anglican, would not stand for sacrilege even when he had been deprived of his benefices. The account of the ruining of Norwich Cathedral's organ is best given in his words:

Lord, what work was here, what clattering of glasses, what beating down of walls, what tearing up of monuments, what pulling down of seates, what wresting out of irons and brass from the windows and graves, what defacing of armes, what demolishing of curious stonework, that had not any representation in the world, but only of the cost of the founder, and skill of the mason, what toting and piping on the destroyed organ pipes, and what a hideous triumph on the market day before all the countrey, when in a kind of sacrilegious and profane procession, all the organ pipes, vestments, both copes and surplices, together with the leaden crosse, which had been newly sawne downe from over the greenyard pulpit, and the service books and singing books that could be had, were carried to the fire in the public market place; a lewd wretch walking before the train, in his cope trailing in the dirt, with a service book in his hand imitating in an impious scorne the tune, and usurping the words of the litany used formerly in the church . . . and the cathedrall now open on all sides to be filled with muskatiers, wayting for the majors returne, drinking and tobacconing as freely as it had turn'd ale-house.[22]

On August 26, 1646, the Presbyterian party in Norwich published in London a pamphlet called *Vox Populi, or The Peoples Cry against the Clergy, Containing the Rise, Progress, and Ruine of Norwich Remonstrance.* Written when only ten of Norwich's thirty-six parish churches had ministers, it accuses eight of them of conspiring with the mayor of Norwich to suppress the freedom of religious worship. More particularly, it accuses the Reverend Mr. Thornback of exhorting the people "to tread out the sparks" of the non-Anglican mode of worship, "and if any wretch should interpose or foe to hinder it, he deserves to be cut in pieces and his house to be made a Jaques."

Strong language like this is matched by a too staunch Anglican, calling himself "S. T." and arguing like a Roman Catholic, in *Truth Vindicated from the Unjust Accusations of the Independent Society in the City of Norwich* (London, 1646). The author "proves" that the Church of England, not the Independent Society in Norwich, is the true church of Christ, and that to separate from the true church in order to join the false communion is consequently a sin.

The middle view, in a pamphlet signed by fifteen leading citizens including Dr. Thomas Browne, pleads for the safety of the ministers. Its title is *Vox Norwici: or, The Cry of Norwich, vindicating their Ministers . . . from the foule and false aspersions and slanders, which are unchristianly throwne upon them in a lying and scurrilous Libell, lately come forth, intituled, Vox Populi . . .* (London, 1646). Since the ministers themselves will not answer the charges against them ". . . in the gentlenesse of their spirits . . . , we their people who have lived under their Minstries, and received so much comfort and benefit from them" cannot remain silent. The purpose of the accusation is to drive them away, "But God knowes, and all Israel shall know, that our City generally (excepting only some malignants and members of separated Congregations) doth honour, love, and reverence them for their works sake."[23] In answering the various charges, the pamphlet asserts that these ministers do not fail to preach against sin, "except only to Recusants and Separatists that never frequent our Congregations"; and in the margin is printed the reason for their absence: "they are in Mrs. Ashwells chamber." That the ministers are carnal or want only richer preferments is refuted by a "character" of each one. Most interesting is that almost all of them had resisted the high Anglican encroachments of Bishop Wren, who, succeeding Bishop Corbet in 1635, was impeached by the House of Commons in 1641 for ordering all ministers to wear vestments.

The character of Dr. Browne's own rector at St. Peter Mancroft church bears quotation in full:

Master Carter hath lived the Minister of St. Peters Parish now these seventeen yeares, except only that time in which he was banished by Bishop *Wrenn*, and his Chancellour, we never could discerne that ever he did seeke after, or affect any worldly preferment; he hath had advantages of raising himselfe, but never improved them so farre, as ever we could see or heare, this we know he hath often been about to leave St. Peters Parish for a lesse people, and lesse means, only as he professed out of the sense of his owne weakenesse, being not able to beare so great a burthen as lyeth upon him: and as for the Prelaticall ceremonies, he hath ever groned under them, declaimed against them bitterly, both publickely and privately, and because his conscience would not suffer him to yeeld to their trash, he was unmercifully persecuted by Bishop Wrenn, and his Chancellour, suspended, deprived and molested: So he was forced to leave Norfolke, and seeke hiding places, he suffered with joy the spoyling of his goods, and counted exile a Paradice, only to be free from the base trash of Prelates: He hath ever been the same, keeping close to his principles; and if he have varied in any thing, it hath been in the increase of his detestation of superstition and Prelacy: We all testifie of seventeene yeares experience of him, that these aspersions of him are foule, and the accusations most false and grosse.[24]

Thomas Browne's is the third of the fifteen signatures which "are to be seen at Hamond Craske's house."

Chapter III

OXFORD AND BROWNE'S TWO TEACHERS

Thomas Browne matriculated at Broadgates Hall, Oxford, on December 5, 1623, and within his first year took part in the inauguration of Broadgates Hall as Pembroke College on August 5, 1624. The man who gave Browne's college its endowment as well as a name was William Herbert Earl of Pembroke, the chancellor of Oxford and a great patron of the arts. It was he who set aside twenty pounds each New Year's Day for Ben Jonson to buy books with, and who sent Inigo Jones on a traveling fellowship to Italy.

Through his generosity, Browne's college was able to combine literature, religion, and medicine. Pembroke graduates distinguished in literature were Edward Dyer, George Peele, Francis and his brother Sir John Beaumont, and Dr. Samuel Johnson. Of all England's literary men, Charles Lamb desired to see in the flesh two men from Pembroke, Sir Fulke Greville and Sir Thomas Browne. Among men of religion were Richard Corbett, himself a poet, head of Christ Church, later bishop of Norwich, and his friend Dr. Lushington. With regius professor of physic Dr. Thomas Clayton as the first master of the new college, Pembroke nourished such famous physicians and anatomists as Edward Dawson, Elisha Coush, Nicholas Lamy, William Quartermaine, George Joyliffe, and John Wyberd.

On that great day when Broadgates Hall became Pembroke College, three students were chosen to give Latin orations before an audience composed of the chancellor of Oxford, the regius professor of medicine Dr. Clayton, the vice-principal Dr. Prideaux, and a large group of distinguished guests. These students were Matthew Turner, M.A., John Lee, B.A., and the youngest, the only "studiosus non graduatus commensalis collegii," Thomas Browne. His address, in youthfully ornamented Latin periods, follows:

I feel, gentlemen of Broadgates (for you still retain this ancient name that is to be abolished anon), I feel, I say, that each man among you has pricked up his ears, eagerly awaiting the tenor of my speech, and, if I may thus say, itching to hear whether 'tis in disfavour or in favour of them of Pembroke that I have risen to speak. Yet what, I pray you, are these evils, as misjudging men deem them, for which you would have me with lamentations unfeigned, and, as he said, having the breath of life, make moan in high tragic vein? Lo! your hall unfixed and ownerless (for what father or founder of the house can we bring to mind?), a most noble Maecenas hath taken under his protection, who from a hall will make it a college, from Broadgates, Pembroke, bestowing thereon his own name, from a hall of brick will make, if I may thus say, aye, and truly too, if one should regard the duration thereof, a college of marble, which not even envy, or only passing envy, shall look upon. Why, shall he who has come forth the founder and author of this benefaction, who has brought about this transformation, shall he be arraigned at the bar on the charge of kind conduct, be impeached for his good will? Shall we look askance at him for granting us that which, if we esteem it aright, is a benefaction?

What man among us is so shameless and brazenfronted as to speak thus? Why, our rights, whatsoever they have been, we retain them all. Although what rights of them of Broadgates, what peculiar interests could we hold to be of such worth that when common advantage is in debate they should not straightway be overthrown and bow before the College of Pembroke? Nevertheless, we have all our rights the same. The same principal and master, the same house, save that it is a nobler one. He of Broadgates is one of Pembroke, and contrariwise, he of Pembroke is one of Broadgates. Trojan and Tyrian have this sole difference: that whereas hitherto I know not by what hap we have borne a title ironically given, we shall now be graced with a name that is truly glorious.

What man of Broadgates, then, when he shall see this Phoenix of Pembroke uproused from the ruins of this ancient hall, which all but happeneth at this very moment, will not vaunt his own loss, and congratulate himself on so profitable a deprivation of his name? Let Pembroke now enter within our gates, aye, and within our hearts. This Broadgates of ours in our hands, most excellent Sir, we deposit as a trust. We cannot bring ourselves to say we *leave* it in thy hands. I say we deposit it with happy omen, to take back anon in the stead of a hall a college, in the stead of a principal a master.[1]

The ceremony over, Browne must have returned to the ordinary college life he was used to by this time. Thomas Crosfield, an undergraduate at Queen's, records in his diary under March 3, 1627, that the "fellows play at ball [and] shitlecock in their chamber."[2] And it was during an Oxford March that he complained of "Childeblaine because of colde & intemperate diet."[3] There was always the town for the more gregarious, and on July 11, 1631, Crosfield noted:

Things to be seene for money in ye City. 1. Playes. 2. dancing upon ye Rope & vaulting upon ye Sadle. 3. Virginalls & organs playing by themselves. 4. a dutch-wench all hairy & rough upon her body. 5. The history of some parts of ye bible, as ye creation of ye world, Abrahms sacrificing his sonne, Ninevah beseiged & taken, Dives & Lazarus. 6. The dancing of ye horse at ye Starre.[4]

But Thomas Browne, morose by his stars, probably frequented the museums, bookstalls, and the churches more than the sideshows. Perhaps the dancing horse at the Star interested him less than the huge statue of the "River Horse and Young" that, like something out of Pliny, had been set up in front of Magdalen over a hundred years before.[5] At the Anatomy Museum, which preceded the Tradescant and the Ashmolean, he could very well have looked at these exhibits among others: No. 180, "Skin of a woman not stuff'd"; No. 45, "a Mermaids hand"; No. 50, "Scalp of an American who was flead alive"; No. 42, "The teat of a Witch"; and No. 210, "Pizzle of a Sea-Dragon."[6] Crosfield remembered[7] "Mr. Camden, Enginer, who bestowed the Dodar (a blacke Indian bird) upon ye Anatomy Schoole," a reference to Tradescant's famous dodo. There is little doubt that young Browne, having graduated from simpling in London's Cheapside, spent many hours in the Physick Garden founded by the Earl of Danby in 1621,[8] for he maintained a professional's skill and an amateur's enthusiasm in botany for the rest of his life.

No one knows how many books Browne bought at Oxford. Yet his early interest in reading and his ultimate large personal library suggest that he may have been an eager customer in the bookstalls on High Street. On March 3, 1627, Crosfield bought a just published first edition of Hakewill's famous argument against the theory of decay, *An Apologie of the Power and Providence of God in the Government of the World* (1627), laconically recorded as "Dr. Hackwells book 6s."[9] College stores in that day as in this sold more than books, however; Crosfield "bought of Mrs Webb a little globe, a dyall, a pair of compasses for 4s."[10]

Besides attending daily chapel in Pembroke College and occasionally going to St. Mary's Church on High Street, the Pembroke men in a body went to "St.

Olds," that is, St. Aldate's Church, next door to the college.[11] Browne was also attracted to Christ Church cathedral; every day of his life at Oxford he could not help seeing its noble roof and tower, the whole of Christ Church dwarfing little Pembroke, its adjacent neighbor across St. Aldates Street. It was the college and the church of Royalists and Laud-men, of Bishop Corbett and later of his tutor Dr. Lushington. As an old alumnus of Pembroke he subscribed the sum of 130 pounds to have Christ Church repaired.[12] But the sermons at Oxford, except perhaps for those of Dr. Lushington, were not very inspiring, if we can take Crosfield's as a typical undergraduate reaction. "Sermons repeated," he complained on April 1, 1627, "all tending to small edification, nugae laboriosae, for indeed the end of all sermons should be to bring comfort to each Christian soule, by redemption through Jesus Christ who dyed & was buried & rose againe for salvation."[13] On June 1, 1630, a Mr. Hinton told Crosfield about a different preacher, "Dr. Donne deane of Pauls, his powerfull kinde of preaching by his gestur & Rhetoriquall expression."[14] Apparently Crosfield while at Oxford never went to hear the famous Lushington, whose sermons were actually applauded by the undergraduate congregation. Browne may have gone through a period of religious jolting at Oxford. The heresies he refers to the time of his "greener studies"[15] are more like those of a college student than of a schoolboy.

The undergraduate curriculum at Pembroke favored the arts more than the sciences. This was due not only to the belief that a liberal education formed the best foundation for anatomy and materia medica, but also to the fact that only the beginnings of medical education in England as we know it today coincided with Browne's Oxford experience from his matriculation in 1623 through his M.A. in 1629. It is unlikely that he had any formal medical training for his B.A. and not much even for his M.A. "Both Oxford and Cambridge," writes one historian, "compelled all who desired to study medicine to proceed in arts before taking a medical degree."[16]

Thomas Browne at eighteen began each rigorous college day with morning prayer at 5:00 A.M. in the chapel. There was a fine of twopence for absence without cause and of one penny for coming or leaving after the *Psalm*. At 6:00 A.M. on Mondays, Wednesdays, and Fridays the first-year students were required to attend a logic lecture. This was followed on Tuesday and Friday by rhetoric for members of the younger classes and by a lecture in natural philosophy for the senior classes. At ten every day except Saturday and Sunday all undergraduates were compelled to hear the catechetical lecture "delivering the sum and foundation of the Christian religion." Then at two in the afternoon every Tuesday and Friday those undergraduates "imbued with Greek" had an opportunity to extend their knowledge of it.[17]

Besides these set lectures, Pembroke demanded regular disputations. For the men qualifying for the M.A. this was a theological exercise; for those still working for the B.A. it was a philosophical one. But though the content differed, the same rules of grammar, rhetoric, and logic obtained. Every Saturday after prayers the undergraduates had to declaim publicly in hall on set subjects of greater variety.[18] It was probably for these exercises that the young Browne read, wrote, and practiced under his tutor Lushington. When on June 30, 1626,[19] Browne received his B.A. degree, he had to appear in hall either to present or to oppose a proposition approved in advance by Dr. Clayton, the master.

Much the same discipline obtained throughout the

three years required for the M.A. degree. The student perforce heard lectures on moral and natural philosophy, disputed *pro forma* once a year "in Augustininensibus" and "in Quodlibeticis," and had to read *lectiones* in logic and natural philosophy. It was only after the M.A. that the serious student could then attach himself to one of the higher faculties of law, theology, or medicine[20]—a significant point for the dating of Browne's practice of medicine during the writing of *Religio Medici*.

Despite the emphasis on required chapel and disputation, however, Browne of Pembroke was well, if informally, introduced to the philosophy and techniques of the physician. In 1613 the medical buildings had been built into the Bodleian Library quadrangle: on the north, natural philosophy on the first floor and anatomy on the second. At the east side the new astronomy building was placed, its tower to be added later. Within a few years of the acquisition of these buildings and their equipment, the teaching of the physical sciences was strengthened by four new chairs: the Savile chairs of geometry and astronomy in 1619; the Sedley chair of natural philosophy in 1622; and in 1623, the year Browne matriculated, the Tomlins chair in anatomy.

Of Browne's teachers at Oxford the two most important were Dr. Clayton and the Reverend Dr. Lushington (both named Thomas): the one, physician and anatomist who lived mainly in this changing world of matter; and the other, Browne's tutor, an amateur mathematician and Neoplatonic divine who lived in the unchanging world of form. Browne himself mentions a few others. Some Latin epigrams years later reminded him bitterly of a pair of proctors at Oxford, John Smith and William Oldis, to the extent of inspiring him to quote:

William Oldis
Silly dimme owl
John Smith
Shyt on him.[21]

Browne was interested in science. Astronomy in
his day was taught by Dr. Bainbridge, and the student
refers to the book on the *Canicularis* by "the learned
Bainbrigius."[22] Again he recalled Mr. Briggs, "in our
time Geometry Professor in Oxford,"[23] and Briggs's
student Ridley, who, as physician to the emperor of
Russia, wrote *On Magnetical Bodies*.[24] By far the
most memorable teacher to fire the young student's
imagination with terrestrial and celestial geography
was not a member of Pembroke at all, but a seventy-
year-old scholar of Christ Church College whom
Browne met as a fellow communicant at St. Aldate's
Church. He was the famous Robert Hues, who had
accompanied Cavendish in a voyage around the world,
had tutored Algernon the son of Henry Earl of North-
umberland, and had been mentioned for his knowledge
of Greek in the preface of Chapman's *Homer* (1611).
He wrote the *Tractatus de Globis et eorum Usu* (London, 1594) on the first pair of globes that had been
made in England, those by Molyneux; and the book is
dedicated to Sir Walter Raleigh, who sought his guidance in navigation for the voyage to Virginia.[25] How
many evenings Browne spent with this learned man,
talking of longitude and latitude, climates and parallels,
altitudes, angles, horizontals, and declinations, we
shall never know. But the student used his master's
book in composing his *Vulgar Errors*[26] and left a
warm appreciation of the man in a letter to his son:

My old freind Mr. H . . . lived & dyed in Oxford, living in
a freinds howse neere Xtchurch & attaining unto great
yeares. Hee writt his book *de globis* for the sake & informa-

tion of one of my Lord of Northumberlands sonnes, whom hee had instructed in that waye. Hee came to church constantly, the parish church, which was St. Aldates, commonly St. Owls, & whether the scollars of Penbrooke colledg also went, & had one Isle for them selves. Hee was [a] very good & playne dealing man, & had read Euclide & Ptolomie very accurately, and also Aristotle, whereof wee should often discourse, and I cannot butt remember him with some content. . . .[27]

Had Hues been younger and more closely connected with Pembroke, Browne might have become an astronomer.

DR. CLAYTON

Thus it was a happy augury that a man like Dr. Thomas Clayton should have been at Pembroke as both the regius professor of physic (the chair was founded in 1546) and the first Tomlins lecturer in anatomy, appointed in 1623. Preceding Clayton as regius professor was Dr. Bartholomew Warner (1556-1619), whose daughter became Dr. Clayton's wife. Richard Tomlins of the City of Westminster did

. . . found constitute and ordayne an Anatomye Lector to be for ever read and performed in the said Vniversitie . . . first and chiefly to the honor and glory of God . . . but also because the knowledge and true understanding of mans body and the parts and faculties of the same . . . is also of great vse to the Professors of Divinitie, Philosophy and all other good Literature and more particularly necessary for the Faculties of Artes of Physicke and Chirurgery, the perfection whereof doth much avayle to the safety health and comfort of the whole Common wealth in the conservation of theire persons: And that there is as yet in neither of the Vniversities of this Kingdome (thoughe otherwise the most flourisshing of the whole Christian world) any such Anatomy Lecture founded or established.[28]

The first lecturer nominated by the founder was "his worthy friend Thomas Clayton," who inspired Browne to become a doctor and to go on, after the M.A., in medicine. That literary amateur physician of Christ Church, Robert Burton, wrote of Dr. Clayton in his preface to *The Anatomy of Melancholy*:

A good Divine either is or ought to be a good physician, a spiritual physician at least, as our Saviour calls Himself, and was indeed. . . . They differ but in object, the one of the body, the other of the soul, and use divers medicines to cure: one amends *animam per corpus*, the other *corpus per animam*, as our Regius Professor of Physick well informed us in a learned lecture of his not long since.[29]

Every spring after the Lent Assizes Dr. Clayton would arrange for "a sounde body of one of the Executed persons" to be prepared and cut up by the barber-surgeon and would lecture out of Galen as follows: on the first day, two hours in the morning and two hours in the afternoon on the organs that decay first—"the partes commonly called Naturall, videlicet Liver Spleene Stomacke Guttes &c." On the next day "the Vital partes videlicet Hart Lunges &c," and on the third and final day "the Animall partes and faculties videlicet the Brayne &c" were demonstrated in the same manner —the professor reading from Galen, the barber hacking, and the students watching and listening. For this three-day session Dr. Clayton received the sum of twenty-five pounds, out of which he had to pay three pounds to one Bernard Wright, who did the cutting, and two pounds for the decent disposal of the remains.[30]

At times the dissection was a sporting event (and in London Pepys would attend an autopsy as though it were a play). In 1650 Doctors Sir William Petty and Thomas Willis (the famous brain surgeon) were surprised by the sudden revival of their female corpse who had been "hanged by the neck till she was dead." The students cheerfully aided her resuscitation and celebrated her subsequent marriage and children. This poem commemorates her:

> Ann Greene was a slippery quean,
> In vain did the jury detect her;—
> She cheated Jack Ketch, and then the vile wretch
> 'Scaped the knife of the learned dissecter.[31]

The anatomical lectures at Oxford can be reconstructed with fair accuracy from the notes in the diary of John Ward from 1649 to 1660.[32] As late as 1665, apparently, there was no mention at Oxford of Harvey's discovery of the circulation of the blood which had been published in 1628. While Milton inveighed against the hopelessly scholastic methods of the universities in the teaching of humane subjects, Marchamont Needham in *Medela Medicinae, a Plea for the Free Profession of the Art of Physicke* (1665) complained that only the ancient medical classics were still being lectured upon:

For here lies the Bane of our Profession, that because a Book-knowledge of Hippocrates, Galen, and the rest are counted Classick, is admitted in the Universities as a sufficient Test to try a man's fitness to become a Doctor of Physick, therefore less ingenious spirits content themselves with that sort of Learning, and seldom seek after the other. . . .[33]

It is little wonder that thirty-five years before this diatribe an ingenious student of medicine like Thomas Browne, along with many others, had to get his real medical education in the great university centers on the continent. Oxford, in spite of good men like Clayton, had barely advanced beyond the zoology of Michael

Scot, which was after all only the Latin from the Greek
of Aristotle on animals.

DR. LUSHINGTON

On April 18 and April 23, 1624, just four months
before Broadgates Hall became Pembroke College, Dr.
Thomas Lushington, Browne's other most influential
teacher at Oxford, preached two sermons at St. Mary's
Church which made history.[34] If the congregation
present at the preaching of the first sermon had been
average in size, the church must have been overflowing
with dons, undergraduates, and townsmen the following Sunday as word got around that Lushington had
to take back his words.

The University could hardly allow Broadgates another *cause célèbre*, since only two years before, William Knight, unfortunately of the same college, had
been imprisoned for just such a sermon.[35] Now, in April
1624, the political situation was even worse. A faction
led by the king and his favorite George Villiers, duke of
Buckingham, was agitating for war with Spain over
the breaking down of the Spanish match for Prince
Charles. Anglicans and Puritans alike were against the
Roman Catholic marriage. Christian pacifist though
Lushington was, his opening paragraph was politically
rash, and his allusion to the Parliament as peasants perhaps illustrated a high church blindness to the growing
democratic feeling in England.

Though the first section of the sermon may be too
dramatic for some tastes, the theology is quite orthodox.
Preaching on the day after Easter, Lushington insists
that one must believe the Biblical account of the Resurrection. The manner of it was so ineffable that bad
words express it best: say it was "stealing," the priests
tell the soldiers. The fact is, Lushington argues, that

the "disciple" that "stole" Christ away from the tomb was Christ's soul. In a sustained passage of a dozen questions raised by hypothetical groups of people about this, the preacher dismisses them all as irrelevant to the fact of the Resurrection. Yet the homiletic virtuosity and the shock of the gibes at the king's Spanish policy and at Parliament overshadowed the theology.

For a long time a form of recantation had been prescribed at the universities. Dr. Pierce, later bishop of Bath and Wells, commanded a copy of the offending sermon to be delivered to him, and a delegation of doctors, in Clarendon's words, "reprehended Mr. Lushington to preach a Recantation on *Acts* 2:1. . . ." Accordingly, the following Sunday in a new sermon Lushington corrected the two offending passages: the one on war and the other beginning "Now the peasant thinks. . . ." The printed version of this recantation sermon from 1659 on had only a brief paragraph of personal recantation, which has obviously been rewritten to put the preacher in the worst light and the authorities in the best. The manuscripts, however, show that what Lushington actually said on that occasion was both more magnanimous and less cringing.[36] The printed recantation, moreover, shows no sign of Lushington's famed wit, but his actual words at St. Mary's in that second sermon were quite in character. The final sentence was memorable: "For, as good men profit the commonwealth because in themselves they are to be imitated, so I happily benefit the Church by making myself a bad example, for by ill preaching others may learn to do well, as a man may much better his horsemanship by seeing a Venetian or a sailor ride." Quite possibly laughter in the church was still audible as Lushington turned toward the altar to intone: "In the name of the Father, the Son, and. . . ."

Neither the listeners nor the preacher of this

famous pair of sermons were conscious of heresy. Yet word got around that the sermons were shocking, the gossip helped by the collegiate pun on Broadgates Hall and that Biblical *broad gate* of perdition. Four months later young Thomas Browne said in his Latin speech: "I know not by what hap we have borne a title ironically given." The Easter Monday sermon was politically indiscreet and it offended some by its wit, that is all. Wood, for example, concluded many years after the event that Lushington ". . . was reckoned more ingenious than prudent, and more apt to display his fancy than to proceed upon solid reason."[37] But the best commentary comes from the preacher himself in one of his passages of self-castigation. Speaking in another sermon of how by obeying one law we inevitably sin against another, Lushington said:

By the law of edification into the law of industry, because it pleased God by the foolishness of preaching to save some, I will come up *ex tempore* and preach foolishly; and by the law of eloquence into the law of edification, because I will show myself mighty in words and extraordinary in composure, I will play the scholar in the guise of a sailor, in the phrase of a soldier, yet speak like Apocalypse, every word a wonder. So I intend it. But the law of zeal would be quite lawless; by that I am deceived in all law, in all human law.[38]

Pembroke College, Pembroke men, worthy Dr. Clayton, and the daring Dr. Lushington, all had a great deal to do with the rest of Browne's life.

Chapter IV

A TRIP
TO
IRELAND

As a young man Browne made two trips abroad: the first, a visit to Ireland with his stepfather; the second, a long sojourn on the continent to study medicine at Europe's leading universities. Actual records of both trips are few, and even the dates are not certain. Although former biographers have concentrated largely on his medical study to the almost complete omission of the trip to Ireland, the Irish experience may have been a turning point in his spiritual life.

The knowledge that Browne did accompany his stepfather Sir Thomas Dutton to Ireland comes from his daughter Mrs. Elizabeth Lyttleton in a single short sentence: "His father-in-law [i.e., his stepfather] shewed him all Ireland in some visitation of the forts and castles."[1] Browne makes two autobiographical references to the island among his several allusions to the common bit of folklore concerning its immunity from snakes. In *Vulgar Errors*, for example, he cites the presence of spiders as one kind of venomous creature there despite its reputation: "Thus most men affirm, and few here will believe the contrary, that there be no Spiders in Ireland: but *we have beheld some in that Country.* . . ."[2] Again, on November 16, 1659, he wrote to Sir William Dugdale concerning anciently burned trees:

"The *like I have often observed in Ireland,* where passing through large *woods I have observed* many hundred trees, burnt at the bottome, the trunke yet standing in many."[3] In addition to these references there is evidence that Browne was never to forget the voyage home.

Still we have to conjecture not only the time at which he went to Ireland but also the length of his stay; and we must somehow fit Browne's Irish journey, his study on the continent, and his medical apprenticeship in England around the dates which are certain in his biography. He got his M.A. from Oxford in June 1629; his M.D. from Leiden in December 1633; in January 1637 he received the Oxford M.D. by incorporation after putting in the four years of apprenticeship required by law, and shortly thereafter moved to Norwich to set up his own practice.

The most likely time for the trip to Ireland would have been after he received his M.A. from Oxford and before he went to the continent, i.e., in the summer of 1629. Sir Edmund Gosse dates it earlier, at the end of 1626, ". . . after the rupture with France, when the coast defences were attracting the attention of a special mission of enquiry."[4] However, Browne's stepfather, in whose company he went to Ireland, was in charge not of coast defenses but of the inland forts. Professor Finch,[5] conjecturing that a year's apprenticeship in Oxfordshire preceded the Irish trip, thinks that Browne must have gone to Ireland in 1630. But we have seen from the account of medical education at Oxford that the M.A. hardly qualified a person to practice medicine anywhere, even as an apprentice. Dr. Johnson placed the trip right after the Oxford M.A.,[6] and so did the careful Wilkin.[7] Leroy[8] follows Wilkin. In short, biographers generally agree that Browne must have gone to Ireland between his Oxford M.A. and his medical education abroad.

How long was Browne in Ireland? The voyage home he himself tells us occurred in late September: "I came once from Dublin to Chester at Michaelmas . . . ,"[9] that is, on or near the English quarter day September 29. A young man intent on studying medicine in Italy would not stay in Ireland for a whole year. Political events in Ireland support my belief that he spent only one summer there, from July until the end of September 1629.

Browne's widowed mother, as we have seen, married Sir Thomas Dutton soon after her first husband's death in 1613; their first child Elizabeth was born in 1622, and another daughter, Lucy, in 1623.[10] In 1629 Dutton was a member of the Royal Council in Ireland under Charles the First as sovereign and Lucius Cary Viscount Falkland (the elder) as lord deputy: he was scoutmaster general in charge of all the inland forts of Ireland. Amidst constant fear of an invasion from Spain in a Roman Catholic country where the English forts were in a state of dilapidation, Browne visited Ireland with his stepfather at a crucial juncture in the relationship between Protestant England and Roman Catholic Ireland. As long before as July 15, 1615, Sir Josias Bodley, then devoting his skill in fortification to the problem of Ireland's defense, complained of lack of money.[11] Nothing was done from London about the ruinous state of the English forts, for on June 19, 1619, the lord deputy started a series of regular petitions to the Crown.[12]

As a key member of the Irish Council Sir Thomas Dutton had been pleading for speedier repair. The May 10, 1620, session of the lord deputy and the council is summarized thus:

Upon receipt of their letters of the 18th of March last, and the proposition there enclosed, presented to His Majesty by Sir Thomas Dutton, concerning the granting in fee-farm the inland forts of this kingdom to the several commanders now holding them, they debated the matter, and now enclose a relation how and by whom the several forts mentioned in their letters are now enjoyed. . . .[13]

There follows an alphabetical list by county of every inland fort in Ireland that Thomas Browne, whatever the exact date, must have visited if we are to believe his daughter's word that he saw "all Ireland on a visitation of the forts" with Sir Thomas Dutton: in the county of Ardmogh, he must have been at Montnorris, Moyrie, and Charlemont; in the county of Cavan, Cloughhowter; in the county of Down, Enishlaghlin, etc. These were all in northern Ireland, Dutton's estate at Roth-cline in Longford, where Browne probably stayed between journeys, being the farthest point south. Though King Charles' Privy Council in London had other worries, Dutton's proposal that all the forts become the individual responsibility of officers motivated by the spoils system seemed to be more successful than his predecessor's method of general complaint.

In 1627, at last convinced of Ireland's strategic importance vis-à-vis both France and Spain, the English Privy Council increased the English forces in Ireland to 5000 foot and 500 horse at a cost of over 64,000 pounds per year. Falkland, more scared than ever of the Roman Catholics, wrote on December 20, 1627: "They account us heretics, and will not lose an opportunity of cutting our throats"[14]—a grimly accurate prophecy. Falkland, the husband of a devout and determined Roman Catholic lady, enclosed a three-page memorandum on "the attempt to convert Protestants to the Church of Rome in Ireland," which ends on this note: "These and other suspicions are now proved true . . . and show the danger we run, unless some alteration of hand be in time held towards the seducer of his

Majesty's people. I mean the traitorous locusts of Rome, by name the Jesuits and Franciscans."[15]

Falkland wanted to banish them. The lords of the established Church of England in Ireland assembled on April 22, 1627, at Christchurch, Dublin, to vote for nontoleration. Dr. Downham, bishop of Derry, read out the judgment from the pulpit and asked the assembly of divines and civil authorities to say "Amen" to it if they approved: "Suddenly the whole Church was almost shaked with the great sound their loud Amens made."[16] The bishop then preached his prepared sermon on the text: "That he would grant us, that we being delivered out of the hands of our enemies might serve him without fear" (Luke 1:74).

The climax of this mounting bitterness in Ireland coincided with the young Browne's leaving Oxford in the summer of 1629. In July of that year orders went out to suppress all Popish colleges and all foreign jurisdiction. These violent measures were made possible through the signing of the Peace of Suza with France in May 1629. In return for the withdrawal of English support of the French Protestants in La Rochelle during the 1627-28 siege, Richelieu abandoned the Roman Catholics in Ireland to their own devices.[17] Only Spain was left, and in the tense period of the cold war Sir Thomas Dutton wrote from Dublin on December 20, 1629, urging the king to maintain situations of strength:

Except for the northern settlements, the whole of Ireland is now more addicted to Popery than it was in the time of Queen Elizabeth. Where there were only two or three Jesuits or Schoolmen in a town, there are now forty or fifty. The nobility and gentry have private priests of their own. If the Jesuits and Schoolmen were well banished the other secular orders would soon conform, especially in Dublin, where the influence of the Pale Protestants is strongly felt. If the captains are made to take the Oaths of

Supremacy and Allegiance often, and if the horse are kept
strong (100 horse here are worth 2000 foot) all may be
well. . . . The Gospel should be planted here [Connaught,
Glins, and Ranelagh] while Spain is so busy abroad that
the ill-affected cannot hope for her or the Pope's aid.[18]

In less than a week after this letter was written,
that is on December 26, 1629, the English civil authorities, backed by the Anglican bishops, conducted a raid
on the Carmelite religious establishment in Dublin.
This so infuriated the Irish that a mob of three thousand
stoned (appropriately enough on St. Stephen's Day)
the representatives of English civil and religious authority. Four days after the riot Browne's stepfather in
Dublin wrote Lord Dorchester in London: "Order is
restored, but the danger of conniving Papists has now
been made clear. A Catholic rebellion now would be
fraught with terrible danger, for both the commoners
and the soldiers in the King's pay are Papists. In Ireland
they are in a majority of 40 to 1. Ireland is the back
door to England and must be carefully guarded."[19] On
April 4, 1630, Dutton wrote directly to King Charles:

Unless the Papists and seminary schools are rooted out
and destroyed, it will be impossible to plant the Gospel
here. The noble families make their sons priests and their
daughters nuns. There are titulary Bishops in every diocese,
and priests in every parish to execute jurisdiction, say mass,
and keep schools. The Bishops remember to take their
tithes, but they allow the churches to fall to the ground.
The clergy in all places lead scandalous lives; they are
ignorant, and, on both sides, so extortionate that they have
beggared the country. The admitting of recusants to be
justices and captains weakens the Government greatly.
These Papists foreswear themselves in juries and sway all
causes throughout the Kingdom.
I hope I may still have my company. When I left
England my debts were 2,500 l. which I hope your Majesty
will confer on me.[20]

Dutton had been promised this company of horse on November 7, 1628, when his majesty ordered his arrears paid "and also the next company of horse or foot that shall be vacant in Ireland."[21] The horse were assigned to him providentially soon when, as we are told in a communication dated December 3, 1628, Sir James Blount drowned in a shipwreck on the Irish Sea, proverbial for its storms.[22] Finally, on May 24, 1630, the council recorded that Dutton had received his company of horse through having been "appointed over the head" of Sir John Clotworthy,[23] who had been indiscreet enough to allow the Presbyterian congregation to hold its meetings in his fort.

Browne's stepfather seemed to be able to get what he wanted without great gifts in diplomacy. He was always in debt, was desperate for favor, irascible. Though he quarreled with Captain St. George over the administration of the fort at Carickdrumrush,[24] however, he did not forget those under him: in a letter written October 24, 1624, for "the payment of his entertainment," he desired a lieutenant's place for the bearer, "his old soldier."[25] He was described by Elizabeth Lyttleton, who must have heard her father often speak of him, as "a worthy person, who had great places."[26]

Hence the biographical custom[27] of connecting Browne's verses on dueling[28] with Thomas Birch's 1760 account[29] of Dutton's killing Sir Hatton Cheke on Calais sands in 1610 seems slightly remote, despite Dutton's apparent habit of telling everyone about it. Surely the religious riot in Dublin on St. Stephen's Day, 1629, following so closely the time that Browne was with his stepfather in Ireland—and his stepfather was mainly responsible for the English—was more important to Thomas Browne, B.A., M.A., Oxon., than a duel fought by a stranger when Browne was a five-year-old child in a comfortable mercer's home in Cheapside, London.

Sir Thomas Dutton returned from this exciting tour of duty in Ireland in June 1631; at least, on December 20, 1630, he wrote to Dorchester that he hoped to return to England the following June.[30] He died on May 16, 1634, just when Browne was composing his first work, *Religio Medici*. That book holds strong views on the toleration of Catholics, as though the young man were repudiating his stepfather's whole reactionary philosophy after a trip to Ireland intended perhaps to let him see how dangerous the Roman Catholics really were. The young doctor's joining one metaphor of risking one's life upon dangerous seas in a worn-out ship to another metaphor of close combat at sword's point is arresting, in a passage that pleads for peace between the two main branches of the Christian communion:

Yet have I not so shaken hands with those desperate Resolutions, who had rather venture at large their decaied bottome, then bring her in to be new trim'd in the dock; who had rather promiscuously retaine all, then abridge any, and obstinately be what they are, then what they have beene, as to stand in diameter and swords point with them: we have reformed from them [Roman Catholics], not against them; for omitting those improperations and termes of scurrility betwixt us, which onely difference our affections, and not our cause, there is between us one common name and appellation, one faith, and necessary body of principles common to us both; and therefore I am not scrupulous to converse and live with them, to enter their Churches in defect of ours, and either pray with them, or for them . . . we being all Christians, and not divided by such detested impieties as might prophane our prayers, or the place wherein we make them; . . . .[31]

Browne had returned from Ireland at Michaelmas, that is, at the end of September, most probably 1629, while the religious crisis just described was mounting. During the voyage home across the Irish Sea he providentially escaped from death by drowning. Well over fifty years later, he recalls the event in a letter to his daughter Elizabeth in Guernsey: "I came once from Dublin to Chester at Michaelmas and was so tossed, that nothing but milk and Possets would goe down with me 2 or 3 days after. . . ."[32] Twice in a context of storms at sea in these letters to Elizabeth he remembers his younger son, the seagoing Thomas, who as far as we know had met death by drowning in the service of his country. The letter just quoted, of September 15, 1681, was written in response to one from Elizabeth that described a shipwreck on her island coast; she had watched several persons lose their lives. Immediately before his recollection of seasickness Sir Thomas writes: "Yr Brother Thomas went once from Yarmouth in the evening and arrived at the Isle of White the next day at one a Clock in the afternoon, but it was with such a wind, that he was never so sick at sea as at that time." Only three months before penning this, that is, in June 1681, Sir Thomas had written to Elizabeth:

You discribed yr voyage very Prettyly; the Casquets are very noted rocks and infamous for many Misfortunes; yr Brother Thomas who had very experimentall knowledge of the Channell between England and France would speak often of them and of Sark and other Islands. Almighty God is omnipotent everywhere in his Mercys; have not a doubtfull opinion of us that we shall ever forget you . . . God Bless you both.[33]

Can we read the association of ideas in these letters: storms at sea, shipwrecks, my son Thomas' death by drowning (God rest the lad's soul), God's providence to me on my voyage home from Ireland?

Thomas Browne composed a poem at the Crow Inn in Chester, not two miles from his paternal ancestors' home, immediately after his perilous voyage in late

September. We have two versions of it. One, in Browne's handwriting of many years later, is headed: ". . . upon a Tempest I was in on the Irish seas. . . ." The other, his daughter's more complete copy of the poem Browne had some difficulty in remembering, is identified as: "writt by my Father at the Crowe Inne in Chester at his Coming from Ireland."[34] Measured by Milton's standards set only a few years later on the occasion of the actual drowning in the same sea of a young man named Edward King, it is not much of a poem. Browne at twenty-four or so had not yet discovered his gifts in prose, and he was far more devout in his doctrine of Providence than happy in his poetic conceits and octosyllabic couplets:

> Whither yea angry winds! what breath
> is this that whistles nought but death?
> what furie or malicious hagge
> hath now let Loose the Aeolian bag?
> the waves swell high, the surges reare
> as though each man a Jonas were:
> the watry Element doth Aspire
> as tho it would be next to fire,
> and mounts aloft at every flash
> as tho t'would give the Sun a dash.
> no more could doubt who this did see
> whither sea or Land the highest bee,
> but Laugh at that Poetick knack
> Of Arion on a Dolpins back.
> all things by the wind were throwne
> as tho the thirtie two had blowne.
> what Paines thou takest, great god, to drowne
> those who are nothing at thy frowne.
> the Careful steersman Looks about
> whither hee be or his Compas out,
> And fearfully beholds in's glass
> how his Latest hower doth Pass.
> In vayne we do the Pilot coart:
> the bottome of the sea's our Port.
> no Anckers in the sea wee cast;

our Ancker is in heaven fast.
our only hopes on him wee Laye
to whom both Seas and winds obeye.

Back from the continent five years later as an M.D.
setting down his thoughts on religion, Browne asserted:
"I have been shipwrackt, yet am not enemy with the sea
or winds; I can study, play, or sleepe in a tempest."[35]
Again he confessed—this young man who had been
born in the leaden hour of Saturn under the deathly
sign of Scorpio (he called it "Watry Scorpio")—that
he was not so much afraid of death as ashamed of it.
This conceit ". . . hath in a tempest disposed and left
me willing to be swallowed in the abysse of waters,
wherein I had perished, unseene, unpityed. . . ."[36]

I conclude that the religious strife he had witnessed
in Ireland with his stepfather, combined with his
miraculous escape from drowning in the Irish Sea,
formed a turning point in his religious experience.
When he saw his *Religio Medici* piratically printed in
1642 with a frontispiece by Will Marshall of a man
falling from a high rock into the sea and the left arm
of God grasping him firmly by the wrist, with the words
"A coelo salus"—salvation from heaven—he was not
displeased. He kept the same bookseller for his authorized version, and in the artist's graphic summary of
the book's doctrine only changed a Latin word to the
variant form "caelo."

Chapter V

MEDICAL
STUDY
ABROAD

Browne studied medicine at the universities of Montpellier, Padua, and Leiden, and received his M.D. degree at Leiden in December 1633. But just when he
started on this journey and how long he stayed at each
of these three universities is left, again, to conjecture. If
a young man entering upon the study of medicine after
his master of arts were to remain at home rather than
go abroad, he would take three years to achieve the
baccalaureate in medicine and four more for the doctorate. The advantage in going abroad was not in a saving
of time but in the superiority of instruction and the
general education gained from travel. According to the
Caroline Code at Oxford, put strictly into operation in
1636 though codifying previous practice, the M.D. degree from a foreign university was considered the
equivalent of the Oxford or Cambridge baccalaureate,
the initial degree in a new field.[1] The absolute minimum
time abroad, then, for the Leiden M.D. to be recognized
in England would have been three years. Browne, however, was slow in maturing; his interest in the languages,
customs, histories, and religious practices of various
countries took him far beyond a narrow professional
degree; and his educational birthright had been guaranteed, apparently in time, by the Orphans' Court.

It seems very probable, therefore, that Browne stayed on the continent for four years instead of the legal three. If so, he started out in the late autumn of 1629 after recuperating, presumably at his mother's home in Isleworth, from his tempestuous voyage on the Irish Sea.

The usual tour called for a crossing to Calais by ship, then an overland trip by coach, with a stopover in Paris, to Montpellier in the south. But Browne ended his European tour at Leiden (whence Englishmen usually came home the shortest way, from the Hook to Yarmouth), and he mentions having been in La Rochelle.[2] Probably he sailed from Plymouth around Brittany, halfway down the French coast to La Rochelle, then proceeded overland to Montpellier on the Mediterranean coast. He must have visited other countries besides France, Italy, and Holland, since he mentions having seen circumcisions performed at Vienna.[3]

Because a man's letters are not usually saved until he becomes famous, those of Browne which we would most cherish are lost. From what we know of his habits of observation and note-taking, this loss is grievous indeed. Partial reparation would be the finding of his own copy of Fynes Moryson's *Itinerary* (London, 1617), which was sold with his library in 1710.[4] This book, a popular guide for the seventeenth-century English traveler, contains Moryson's account of ten years of travel through Germany, Switzerland, Holland, Denmark, Poland, France, and Italy. Browne also owned[5] a 1629 octavo published in Rouen called *Description de la France, Allemagne, Italie & Espagne*. Since he casually notes that he could speak six languages,[6] he must also have bought dictionaries during his trip. Among the many left in his library was a 1598 copy of John Florio's *A World of Words, or most copious and exact Dictionary in Italian and English*. One of his favorites must have been John Minsheu's *Dictionary of Nine Lan-*

guages, of which he owned the second, folio, edition (1627).[7] This polyglot contained words in English, Dutch, German, French, Italian, Spanish, Latin, Greek, and Hebrew. And apropos of his lingual boast, he owned[8] a 1631 octavo published at Rouen entitled *Le Dictionnaire des 6 Langages Lat. Flam. Franc. Esp. Ital. & Anglois.*

That the young Browne was a sober, God-fearing expatriate comes to us from a letter to his daughter Elizabeth of October 1681: "When I travaild beyond sea I resolved to my best Power to doe nothing that should trouble my mind when I returnd in to my own Country."[9] This experience of the wider world seemed quite natural to him and nothing to be particularly proud of:

I have not onely seene severall Countries, beheld the nature of their climes, the Chorography of their Provinces, Topography of their Cities, but understand their severall Lawes, Customes and Policies; yet cannot all this persuade the dulnesse of my spirit unto such an opinion of my self, as I behold in nimbler and conceited heads, that never looked a degree beyond their nests.[10]

Boasting and not boasting in the same breath, Browne says that he became so much a *citoyen du monde* that he could digest with no insular qualms all foods, customs, and languages:

. . . I am of a constitution so generall, that it consorts and sympathizeth with all things; I have no antipathy, or rather Idiosyncrasie, in dyet, humour, ayre, any thing; I wonder not at the *French* for their dishes of frogges, snailes, and toadstooles, nor at the Jewes for Locusts and Grassehoppers, but being amongst them, make them my common viands; and I find they agree with my stomach as well as theirs. . . . Those national repugnancies doe not touch me, nor doe I behold with prejudice the *French, Italian, Spaniard, or Dutch;* but where I finde their actions in ballance with my Countreymens, I honour, love, and embrace them in the same degree; . . . .[11]

Only a long residence abroad could lead such a man to inveigh against the easy stereotypes with which many people prejudge their fellow men of a different country: ". . . wherein by opprobrious Epithets wee miscall each other, and by an uncharitable Logicke, from a disposition in a few conclude a habit in all."[12]

Of Browne's actual life in France we know very little. The Pembroke manuscript of *Religio Medici* contains an autobiographical passage: Browne argued against the conclusion that Sarah showed unusual respect to Abraham by calling him "Lord" on the grounds that this is no more than "Seignior" or "Monsieur": ". . . the ordinary languages all civill nations use in their familiar compellations. . . ."[13] Browne advised his fourteen-year-old son Thomas on his first trip abroad to put off that *pudor rusticus*—as well as to learn French and attend Protestant churches— ". . . and Practise an handsome garb and Civil boldness wch he that learneth not in France travaileth in vain."[14] Again, in *A Letter to a Friend* he mentions having seen children in the south-France province in which Montpellier is located suffering from the disease of "Morgellons": ". . . as I long ago observed in that endemial Distemper of little Children in Languedock. . . ."[15] And he cites the Provençal name for the praying mantis, "Prega Diou."[16]

At the University of Montpellier, well described by Leroy,[17] Browne must have listened to the great Lazare Rivière, professor there from 1622 to 1655, whose *Praxis* was for years a leading textbook in diagnostics in Europe.[18] In 1646 Browne referred to him as Riverius in his letter to Power on how best to lay a foundation for the study of medicine.[19]

Padua was the attraction that was drawing this young student to the continent, particularly for the study of anatomy—in the great tradition of Vesalius, Fabrizio d'Acquapendente, and Harvey.[20] It is most likely that he was at Padua for the longest time during his stay abroad, despite the plagues that raged intermittently in Italy. But no more than at Montpellier is there any record even of his name in the registers there. Thomas Coryat, visiting Padua in 1608, casts some light ɔn the spirit of the place:

I heard that when the number of the Students is full, there are at least one thousand five hundred here: the principall faculties that are professed in the University being Physicke and the civill law: and more students of forraine and remote nations doe live in Padua, then in any one University of Christendome. For hither come in many from France, high Germany, the Netherlands, England, &c. who with great desire flocke together to Padua for good letters sake, as to a fertile nursery of learning. For indeed it hath bred many famous and singular learned men within these hundred yeares, and a little more . . . that have greatly beautified the CommonWeale of learning.[21]

While obviously applying himself well to the study of physic at Padua, Browne never gave up his interest in religion:

I remember [he wrote in *Religio Medici*] a Doctor in Physick of Italy, who could not perfectly believe the immortality of the soule, because *Galen* seemed to make a doubt thereof. With another I was familiarly acquainted in France, a Divine, and a man of singular parts, that on the same point was so plunged and gravelled with three lines of *Seneca*, that all our Antidotes, drawne from both Scripture and Philosophy, could not expel the poyson of his errour.[22]

It seems likely that a friendly argument on the interpretation of Acts 12:15 also took place either in Italy or France: "This exposition I once suggested to a young Divine, that answered upon this point to which I remember the *Franciscan* Opponent replyed no more, but, That it was a new, and no authentick interpretation."[23] Another argument on textual interpretation seems to have taken place during his student days abroad: ". . . t'is an absurdity, and an affirmative that is not expressed in the text. . . . With this paradoxe I remember I netled an angrie Jesuite who had that day let this fall in his sermon, who afterwards, upon a serious perusall of the text, confessed my opinion, and prooved a courteous friend to mee, a stranger, and noe enemy."[24]

Besides this amateur interest in theology, the young Englishman must have satisfied in Italy his lifelong passion for the visual arts. Not given to quoting Spenser or Shakespeare (though he quotes Dante often), Browne nevertheless was certainly not blind to beauty. The passage on music is famous.[25] But it was with painting and sculpture that he seemed most to satisfy his aesthetic hunger. And here he held, in common with many others in the Renaissance, a double view: when the artist depicts nature, he must be true to it, but shining through that truth is another truth—in the spirit of the artist and even of God the creator. For example, Sir John Davies (a Winchester man) connected optics, painting, and the mystic conceptions of light in *Nosce Teipsum* (1599):

> Thus we see how the Soule doth vse the eyes,
> As instruments of her quicke power of sight;
> Hence do th'Arts *opticke* and faire *painting* rise:
> *Painting*, which doth all gentle minds delight.[26]

Exact representation came first, and the Renaissance joined great art with anatomy. In Germany Dürer had produced his *Vier Bücher von Menslicher Proportion* (1528); Professor Panofsky, commenting on it, implies that since in the Renaissance art became the imitation of nature rather than of other art, the artist is the first true natural scientist.[27] Dutch painters reflected the manners and tastes of a people interested in medicine: the sick room, the surgeon, the alchemist, and the quack. Later, in England, Christopher Wren was hired to make the drawings for Dr. Willis' epochal book on the human brain. In Italy, Leonardo da Vinci collaborated with Della Torre; Michelangelo took lessons from Columbus Realdus; Paolo Veronese designed the frontispiece for Realdus' *Anatomy*, and De Calcar, Flemish pupil of Titian, did the plates for Vesalius. De Musis of Venice illustrated Eustachius' tubes; and Giulio Cesario, one of Harvey's teachers at Padua's medical school, hired Correggio (some say) to illustrate his *Tabulae Anatomicae* (1627). "I can looke a whole day with delight upon a handsome Picture," cries Browne, "though it be but of an Horse."[28] Leonardo made his horse only after months of anatomical dissection.[29] In Italy the young English medical student could see with his own eyes the truth of the horse's skeleton or of the human body and behind that truth the creative wonder.

As Galen had written to a young man, "I notice indeed that you do not venture to lay out anything in things of beauty . . . ,"[30] so Browne filled his later letters to his children with encouragement to sketch whatever they saw and to "limn with colours." In 1679 he congratulated his son Edward on being able to visit Cobham Hall, whose ". . . gallery with so many excellent pictures must needs bee recreative. . . ."[31] When the same boy was traveling through Europe, he was advised by his father to be sure to see ". . . the green jaspar color'd Tomb at Larissa in the barbers shop."[32] His family was friendly with that of the Earl of Arundel, owners of the Arundel marbles. Browne himself loved medals, coins, and plaques not merely for their history but for their beauty; and he pored over the title pages of his books, especially when they were "adorned with sculptures." God to him is often the artist, poised with a pencil in His mighty hand. He loved Hermes Trismegistus' description of this world as a picture of the invisible, ". . . wherein, as in a pourtract, things are not truely, but in equivocall shapes, and as they counterfeit some more reall substance in that invisible fabrick."[33] The very metaphor he used for the human body, *fabric*, not only echoes Vesalius' title *De Fabrica Corporis Humani* but means God the creator as a builder, an artist, a technician; hence "these walls of flesh" starts an image of architecture. As Bulwer-Lytton remarked, it is in the "poetical spirit of painting thoughts that Browne often conveys to us his meaning."[34]

From Padua Browne went to Leiden, as the custom was, to take the medical degree from a Protestant university, since he intended to practice in England. Although some previous biographers give Leiden as much importance as Padua in Browne's growth, a recent tendency has been to minimize it to a mere formality.[35] He did matriculate there on December 3, 1633,[36] and only eighteen days after was examined for the degree: "Acta Sen. 1633. Dec. 21. Visus est dignus Thomas Browne, cui supremus in Medicina gradus conferatur, quem illi tribuit Adolphus Vorstius."[37] There is little doubt that Browne, as well as many other Englishmen, was given the degree for work accomplished elsewhere. Yet it seems likely that, though he did not stay at Leiden as long as he stayed at Padua, nevertheless he stayed there much longer than three weeks. For one thing, a student might go through with the matriculation and pay his fee not at the beginning of his residence but toward the very end in final candidacy for the degree itself. And too, Leiden was the child of Padua in medicine and coming up fast: Browne could profit from a stay there of some duration. Finally, the atmosphere was congenial. He seems to have absorbed more of its Protestant and democratic air than any student could possibly absorb in only three weeks.

John Evelyn, matriculating at Leiden on September 6, 1641, described the event in these terms: ". . . I . . . was matriculated by the then Magnificus Professor who first in Latine demanded of me where my Lodging in the Towne was; my Name, Age, Birth; & to what faculty I addicted my self; then recording my Answers in a Booke, he administered an Oath to me. . . ."[38] That the custom may have been to postpone this formality until the end of one's stay may be shown by the example of John Spenser, who matriculated on September 14, 1634, and received his M.D. two days later on September 16, 1634. Browne had been in town long enough to acquire a residence, first discovered for us by Leroy in 1931. He lived at the home of Richardus Monck in the "Son-neveltsteeg." The *rector magnificus* who administered the oath to him was Antonius Thysius, who died in 1640. Among Browne's medical student friends may well have been three contemporary Londoners: William Smith, John Buggs, and John Hinton. The last one was later knighted, and the first two practiced medicine in Norwich after Browne had become established there. Two other English contemporaries at Leiden's medical school were Samuel Remington, a Norwich man, and John Robinson, Jr., the son of the pastor of the Pilgrim Fathers' church in Leiden. It was this junior Robinson who later animadverted on Browne's *Vulgar Errors* in *Endoxa . . . A Calm Ventilation* (1656).

Founded as late as 1575, Leiden's medical school drew two professors from Padua, Peter Forrest and Gerard de Bontius, to establish the medical library and the herbal garden. Their earliest English student, John

James of Cambridge, received the second medical degree the university granted, in 1578.[39] A pupil of Acquapendente at Padua, Pieter Paaw (1564-1617), taught both anatomy and botany at Leiden and built the anatomical theater there in 1597. Years later Browne remembered to write his son Edward that "Peter Pau, a famous professor of Leyden," had dissected a *gulo*.[40] Paaw's pupil, Dr. Tulpius (1593-1674), posed for the central figure in the famous anatomical scene painted by Rembrandt in 1632. Leiden attracted so many medical students from England that by 1607 the university began to publish in English a list of the chief rarities in the public theater and anatomy hall. The school was visited by such famous professors as the Danish Olaus Wormius (1588-1654), whose *Monumenta et Antiquitates* Browne relied upon in the second chapter of *Urn Burial*. Bauhin (1560-1624), who taught at Basel, also visited Leiden, and Browne owned several of his books on botany.[41]

This was an age of versatile men in medicine. Kaspar Bartholin (1585-1629), for example, like Wormius a Dane, studied under Acquapendente at Padua and under Bauhin at Basel, became professor of philosophy at Basel, of anatomy at Naples, of Greek at Montpellier, and at Copenhagen professor first of eloquence, then of medicine, and finally of theology.[42] Bartholin's *Controversiae Anatomicae ac affines nobiliores ac rariores* Browne owned [43] in the 1631 Gosling edition, but his favorite copy of this book—"Bartolinus his [six] *Centuries of rarer Observations*" was "in 3 volumes in 12° or a small octavo ... I cannot bee without [them]."[44] That Browne kept up with the medical faculty at Leiden is shown by his citation of a 1636 operation by the Leiden professor Daniel Beckerus, who removed an iron knife from a man's stomach after allegedly attracting it into a convenient position by means of a powdered loadstone poultice.[45] And one reason why Browne early accepted Harvey's hypothesis on the blood might have been that Waleus, or Jan de Wale (1604-49), only one year Browne's senior and a celebrated professor of anatomy at Leiden, experimentally, though partially, confirmed Harvey's findings.

Browne received the degree of M.D. at Leiden from Professor Adolph Vorstius on December 21, 1633, after defending a thesis in public. The formalities that accompanied the degree were expensive. According to John Ward's *Diary*: "Mr Burnet had a letter out of the Low Countries of the charge of a doctor's degree which is at Leiden about L 16 besides feasting the professors; at Angiers in France not above L 9, and feasting not necessary either."[46] This merrymaking may have given James Howell the amiable impression that Leiden was all play and no work; in his May 30, 1619, letter to Dr. Thomas Pritchard of Jesus College, Oxford, he described the various *nationes* there, the largest one being German, and added: "A small time and lesse learning will suffice to make one a Graduate. . . ."[47]

Certainly the M.D. thesis was slight, with a fulsome dedication to the professor and a modest vita of the student. The British Museum has a whole volume of such theses, mostly with Vorstius' name on them as the examining professor. One such is *De Lue Venerea* defended by a Mr. Libergen of the Hague on December 1, 1621; it consists of twenty-six propositions printed on five pages. The thesis of Thomas Browne is lost, Innes Smith thinks in a fire; but ironically that of his future adversary John Robinson is in the British Museum: *De Purgatione quas favente D.O.M.*, dated March 22, 1628/9, presided over by Professor Ewaldo Schrevelio, and consisting of four printed pages of seventeen separate propositions.

We do not know what Browne's thesis subject was.

For a time it was thought to be *De Lue Venerea* because Gui Patin in France, after reading the Latin *Religio Medici* of 1644, said that this Englishman Browne had written his thesis at Leiden on syphilis.[48] But in 1703 Jean Astruc could remember no one except Patin ever mentioning such a thesis by Browne.[49] Dr. A. Kessen, bibliothecary at Leiden, writes in a personal letter on May 16, 1953: "I do not know anything of a fire that destroyed theses, but the Senate's secretary from 1610 to 1654, Daniel Heinsius, being very careless in keeping them, there are hardly any theses preserved from this period." I believe the Patin suggestion to be a case of mistaken identity. Two years before Patin could have read the Latin *Religio Medici*, that is in 1642, a young Englishman named Robert Wright, protégé of Dr. Baldwin Hamey of London, had defended his thesis *De Lue Venerea* with such brilliance that Professor Vorstius wrote to Hamey about it.[50] Patin may very well have heard this piece of medical faculty gossip and have confused two Englishmen, one who had recently received a brilliant degree from Vorstius for a thesis on syphilis, and one who, having become a *doctor medicinae* under Vorstius eleven years before, was the author of the interesting book he had just read on a doctor's religion.[51] If Browne's thesis still exists, a good place to look for it might be among works on generation.

In addition to the student life and good instruction at Leiden, Browne must have relished its theological and political atmosphere. Arminius, whose thoughts *contra* Calvinism had crept into Browne's mind at Oxford, had been a student of Zabarella at Padua before he taught theology at Leiden. Hugo Grotius, whose views *contra* Socinianism had helped protect Browne's English religion, had returned in 1631 from his exile in France to the accompaniment of Dutch national rejoicing. A theologian at Leiden in Browne's own day was Joannes Polyander a Kerckhoven (1558-1646), who not only was a Remonstrant *contra* Calvinism but also wrote a book *contra* Socinus. Browne composed a memorial poem in five stanzas for this religious teacher, whom he must have known for more than three weeks:

> Difference in Church or State
> hee did calmely Temperate,
> and quarrell'd with the same mind
> with which other men are kind.
>
> . . .
> to Rich and poore an equall freind
> who lov'd all, yet lov'd none for end.
> Peace hee gave oft the wounded Mind:
> Peace now lett his Ashes find.[52]

Had Browne gone to him for his own "wounded mind"? And if it were not the theological atmosphere of Protestant Holland, would not Browne have drunk in Holland's air of political liberty? And can anyone imagine Browne's passion for languages satisfied with a mere three-week stay among people who spoke, thought, and felt more like Englishmen than any he had associated with for three years?

On the continent Browne went to various places, met people, learned their customs and languages, watched with emotion their religious processions, and engaged in friendly disputes on the usual student topics. But the *raison d'être* of his four years abroad finally was to acquire the fundamentals of medicine which he could not get at Oxford, but which he did get at Montpellier, Padua, and Leiden. Perhaps the best way to demonstrate this is to read again the letter[53] which he wrote after he had been engaged for ten years in successful medical practice in Norwich to young Henry

Power on how best to prepare oneself to become a doctor. Read first, Browne said, "the fathers and fountains of the faculty"—Hippocrates and Galen, whom he had well begun at Oxford. Next, he advised, learn your anatomy. The texts he cites were all in his library: Galen and Hippocrates, of course; Vesalius' *De Fabrica*, the 1555 edition with plates as well as the 1551 edition published at Leiden by Fuchsius; Adrian van Spieghel, known in Padua as Spigelius, the *De Humani Corporis Fabrica* with plates of 1627; Kaspar Bartholin, the *Controversiae Anatomicae* of 1631; and Harvey's *De Motu Cordis*, popularly known as *De Circulatione Sanguinis*, of 1628. All these for anatomy, the "fidus Achates" of the physician. There follows a long bibliography in botany and *materia medica*: Dioscorides and Theophrastus, two classics Browne owned in sixteenth-century editions; Matthiolus' *Epistalae Medicinales* (Leiden, 1564); Dodonaeus' *Herbal*, which he owned in a 1574 edition; Spigelius' *Isagoge in rem herbarium*, in Browne's library both as a 1606 quarto and a 1633 octavo; and Wecker's *Antidotarium Generale*, which he owned in a 1585 Basel quarto.

All this time Power should be reading Fallopius (Browne owned the 1600 Frankfort edition of *Omnia Opera*) and Fabricius d'Acquapendente of Padua: of the latter Browne owned the 1600 work on the eyes, voice, and ears; the work on surgery of 1619; the work on breathing of 1625; and the collected anatomical works of 1625. In chemistry, which Browne had come upon at Leiden, Power should concentrate on the *Tiroconium Chymicum* and then read the *Institutes* of Daniel Sennertus (d. 1637) two or three times over. Useful in chemistry also are Henricus Crollius (1611) and his contemporary Johann Hartmann of Marburg. For learning how to apply all this theory to practice, Browne recommends that Power read Sennertus again, whose *De Chymior consensus et diffensu* Browne owned in a Paris 1633 folio. Next read Jean Fernel, "the French Galen," whose *Cosmotheorie* of 1528 he owned; and Rivière, Browne's professor at Montpellier. For reference he recommends Matthias Moronus' *Directorum Medico Practicum*. And be sure to learn Greek, Browne adds, with some help from Gorreus' medical dictionary, which he owned in a 1625 folio.

It may well be that Dr. Browne was old-fashioned; indeed young Power wrote back that Descartes and Du Roy, called Regius in Latin (neither of whom Browne mentioned), were the only two that answered his doubts on anatomy. The point is that most of the books Browne prescribed from his own library in 1647 are—by their authors, titles, and dates of publication—books which he himself could have learned medicine from at Montpellier, Padua, and Leiden between the fall of 1629 and December 1633.

This is his own summary of the years of formal medical training on the continent. The real impact emerges informally from the rest of his life and work.

Chapter VI

BROWNE AND THE WORLD OF SCIENCE

Most scientists since Newton have separated their problems from those of ultimate causation, but in the seventeenth century men of science still posited God as primary cause and nature as a series of secondary causes. Browne never pursued science to the point of pushing God out of the universe he so passionately contemplated. Hence so much argument about why Dr. Browne was not a member of the Royal Society[1] hardly gives us a view of the impact science made upon the man. This we shall try to assess first by describing how the two major sciences, astronomy and biology, appealed to him as avenues to the macrocosm of God's great universe and the microcosm of himself; then by discussing the reputation for atheism that medical science had; and finally by seeing how Browne as a Christian accepted both the knowledge and the means of knowing that the "new philosophy" gave him.[2]

ASTRONOMY

Not piety, as it is commonly believed, but common sense made many people doubt the Copernican theory.[3] The Ptolemaic system accounted for all the known celestial phenomena with just as high a degree of accuracy. And if science insisted on observation, sensory testimony favored the earth's being the more massive and the heavens the more ethereal. Before Galileo's telescope showed these heavenly bodies to be also heavy masses like the earth, one would well conclude that the earth stays still, and "airy" forms float around it. Such a view was strengthened by the hierarchical system of the four elements, from earth, through water, through fire, through air, up to the quintessence—almost an airy nothingness.

That people changed their minds was a victory for the new science as it was for the essential rightness of some traditional views. Aristotle's law that nature performs her work simply and efficiently (*natura nihil agit frustra*)—to Browne the only "indisputable axiome" in philosophy[4]—argued for the Copernican thesis. A reduction from the eighty epicycles of the Ptolemaic system to the thirty-four of Copernicus appealed to simplicity and harmony.

To accept the mathematical reasoning of Copernicus against the testimony of the senses, however, meant that there must have been an alternative to the prevailing Aristotelian interpretation of physical phenomena. There was just such an alternative, in the rising tide of Pythagorean and Neoplatonic mathematics. Geometry had dealt with shapes that could be drawn and seen to be real. But with algebra, the sides that "squared" a given line were taken away and a small superscript "2" placed there instead. When a given line went down before an "x" and "x^2" represented what used to be an actual square, the reasoning mind was set above the seeing eye. During the growth of Neoplatonism the most popular work of Plato was the *Timaeus*, which is mathematical. Copernicus the Pole, thinking that the universe might be fundamentally mathematical in its structure, went to Italy in 1496 to

work with the bold Pythagorean Dominico Novara
(1454-1504). Soon mathematics and Christian Neoplatonism joined in Nicholas of Cusa, Marsilio Ficino,
and Pico della Mirandola.

To Galileo (1564-1642), who criticized Gilbert
the father of magnetism for being insufficiently grounded in mathematics, the Copernican theory was the
prime example of the victory of pure reason over sense
perception:

I cannot sufficiently admire the eminence of those men's
wits, that received and held it to be true, and with the
sprightliness of their judgments offered such violence to
their own senses, as that they have been able to prefer that
which their reason dictated to them, to that which sensible
experiments represented most manifestly to the contrary
. . . I cannot find any bounds for my admiration, how that
reason was able in Aristarchus and Copernicus to commit
such a rape on their senses, as in despite thereof to make
herself mistress of their credulity.[5]

When Galileo used the word "nature," he gave it a
religious meaning imparted to it by Christian Neoplatonism: God the creative geometrician thought into
this universe a rigorous mathematical necessity. Thus
Galileo still set theology above science:

Profound considerations of this sort belong to a higher
science than ours. We must be satisfied to belong to that
class of less worthy workmen who procure from the quarry
the marble out of which, later, the gifted sculptor pro-
duces those masterpieces which lay hidden in this rough
and shapeless exterior.[6]

Kepler in 1609 as a mathematician studied the
Copernican theory to discover other harmonies and the
"fuller knowledge of God through nature." Convinced

that God had created the universe in accordance with the principle of perfect numbers, Kepler worked in favor of the Copernican hypothesis in order to furnish the cause of things in a Mind that thought creatively in number, size, motion, and harmony. His "new science" was not unmixed with an ancient Zoroastrian tradition concerning the centrality of the sun.

Between the Ptolemaic system, based on ordinary observation as far as it went, and the Copernican system, almost purely mathematical, lay, as it were, the Tychonic. Tycho Brahe (1546-1601) kept accurate records of his telescopic observations, but at the same time held on to Pythagorean notions of perfect spheres. He made the earth central only to the orbits of the sun, moon, and fixed stars. The sun revolves around the earth each day carrying in its own train all the planets. The sun, therefore, he conceived as central to Mercury, Venus, Mars, Jupiter, and Saturn, a picture that seems to lie behind Vaughan's "I saw Eternity the other night/Like a great ring of pure and endless light."

Despite these bright visions, however, the new astronomy worked against poetry and religion. It implied that the real world is quantitative and that what people thought was the real world—this earth, this animal, this star—is only a qualitative imitation of that which Browne, in his Pythagorean moments, termed "the numerical self." Although his constant references to astronomy show that he probably knew as much about it as any layman in the seventeenth century, yet

the hesitation with which he refers to the Copernican hypothesis and the comfort he takes in returning to the Ptolemaic view in spite of his acquaintance with Galileo's work serve as a gauge of the understandable scientific caution which the 'new philosophy' had to overcome in Galileo's time.[7]

Galileo was a physicist; Aristotle, Galen, and Browne were biologists. Their study, man, is a creature of sights and sounds and other qualitative characteristics which cannot easily be reduced and manipulated as pure numbers. The telescope pointed outward and reduced man to a nonquantitative substance apart from his environment; the microscope, which followed, pointed inward to uncover the wonder of man's visible, not mathematical, functions. As it was the ancient stream of Neoplatonism that informed the new astronomy, so it was the ancient tradition of Hippocrates, Aristotle, and Galen that in Browne's Italy, at least, furnished forth the new biology. An interesting survival of the ancient bond between astronomy and medicine is the sign for Jupiter, ℞, which, once associated with the eye of the Egyptian medicine-god Horus, even today begins every drugstore prescription.

In ancient times there were three prominent schools of medicine: the Empirics, who affected the Epicurean philosophy; the Methodists, who took their philosophy from the Skeptics; and the Rationalists, who felt themselves bound closely to the Stoic thinkers. In the seventeenth century, Samuel Sorbière's "Advice to a Young Physician" (*Avis à un Jeune Medicin*, 1672) describes four schools of medicine common at that time—three of them by the same names as the Greeks and Romans had used, and a fourth, startling interloper that it was, the Chemiatrist, Spagyrist, or Paracelsian school in Germany.

In Italy the Renaissance in medicine flowed smoothly from ancient into modern, but in Germany the "reformer" Philip Aureol Theophrast Bombast von Hohenheim, called Paracelsus, by himself, that is "beyond Celsus," began his explosion by publicly burning the works of Galen. Italian medicine was devoted to Aristotle and Galen; but Paracelsus, imbued with Neoplatonism at Ferrara, brought to his medicine such notions as *aurum potabile*, macrocosm-microcosm, and the melothesia or zodiacal man.[8] The doctrine of signatures, by which a remedy was applied because of its resemblance to the disease—for example, the yellow turmeric (*Curcuma longa*) for jaundice—was developed by Paracelsus. John Donne, quite in style, put Paracelsus in his place as an innovator in *Ignatius His Conclave*, but at the same time recognized the tradition in much of his thinking as stemming from Hermes Trismegistus. In his letter to Sir Thomas Lucy of October 9, 1607, which describes medicine from Hippocrates to Galen, Donne adds that now ". . . we see the world hath turned upon new principles which are attributed to *Paracelsus*, but (indeed) too much to his honour."[9] Browne, too, opposed some of the Paracelsian techniques but was attracted to his Hermetic way of thinking. To him Paracelsus and Van Helmont were untrustworthy innovators yet with a possibility of good: some, he says, discontent to "sing the same song in all ages . . . would be content [to] . . . write like Helmont or Paracelsus; and be willing to endure the monstrosity of some opinions, for divers singular notions requiting such aberrations."[10] To be an out-and-out Paracelsian, like Elias Ashmole (1617-92), you had to uphold your views by attempting to prove that the Chemiatrists had brought their "chemick learning" out of Ancient Egypt.

Of the traditional schools of medicine (the Chemiatrists being new), the Empirics emphasized observation more than theory; and the Methodists, theory more than observation. By Browne's time the Empirics were synonymous with quacks. "It is accounted an errour," Bacon could say, "to commit a naturall bodie to Empyrique Physitians";[11] and Burton, ". . . there be many

Mountebanks, Quacksalvers, Empiricks, in every street almost, and in every village, that take upon them this name, make this noble and profitable Art to be evil spoken of. . . ."[12] Similarly the Methodists, nicknamed "abbreviators" for their fatally lengthy diagnoses, were supposed to "kill with Hellebore" without even looking at the patient. On the theory that morbid conditions come about in the body's humors in only three forms—loose, tight, or loose-and-tight—the Methodists prescribed clysters and leeches as needed, often diagnosing the patient's requirements from the next room—as one can well imagine from seeing Dr. Argan in Molière's *Le Malade Imaginaire.*

The Hippocratic-Galenist school, the "Rationalists," combined the best features of the other two. Sometimes they were called "Pneumatists" after Galen's *pneuma,* sometimes "dogmatists," depending upon one's point of view. The "new" anatomy taught by Vesalius, Aldrovandus, Spigelius, Realdus, Bauhin, and Laurentius—which produced Harvey the scientist and Browne the scholar-physician—grew quite naturally out of Galen and the "rational" school.[13] Primarily teleological, Galenic medicine starts with the Aristotelian assumption that man's organs are perfectly fitted for their particular ends.[14] Meditating on the structure and the functions of the human body, Galen composed perhaps the most splendid paean in medical literature of the divine intention *"in creatoris nostri laudem."*[15] Passages like this in Galen made Browne cry out: "In our study of Anatomy there is a masse of mysterious Philosophy, and such as reduced the very Heathens to Divinitie . . .";[16] and ". . . there appears to mee as much divinity in *Galen* his Books *De usu partium,* as in *Suarez* Metaphysicks. . . ."[17] Browne's first critic, Sir Kenelm Digby, accurately read his movement from the macrocosm of the outer world to the microcosm of man's body: "He hath reason to wish that Aristotle had been as accurate in examining the causes, nature, and affections, of the great universe he busied himself about, as his patriarch Galen hath been in the like considerations upon his little world, man's body, in that admirable work of his, *De Usu Partium*."[18] In Galen's account of the muscles of the hand, accomplished during a period of Stoic determinism when Galen was physician in the court of the Emperor Marcus Aurelius, there is the implication that all further research is really futile except to verify a great religious hypothesis.[19]

If the biology of Browne's day received its sense of wonder from Galen's *De Usu Partium*, it was from his *De Facultatibus* ("On the Natural Faculties") and from his *De Administrationibus Anatomicis* ("On Anatomical Procedures") that it received the major impulse to examine as closely as possible every anatomical organ for its true function. Whereas in *De Usu* Galen felt himself called upon to be the apologist for nature, in the other two works he was more the unprejudiced observer.[20] Hence Vesalius did not have to break away from Galen as Copernicus and Galileo had to break away from Ptolemy. "The way from Galen to anatomical research is beautiful and smooth," writes Arturo Castiglione, the medical historian, "and never in Vesalio's book is there a disrespectful comment on the classics, no word that might seem critical."[21] One cannot call Browne "unscientific" because as late as June 1676 he wrote to his son Edward: "[Galen's] *De administrationibus Anatomicis & De usu partium,* &c. are to be . . . [read] upon all occasions."[22]

And yet Galen—who must have known that Seneca died by having his veins, not arteries, opened—failed to grasp the principle of circulation. According to Galen, sometimes *pneuma* is the air "inspired" into the left ventricle to be turned into heat, but more often in

Galen the *pneuma* is a vital principle conceived of as matter in its subtlest state. This vital principle resolves into *spiritus naturalis* (vegetative, in the liver), or into *spiritus vitalis* (in the heart), or into *spiritus animalis* (in the brain). Carrying the *pneuma* to these parts, the blood, Galen believed, ebbed and flowed like the tides of Euripus, while a little of it, mixed with air, came and went in the arteries. To explain how the blood gets from one ventricle to the other, Galen assumed that the septum, the central solid wall of the heart, was pierced with invisible pores through which some of the blood seeped.[23] He had grasped the concept of anastomosis or the connection between the branches of the blood system,[24] but he misread the morphology and the function of the septum.

Fabricius d'Acquapendente, Harvey's teacher at Padua, who published "On the Little Valves in the Veins" (*De Ostiolis Venarum*) in 1603, was closer to the truth, yet he missed the real function of the valves. Following Galen, he asserted that the valves exist to prevent an excess of blood from reaching the periphery.[25] Little wonder that Donne should ask in his *Second Anniversary* (1612), "Know'st thou how blood, which to the heart doth flow, / Doth from one Ventricle to th'other goe?" (Lines 211-12.)

The most important contribution in biological science in the seventeenth century was Harvey's discovery of the circulation of the blood.[26] Announcing his discovery in a series of lectures in London in 1616, he then waited twelve years before publishing it in 1628 as *Exercitatio Anatomica de Motu Cordis et Sanguinis in Animalibus*. This student from Padua did not begin by burning Galen's works, as Paracelsus had done. In chapter VII of his book he quotes Galen's *De Usu Partium* on the function of the lungs and in his *Praelectiones* (1616) he even credits Aristotle with the suggestion of the circulation of the blood.[27] His *Opuscula Anatomica Nova* (1649) gives thoughtful consideration to Galen. Harvey did not so much discover the circulation as demonstrate, finally, a hypothesis by means of quantitative experiment. His predecessors had shown that the heart is really a muscle. From its continual beat in contraction and expansion, Harvey concluded that the blood flows through it in one continuous direction from the veins to the arteries. If there is no passage for the blood through the septum, how does it continue to flow? The valves keep it from flowing backwards. "I began to think there was a sort of motion as in a circle," he announced in chapter VIII. This hypothesis he then proved experimentally by pinching the *vena cava* of a small snake until its heart became pale and empty, then pinching its aorta with the forceps until the heart filled with blood almost to the bursting point. Demonstrations with ligatures on the arms of a man illustrated the same principle. Anyone can make the veins swell in his hand at the valves by pressing with a finger. Measuring the flow of blood, Harvey proved that it flowed about three times the weight of the body per hour. There is only one explanation, and Dr. Browne immediately grasped it!

From the left ventricle when the walls are contracted, the blood is forced into the aorta, whence it flows through the arteries to the upper and lower parts of the body, thence it is carried by the veins into the right auricle of the heart, into the right ventricle, thence by the pulmonary artery into the lungs, where, freshened by new oxygen, it enters the left auricle—to begin once more its circulatory journey. The septum or solid wall of muscle dividing the heart is shaped that way in order to perform that particular function. Harvey, therefore, combined Aristotelian-Galenic doctrine with quantitative measurement for the demonstration of a hypothesis of overpowering imagination. But it took almost as long for the world of biology to accept his thesis as it did for people to believe that the sun and not the earth is the center of the universe.

The two great names, Copernicus and Harvey, began to be connected by the metaphor of the circle and by the poetic proportion of the sun-is-to-the-universe-as-the-heart-is-to-man.[28] In these very terms Harvey dedicated his great discovery to Charles I: *"Serenissime Rex, cor animalium fundamentum est vitae*; Most illustrious Prince, the heart of animals is the foundation of their life, the sovereign of everything within them, the sun of their microcosm, that upon which all growth depends, from which all power proceeds." "So the heart," he continues in the center of his main argument, "is the center of life, the sun of the Microcosm, as the sun itself might be called the heart of the world. . . ."[29] Henceforward this became a seventeenth-century commonplace. Baldwin Hamey, for example, concluded a brief life of Harvey with this epigram:

That according to the opinion of Copernicus as to the motion of the earth and of Harvey as to the movement of the blood we are here—

Ἐν τῷ τροχῷ παντες και ενι πασι τροχός;
Tunc agit atque agimus nos rota nosque rotam;
Then are we all in a wheel and a wheel in us all.[30]

Thus Browne's first mention of the theory of the circulation of the blood, to Dr. Henry Power of Halifax in 1646—"And be sure you make yourself master of Dr. Harvey's piece *De Circul. Sang.*; which discovery I prefer to that of Columbus"[31]—contrasts the microcosmic circle of blood in the human body to the "great circle" voyage around our earthly macrocosm.[32]

Peering at the stars through a telescope was shocking enough to some people, without prying into the inmost secrets of the body of man who is made in God's own image. Biology challenged religion in a double-fronted war waged on the suspicion that doctors could not be religious. Part of the battle was fought between the physicians and the divines: according to the medieval proverb, *Tres medici duo athei* ("where you find three doctors, two of them will be atheists"), with which Browne ironically begins his *Religio*. Chaucer's Doctor of Physicke, we remember, was a Paduan well grounded in Avicenna and Averroes "but litel on the Bible."

One of the main targets for the pious was that amiable physician Pliny. No less than thirty-eight editions of Pliny's *Natural History* had been published between 1469 and 1532, so that a great English translation, Philemon Holland's in 1601, was a necessity. Like Aristotle, Pliny held the world to be immortal, contrary to the Christian assurance of its total destruction by fire in God's good time. Indeed, Philemon Holland had to be on constant guard in translating this popular rationalizer; in his "Preface to the Reader" he wrote:

In attributing so much unto Nature, Plinie seemeth to derogate from the almightie God . . . and therefore . . . daungerous (saith one) to be divulged. Farre be it from me, that I should publish any thing to corrupt mens manners, and much lesse to preiudice Christian religion.[33]

Holland then appends a letter written by a "learned preacher":

And though Plinie and the rest were not able by natures light to search so far as to find out the God of Nature, who sitteth in the glorie of light which none attaineth, but contrariwise in the vanitie of their imagination bewrayed the ignorance of foolish beasts, some doting upon Natur her self, and others upon speciall creatures, as their God: yet feare we not that Christians, in so cleare light, should be so farre bewitched by such blind teachers, as to fall before those heathen idols.

The English translator wishes those parts wherein Pliny has spoken "dishonourably" of the only true God and of His providence could be omitted "if it might stand with the lawes of Translation," but with this warning he must let them stand. He alludes to those infamous ideas of Pliny on God, for example, as: "I suppose therefore that to seeke after any shape of God, and to assigne a forme and image to him, bewraieth mans weaknesse" (II, vii); and on providence: "Now, That the sovereigne power and deitie, whatsoever it is, should have regard of mankind, is a toy and vanitie worthie to be laughed at" (same chapter).[34] Here Holland must write in his margin: ". . . let Christians take heed, and bee thankfull to God for the light revealed unto them out of the holy scriptures." Pliny was a physician and well thumbed by most doctors. Sir Thomas Browne owned the Latin Pliny with Galen's notes published in Geneva in 1631;[35] Amyot's French translation published in two volumes in Lyons in 1566;[36] and, naturally, Benedictus' castigation of Pliny in 1496.[37]

None of the fathers of medicine—Hippocrates, Aristotle, Galen, and Averroes—were Christians. The pious Dr. Thomas Newton even warns us against Apollo in the Hippocratic Oath: "Mervaile not thou at the hethenish names of those putative Gods, by whom hee sweareth . . . but rather feare & tremble, and take thereby occasion to yeeld most humble and hartie thanks unto almightie God for enlightening thee with a better knowledge. . . ."[38] The Averroistic Aristotelians at Padua were scored for their non-Christian view of the immortality of the soul and the eternity of the world. The Paduans taught that virtue is its own reward, and that there is no need of a promise of personal afterlife to make a man good. These dangerous views were popularized in France by Vicomercato (1500-1570), royal physician to Francis I, and by his disciple Jean Fernel (1493-1558), both of whose scientific contributions are mentioned by Browne with approval.[39]

The preachers' most vulnerable target, however, was Galen, because he had lived in second-century Rome without adopting Christianity. In his commonplace book Henry Oxinden wrote: "Galen will not approve of the Christian Religion *quia demonstratione caret*. He was an Atheist."[40] And R. Bostocke, a Paracelsian with clerical connections, wrote in *The Difference betwene the Auncient Phisicke . . . and the latter Phisicke* (1585): ". . . Galene the prince of that phisicke in his workes hath blasphemed [Christ] of set purpose, and by expresse words."[41] The English translator of Juan Huarte's *Examen de Ingenios* (1594), in the margin of a passage scoring Galen for questioning the immortality of the soul, adds, without giving the source of his information: "Galen dying, went to hell, and saw by experience that materiall fire burned the soules and could not consume them: this Physitian had knowledge of that Evangelicall doctrine, and could not receive it."[42] Henoch Clapham in *An Epistle upon the Present Pestilence* (1603) affirms that, the plague being from God, to seek only natural rather than spiritual means of relief from it is ". . . of Christians to become Galenists, and of spiritual to become carnall. . . ."[43] Hence it was necessary for all Christian doctors, of whom Browne was one, to uphold their study of Galenic medicine by constant reference to Galen's pre-Christian argument for God through design.

This failing, doctors could cling to the Galenic source of their art and leave the doctrines of the soul to divines. Such a withdrawal of the medical profession from religious controversy was abetted by the skirmish on a second front, not between physicians and divines, but within their own ranks—between the Galenists and the Paracelsians. Those doctors who deplored Galen's lack of Christian dedication upheld the new doctrines of Paracelsus not so much for scientific reasons as on the ground that Paracelsus derived his new chemistry straight out of the hieroglyphical and Mosaic accounts of creation. Here again many doctors, but not Browne, withdrew from the quarrel by separating their science from their religion.

BROWNE AS SCIENTIST

After this brief view of Browne's scientific world in astronomy and biology, and the challenge both of them gave to religion, we can now ask ourselves, "Was Browne a scientist?" by asking in turn three questions concerning the meaning of the term.

The first is: Did Brown accept the scientific method? Here he outdoes Bacon if to use the scientific method means to combine hypothesis and experimentation. Bacon's call for method was noble, and he urged experimentation though he himself was without a laboratory. Browne's motto in *Christian Morals* was "Let thy studies be free as thy thoughts . . . join sense unto Reason." But Browne was not mathematically oriented, and resisted the abstractions of mathematics for the concrete "realities," to him, of anatomy, physiology, generation, botany, and magnetism. In Joseph Needham's words: "Just as the interference of science with the course of Nature weakens the appeal of the mystical attitude towards life, so the habit of abstraction common to all scientific procedure weakens that attention to the individual and unique which always and probably always will be an essential part of religion."[44] Science's preoccupation with the quantitative excludes the realm of qualities inhabited by poetry and religion. It has often been noted that the farther science gets from those things which are most important to us as human beings, the more mensurably exact it is: natural science, in ionosphere or neutron, is most exact; social sciences are less exact; and the humanities, which deal with love and God and beauty and truth and the impact of life and death, abhor the exactitude of numbers. As long as Browne held to that "other world" of affections, he was not a wholehearted user of this aspect of the "scientific method."

A second question might be: To what extent was Browne willing to surrender theological positions in order to accept new scientific theories? Neither Bacon nor Browne wholeheartedly accepted the Copernican hypothesis. Bacon, without any sensible proof, flatly rejected heliocentrism: "The introduction of so much mobility into Nature . . . and the making the moon revolve around the earth in an epicycle, and some other assumptions of his [Copernicus] are the speculations of one who cares not what fictions he introduces into nature, provided his calculations answer."[45] When Browne, on the other hand, casually refers to cosmography he treats the world as Ptolemaic, but when he regards the thesis as a problem he is at least open-minded about it: ". . . some have held that Snow is blacke, that the earth moves";[46] "there is no happiness under (or, as Copernicus will have it, above) the sunne . . .";[47] ". . . if any affirm, the earth doth move, and will not believe with us, it standeth still. . . ."[48] In a nonmathematical field of science which was closer to him, he kept apace of the newest discoveries, like

Harvey's circulation of the blood. But the reason for doubt in the first instance and acceptance in the second was not so much theological or ethical as it was his biological rather than mathematical training and his concrete imagination, which may or may not denote that he was a "true scientist."

Finally: Did Browne look as a scientist upon research as a means to the advancement of material welfare, or, more nobly, as an end in itself? In an age of growing pessimism fed by Calvinism, and Goodman's *The Fall of Man* (1616), the optimistic view that supported Goodman's antagonist, Hakewill, was largely scientific.[49] The Royal Society for the Advancement of Science chartered by Charles II in 1662 and hailed by Thomas Sprat in 1667 was dedicated to utility. To be sure, man's control over nature is only one attribute of science, and utility is more in the popular mind than it is in the mind of the true scientist. Browne never preached science for utility, except as medicine is an art that co-operates with nature to heal the ills our flesh is heir to. And as for knowledge being an end in itself, this too for him was almost a heresy:

The wisedom of God receives small honour from those vulgar heads that rudely stare about, and with a grosse rusticity admire his workes; those highly magnifie him, whose judicious enquiry into his acts, and deliberate research of his creatures, returne the duty of a devout and learned admiration.[50]

To Browne the end of science is the glory of God. Nothing that the "new philosophy" revealed was really "new"; it brought out "embryon truths" which before existed to us as a kind of chaos until God in His grace allowed us to know.

The inward science of anatomy, contrasted with the outward science of astronomy, led man more and more to look in upon himself. The period is characterized by a series of "anatomies," which like Stubbes' *Anatomy of Abuses* (1583), Donne's *Anatomy of the World* (1612), and Burton's *Anatomy of Melancholy* (1621) reveal an almost pathological introspection. The Shakespearean play that opened the seventeenth century was Hamlet's anatomy of himself. The single question the Christian anatomist might ask himself was "What is man that Thou art mindful of him?" As Browne was skeptical even of skeptical philosophy, so he was skeptical of the popular ends of science.

In fine, "Was Browne a scientist?" depends on what we. mean by science. In his day the term bore a closer relationship to its etymological intention in *"scientia"* than it does now, and thus included more. At present nothing is science that is not exact, mathematical, impersonal, objective, capable of laboratory repetitions, and univocal in terminology. In the seventeenth century, however, interesting, penetrating, at times disconnected intuitive insights into the nature of phenomena were exciting additions to man's knowledge of his world and of himself.[51] How Browne actually worked within this realm of thought and feeling, we shall see in a later chapter on his *Vulgar Errors*.

Chapter VII

APPRENTICESHIP IN MEDICINE AND THE BIRTH OF *RELIGIO MEDICI*

OXFORDSHIRE OR HALIFAX?

After returning to England in December 1633 from Padua and Leiden, Browne spent the following four years required by law to get his Oxford M.D. by "incorporation." After the B.M. at home or the M.D. abroad, a young man, usually between the ages of twenty-six and twenty-eight[1] (and Browne was twenty-eight and a half), was licensed to practice only under the supervision for four years of an older and well-established doctor from Oxford or Cambridge. For example, Dr. William Denton (1605-91), who was exactly Browne's age but whom he called "old Dr. Denton of Oxford,"[2] ". . . was initiated into the practice of medicine by a noted physician, Dr. Henry Ashworth,"[3] onetime Fellow of Oriel. Unfortunately there is no record of the name of Browne's medical sponsor, and two traditions exist concerning the place where he was engaged. The problem is important because it was during the leisure of his early apprenticeship in medicine that he composed his first book.

In his "To the Reader" added in 1643, Browne tells us that he wrote *Religio* away from any city or university library: "It was penned in such a place and with such disadvantage, that (I protest) from the first setting of pen unto paper, I had not the assistance of any good booke, whereby to promote my invention or relieve my memory. . . ." Passages within the text make it clear that the book was written after he had returned from the continent and before he was thirty years old:[4] that is, between the Leiden degree of December 1633 and his thirtieth birthday on October 19, 1635. He was practicing medicine at the time:

. . . I cannot goe to cure the body of my Patient, but I forget my profession, and call unto God for his soule. . . .[5] Let mee be sicke my selfe, if sometimes the malady of my patient be not a disease unto me; I desire rather to cure his infirmities than my owne necessities. Where I do no good me thinks it is scarce honest gaine, though I confesse 'tis but the worthy salary of our well-intended endeavours: . . . .[6]

Anthony à Wood, that indefatigable antiquary of Oxford, tells us that Browne ". . . practiced for some time in Oxfordshire,"[7] presumably when he was composing *Religio Medici*. But in his "Supplementary Memoir" prefixed to the edition of Browne's works in 1835-36, Simon Wilkin, a conscientious scholar, announced rather magisterially that Browne had written *Religio* while practicing medicine in Halifax, Yorkshire. Ever since, unquestioning biographers have either split Browne's apprenticeship between two places or scheduled his Oxfordshire sojourn between his M.A. from Oxford in liberal arts in 1629 and his study of medicine on the continent.[8] We shall have to examine Wilkin's original evidence and his reasons for believing it.

In 1708 there appeared in Halifax an anonymous book entitled *Halifax and Its Gibbet-Law Placed in a True Light*. It was thought by some to have been written by Samuel Midgeley, who "practised physick" though in and out of jail for debt; but it is generally agreed that its author is William Bentley, who published it. Halifax, a great mercers' town where cloth had to be hung outdoors, had adopted a severe penalty for stealing: a municipal guillotine on market days cut off the head of any trifler convicted of making off with more than thirteen pence worth of goods. After describing the gibbet in the spirit of a member of the Chamber of Commerce and upholding its legality, the author boasts of the notables who have resided in Halifax:

And unto whom I cannot forbear adding the Learned Dr. *Brown*, (who for his Worth and Fame, was thought worthy of Knighthood by his Prince) because in his Juvenile Years he fixed himself in this Populous, and rich Trading Place, wherein to shew his Skill, and gain respect in the World: And that during his Residence amongst us, and in his vacant Hours he writ his admired Piece called by him *Religio Medici*.[9]

Introducing this evidence, Wilkin asserts that Browne, after he had received his Leiden M.D. in December 1633, ". . . settled as a physician at Shipden [*sic*] Hall, near Halifax. None of his biographers, indeed, have mentioned this fact; but I cannot see the slightest reason for refusing the testimony of Bentley, who published the . . . account of him during the life of his son, Dr. Edward Browne."[10] Wilkin supports the testimony by Wright's history of Halifax, written in 1738 ". . . for the express purpose of revising Bentley's work and correcting its errors. . . ." Wilkin also cites Dr. Watson in *Antiquities of Halifax* among those scholars who ". . . have adopted the statement." Finally, he believes it to derive additional countenance from the fact that Power and Brearcliffe, both of Halifax, were among Browne's correspondents.

Now, that the book was published "during the life of Dr. Edward Browne" was as indeterminable for Wilkin as it is for us. Edward died on August 28, 1708, and was buried in Kent. The book was published in Halifax with "1708" on its title page. Browne's son probably never saw it. As for Wright, the Halifax historian, there is little evidence that he wrote expressly to correct Bentley's mistakes. He added, thirty years later, the name of the house, Shipden Hall (i.e., Upper Shibden Hall), to the name of the city which Bentley had identified with Browne:

Neither must I omit in this Place Sir Thomas Browne, Doctor of Physick, who, tho' born in *London* Oct. 19, 1605, yet practis'd here as a Physician in his younger Years. About the year 1630, he liv'd at *Shipden* Hall nigh Halifax, at which time he wrote that excellent Piece, intitled, *Religio Medici*, before he was thirty Years of Age: . . . .[11]

The error of four years (1630 instead of 1634, which Wilkin corrects) does not enhance Wright's credibility as a historian, and the only reason for naming the particular house is that some of Browne's later correspondents lived there.

Wilkin's next witness, John Watson, the most trustworthy of Halifax's three eighteenth-century historians,[12] actually damages Wilkin's claim. Referring to the two passages in Bentley and in Wright, Watson says:

Whence these Anecdotes were obtained I cannot say, for little or no tradition of this sort remains there now [i.e., in 1775] . . . [he quotes from the monument in St. Peter Mancroft Church in Norwich]. Here is nothing in all this, nor in Anthony Wood's account of him, in his *Athenae* . . . , nor in any other Author, but the above which, as far as I have seen, takes notice of his having been resident in

Halifax parish, and yet the silence of Authors proves nothing against positive assertions of this kind.[13]

Surely Wilkin misread him.

The 1708 evidence that Browne wrote *Religio Medici* in Halifax, of suspicious origin and standing alone, describes an event seventy-three years after it was supposed to have occurred. None of the early biographers—including Whitefoot, the 1712 "Life," Wood, Aubrey, Johnson—mention it. Browne's biography-conscious daughter Mrs. Lyttleton omits it. In spite of the fact that the beheading prescribed by the notorious "Gibbet Law" at Halifax would have interested a young doctor, Browne himself is silent,[14] although years later he advised his son Edward while traveling ". . . to see the manner of the executions in all places."[15] More conclusively negative is the failure of more recent local historians of Halifax[16] to turn up a single bit of corroborative testimony, despite the traditional diligence of England's county antiquarian societies. This includes men such as John Lister, Bryan Dale, J. Horsfall Turner, and T. W. Hanson. Most singular is the absence of any proof by James Crossley of Manchester, who, born in Halifax and an early admirer of Sir Thomas Browne (his interest led Wilkin to begin the monumental edition), would have liked to be certain that *Religio Medici* had been written in Halifax.[17]

From this analysis of Wilkin's evidence I am inclined to credit Anthony à Wood's "he practised for some time in Oxfordshire" above the rather shaky account of an externship in Halifax. Wood's is the older and more responsible evidence. It is disinterested biography. Some place in Oxfordshire would be nearer not only to Browne's mother's home in Isleworth but also to Oxford, though the candidate for the English doctorate in medicine by incorporation was wont to maintain only a nominal relationship with his university.[18]

How did the Halifax legend get started? Bentley in 1708 must have been led by more than sheer invention to boast that Sir Thomas Browne had "writt Religio Medici" in his fair city. Since the only conclusive evidence of any connection between Browne and Halifax is the friends he had there, it is difficult to resist this hypothesis: that Browne, while practicing physic in Oxfordshire, wrote *Religio Medici* for someone dear to him in Halifax.

Though Browne begged his readers to believe that he had written his book ". . . for my private exercise and satisfaction," at the same time he confessed that "being communicated unto one, it became common unto many." The *Religio* is not completely innocent of rhetoric, even in the 1642 version. Woven into its pages is the portrait of a friend who seems to be less of a Renaissance abstraction than a Charles Diodati to a John Milton: ". . . I have loved my Friend as I do vertue, and as I do my soule, my God."[19] Unmarried, Browne looks upon friendship as a nobler union by far. This is not true of the vulgar but only of "such as are mark'd for vertue" and so more chary of their love: ". . . he that cannot love his friend with this noble ardour, will in a competent degree affect all."[20] God is the pattern of such love, and examples in the great epics of the love between two men-friends—Nisus and Euryalus, Damon and Pythias, Achilles and Patroclus—are but imitations of it, containing nothing ". . . which mee thinkes upon some grounds I could not performe within the narrow compasse of my selfe."[21] This kind of love is stronger, Browne maintains, than the ties of blood. At the very end of *Religio* he wrote: "Blesse mee in this life with but the peace of my conscience, command of my affections, the love of thy selfe and my dearest friends, ..."[22] The "thy selfe and" was added in 1643; the Pembroke manuscript at this point has simply: "Blesse mee in this life with the peace of conscience, command of my affections, the love of my dearest friend [singular], and I shall bee happie enough to pittie Caesar."[23]

Browne's friend to whom he "communicated" the manuscript must have been absent from him at the time of writing; otherwise, conversation would have taken the place of these semiprivate, witty, and graceful sentences. One "misery" of friendship, Browne complains, is that we often forget the looks of the person we most dearly love.[24] But in his dreams Browne can be ". . . in heaven though on earth, enjoy my friend and embrace him at a distance; without which I cannot behold him; . . . ." This sentence exists in all the manuscripts and in the 1642 pirated edition, but not in Browne's first authorized edition of 1643.[25]

Bryan Dale rightly asserts that the correspondence ". . . makes it certain that Dr. Browne was well acquainted with several of the most respectable families of Halifax and enjoyed the friendship of its most worthy men."[26] On August 21, 1669, Mr. W. John Brearcliffe of Halifax wrote to Browne concerning some Roman coins.[27] Henry Power passed on to Dr. Browne the sad news of the death in Halifax ". . . of some of your acquaintance, vz. Mr Waterhouse & Mr Sam. Mitchell."[28] Browne's most intimate Halifax friends were the two Powers, father and son, and the family united by marriage to the Powers, named Foxcroft. Young Henry Power (1624-68), though only a boy of eleven when Browne wrote *Religio Medici*, became Browne's most distinguished disciple.[29] He married Margaret, daughter of Anthony Foxcroft, who in turn was related to the Foxcrofts of Upper Shibden Hall—the initial fact which in 1738 connected Browne's name with the name of that house.

Henry's father, Mr. John Power, was an English merchant of Spanish heritage. Little else is known of him except that he lived in Multure Hall, since demolished. The Bankfield Museum has part of the ornamental ceiling of the front hall with the initials in it "I. P." for John Power.[30] We do not even know how Thomas Browne and John Power met, or where. But the two were firm friends and had had conversations with each other on serious subjects. In token of their friendship, young Power in 1658 presented to Dr. Browne ". . . three old Spanish books" which once belonged to his father, ". . . who . . . did much honour you."[31] And on June 8, 1659, Browne expressed to Henry Power the wish that ". . . I might continue the delight I have formerly had by many serious discourses with my old freind your good father, whose memorie is still fresh with mee, & becomes more delightfull by this great enjoyment I have from his true & worthy sonne."[32]

If the evidence for Browne's having written his first book in Halifax is as slight as it seems to be, and if we have correctly read the indications in *Religio Medici* of its having been born of conversations with a friend which it seeks to perpetuate by being "communicated unto one," and if that one is Mr. John Power of Halifax—then Browne could have been learning how to practice physic in Oxfordshire and writing down his thoughts on religion for his Yorkshire friend. But we do not know the name and location of Browne's medical supervisor, or when and where Browne and John Power had had their conversations.[33]

His apprenticeship in medicine finished, Browne went through the formalities at Oxford for the degree of M.D. by incorporation—the cap, the ring, a book, and a kiss from the regius professor. He received this degree on July 10, 1637, and at the age of thirty-two was at last ready to begin his career.

In that year, now a full-fledged doctor, he moved to Norwich, attracted there by Pembroke College friends, including the Reverend Thomas Lushington. Whitefoot said that he first knew Browne when Browne was thirty-two years old, and this would place his Norwich sojourn from 1637. The monument in St. Peter Mancroft Church says that he practiced physic in Norwich forty-six years: since he died in October 1682, this, too, would make his "first year" in Norwich the months from July to December 1637.

In 1641 he married Dorothy Mileham, the fourth daughter of Edward Mileham, Esq., of Burlingham St. Peter, Norfolk.[34] Of the couple Whitefoot remarked that they must have been drawn together by magnetical attraction, so perfectly did they seem to be mated. Thomas and Dorothy had a dozen children, only four of whom, such was the mortality rate even in a physician's family, survived their parents.[35]

ANDREW CROOKE AND WILL MARSHALL

In 1642, seven years after Browne had sent his manuscript to a friend, there suddenly appeared in London an anonymous book called Religio Medici, published by Andrew Crooke, with an engraved frontispiece by Will Marshall.[36] It was an insignificant looking octavo, of one hundred and ninety pages of text; the many misreadings showed that it had been set up in some haste. The bad first edition was partially corrected by the second, still unauthorized; thirty-one pages shorter, this so improved the text that Browne retained many of the corrections in his authorized edition of 1643.[37] The book was probably first published in December 1642, since Digby's letter about it, dated December 23, 1642, implies that it was very recently available. As for the number of copies, by Fredson Bowers' test according to the number of "skeletons" used, there must have been about 1250 copies of each of the 1642 editions, the number allowed by statute.[38] What made Andrew Crooke print it?

Thanks partially to the good sale of *Religio Medici,* Andrew Crooke's fame as a bookseller grew until in 1665 he became master of the Stationers' Company. From 1630 to 1674, when he died, he had kept his shop under the sign of "The Green Dragon" in St. Paul's churchyard within a stone's throw of Browne's boyhood home. He knew a good style when he read it, for he loved good language and talked well. John Dunton, his garrulous successor, wrote of him:

He was well acquainted with Mr. Hobbes, and published many of his books. He got a good estate by his trade, and was a man of extraordinary sense, which he had the happiness of being able to express in words as many and apposite as the sense included under them.[39]

Crooke published a variety of titles. His character books, such as John Earle's *Microcosmography* (the seventh edition, 1638) and Overbury's *Characters* (the sixteenth impression in 1638), were very successful. Richard Tarlton's *Jests*, in the same year, bore his imprint. A best-selling travel book for the decade was the Crooke-sponsored *A Voyage into the Levant* by Sir Henry Blount. As early as 1637 Crooke had the temerity and foresight to publish Hobbes' *Art of Rhetorick*. In drama he published the Reverend Henry Killigrew's *Conspiracy* (1638) and the following year Beaumont and Fletcher's *Wit without Money* and George Chapman's *Chabot Admiral of France*. In 1640 he got out Robert Chamberlain's *The Swaggering Damsell* and John Fletcher's *The Night-Walker or the Little Thief*.

The famous *Works of Benjamin Jonson* in 1640 had
on the title page "and are to be sold by Andrew Crooke
at the signe of the Green Dragon."[40] But of all drama-
tists James Shirley was most closely identified with this
shop. Crooke meanwhile kept up with the growing demand for works in religion and practical piety. Over
two-thirds of the books mentioned by William London
in his *Catalogue of the Most Vendible Books in England* (1658) are works of "divinity"—among them
Religio Medici. The public read Crooke's edition of
Du Bartas' *Divine Weeks and Works* in 1637 and a
Paraphrase upon the Psalms of David (1636) by George
Sandys, the poet famed for his translation of Ovid.
Thomas Hooker's *The Soul's Humiliation,* which
Crooke first published in 1637, had reached its fourth
edition by 1640 with the spread of its author's fame
as a preacher in America. One of the three most popu-
lar devotional works of the century[41] was acquired by
Crooke, Bishop Lewis Bayly's *The Practice of Piety.*
Though the bishop died in 1631, there was no stopping
edition after edition of his book.[42] John Dunton, book-
seller, in looking back over a life not so successful as
Andrew Crooke's, projected a dream book of his own
to be called by two of his rival's leading items: *The
New Practice of Piety, Writ in Imitation of Dr. Brown's
Religio Medici.*[43] So much for Andrew Crooke.

If we can judge from the number of engraved
frontispieces and decorative title pages for new books,
the engraver was almost as important as the bookseller
in calling the attention of the browser in St. Paul's to a
new work entitled *Religio Medici.* Here was the picture
of a tall rock rising from the sea, with a man falling
from it saved by the hand of God. Beside the words
"Printed for Andrew Crooke" were the words "Will:
Marshall scu."

The "sculptor" of this engraving for Browne's

first book was not the best artist of his time but certainly one of the best known. Joseph Strutt denounced Will Marshall's "want of taste": "He was one of those laborious artists, whose engravings were chiefly confined to the ornamenting of books. And indeed his patience and assiduity is all we can admire, when we turn over his prints, which are prodigiously numerous."[44] "No other craftsman," Sir Sidney Colvin writes, "was half so frequently employed by the booksellers of the day," and adds that in the large amount of work he produced there is bound to be unevenness of quality.[45]

Will Marshall made one of the most famous engravings of the century, which must have been seen many times by Dr. Browne, the portrait of Francis Bacon prefixed to the 1640 *Advancement of Learning*. Another inevitable association, at least for all who believed Charles I to have been a martyr, was Marshall's frontispiece for *Eikon Basilike* (1649) of the king kneeling, with a crown of thorns. The design exists in seventeen different versions.

As an engraver of literary men's portraits, Marshall began with his bust of Ovid prefixed to Sandys' verse translation of 1626.[46] The portrait of John Donne at age eighteen, with eight lines of verse by Izaac Walton, was engraved by Marshall in 1635. An even more popular picture of Donne was Marshall's design of the dean of St. Paul's in his winding sheet, prefixed to *Devotions upon Emergent Occasions*, printed by A. Matthews in 1634.[47] Marshall furnished the title pages for the 1633 edition of Phineas Fletcher's *Piscatorie Eclogs* (published with *The Purple Island*), for the sixth edition of Feltham's *Resolves* (1636), and for Ben Jonson's translation of Horace's *Ars Poetica* in Crooke's 1640 edition of the *Works*.[48]

Famed as a "wit" was James Howell, who had started the joke about Browne's naïve desire, expressed in *Religio Medici*, to conjoin sexually like trees.[49] The 1655 edition of Howell's letters, *Epistolae Ho-Elianae*, published by Moseley, had the heads of several famous Romans and the portrait of the author by Will Marshall.

Marshall had engraved an illustration for Dr. Daniel Featly's *The Dippers Dipt* in such execrable taste that Milton, punning in the Tetrachordon controversy, had said, "I do not commend his *marshalling*." When Moseley hired the same artist to do a head of Milton for the 1645 *Poems*, the poet may have given him a sitting or two and then asked him to work from what is now known as the Onslow portrait. The result is Marshall's worst picture. Entitled "at the age of twenty-one," the portrait makes Milton look at least sixty; one hand is stuck awkwardly inside his shirt, and the whole is cornered by four unidentifiable muses. Milton offered to furnish a "motto" in Greek, which Marshall ignorantly etched into the copperplate, the meaning being:

> That an unskilful hand had carved this print
> You'd say at once, seeing the living face;
> But finding here no jot of me, my friends,
> Laugh at the botching artist's mis-attempt.[50]

These are a few of Will Marshall's literary associations.

With frequent contract under Andrew Crooke, Will Marshall also illustrated popular works of religion. He had made the title page for the King James translation of the *Psalms* in 1631 and for William Fulke's text of the *New Testament* (fourth edition, 1633), the latter reviving memories of a religious controversy that had flamed in Elizabeth's day. He had signed the title page for the first edition (1631) of Peter Heylin's *The History of St. George of Cappadocia*. In 1637 his name became linked with John Preston's *The Doctrine of the Saint's Infirmities,* and in 1638 with Andrew Crooke's edition of Bishop Bayly's *Practice of Piety.*

There was no mention of the author of the 1642 *Religio Medici,* only of Crooke and Marshall. Even had there been, few could have known him. As soon as possible, Thomas Browne acknowledged the book as his and furnished a truer copy of it than that which had been surreptitiously printed. He also made certain discretionary emendations, though he left the whole surprisingly frank.

Chapter VIII

RELIGIO MEDICI: SUBSTANCE AND FORM

Browne's first work, "The Religion of a Doctor," is the paradox of one man's mind, set down with the apparent assurance that it would be sympathetically understood.[1] It was not intended to persuade an audience to his way of thinking, but a rhetorical flourish is there, out of pride, perhaps, and to please a friend.

Critics[2] used to dismiss the philosophy while praising the style. Professor John Nichol of Glasgow wrote:

But the greatest master of the quaint style of this, or I may add, of any age, was Sir Thomas Browne, the eccentric physician of Norwich, author of the 'Religio Medici.' He seems to have lived wholly in the past among traditions and mysteries, and medieval theories of life and death, mingling the moderate scepticism of his science with a credulity that embraces Astrology, Alchemy, and Witchcraft, in a train of desultory thought, which often vents itself in bursts of thrilling eloquence. Turning from the history of his age to his own books is like retreating from a battlefield to the interior of a Minster, where an organ is sounding to the chant of ancient Litanies.[3]

Charles Whibley saw Browne as only slightly less "quaint":

Sir Thomas Browne's *Religio Medici* is less a theological treatise than a work of art. Those who look to its pages for guidance in religion will be disappointed. . . . Its ostensible theme, indeed, is of less interest than the style in which it is composed, or than the ingenious epigrams which give a lustre to its pages. Though the Doctor sets out to tell us of his religion, he very soon wanders by the way and discourses at hazard of all things that touch his curiosity, and most especially of himself. The book is various and wayward. No secure thread of thought holds the argument together.[4]

And yet that *Religio Medici* is no great contribution to theology does not mean that its content or even its structure can be summarily overlooked. Walter Pater, despite some aberrations on Browne, was near the truth when he said that what really tells in the book is the witness Browne brings to men's instinct for survival, to their intimations of immortality. The modern view is well expressed by Professor Hardin Craig:

Browne suffers from the reputation of being the writer of possibly the most beautiful English prose that has been written, and of being that only. . . . Browne needs to be brought to life as a man and a thinker. No man's prose style can be divorced from his thoughts, since all prose writing is a matter of ideas or nothing.[5]

DUALITY, DOUBT, CERTITUDE, AND IRONY

The doctor of *Religio Medici*, like most of us, is afflicted with a polarity of doubt and certainty.[6] There are many affirmations of belief, such as: "I believe that," "Yet do I believe all this," "I know," "Surely there are," "Yet is all this an easy possibility," "I do not question," "I grant that," " 'Tis a postulate unto me that," "To speak properly, those are true," "There are questionless. . . ," "I hold that God can do all things," "I do believe," "I have ever believed and do now know," etc. Though many of these, like "I can neither prove nor absolutely deny," shade into some doubt, doubt becomes explicit in innumerable phrases: "I find it very fallible," "We are ignorant of," "I cannot justify," "This bids me mistrust," "He would inveigle my belief," "I can no way grant," "This makes it improbable," "That seems to overthrow it," "I could wish it were true," "I have no confidence in," "I cannot but wonder," etc. Both religious faith and doubt express themselves in a double action. First comes the cognition or statement, and then the volition or relishing of it: an affirmation and then a surrender.

Some people warn us against dualism: we live in a pluralistic universe, they say, and dualism oversimplifies things to the extent of jeopardizing our sanity. And yet the dualistic is not a simple view so much as it is an all-inclusive one, often in experience both the beginning and the end of the choices we make. All the essential Christian doctrines are dichotomies: man and God, the Fall and the Redemption, body and soul, visible and invisible, mortal and immortal, the "Word become Flesh."

St. John and St. Augustine Christianized Plato's double view and Browne, torn between doubt and certainty, pride and humility, adds to the vision a deep irony. To love our neighbors as ourselves, we must love ourselves; he cannot truly love others who does not look upon himself as a son of God. But the moment he thinks this, he suspects that he is not really a son of God, and such a Lepanto humbles and chastens. Again, constant self-qualification defines as precisely as possible one's concepts of God, the universe, and time. For if man's greatest source of pride is his reason, which lifts him above the animals, he must humble this reason before the mind of God. Such tensions in an age like the seventeenth century when the ideal and the real were so far apart (as they are perhaps today) and in a man like Browne, make for a profound irony—forever inseparable from the double vision.

THE TWO PARTS OF *Religio Medici*

Browne cast the *imitatio* of his own life[7] into two major parts, antithetical and correlative to each other. There are practical, philosophical, and theological reasons for this. The study of anatomy for him had been morphology and function. As a physician he knew that medicine's theory and practice, diagnosis and cure, parallel in religion, faith and conduct or belief and action. The Hippocratic Oath enjoins *love* of one's patients as requisite to the *wisdom* of the art. Further, the philosophical problem of the *one* in the first part is thrown against the problem of the *many* in the second. The first part is substance; the second, accident; or forms and operations, intellectual and sensible worlds, unity and diversity.

Behind such a dual structure lies the Christian division of the ten Hebrew commandments into two, the love of God and the love of man. Where there is a triple division like "faith, hope, and charity," sooner or later two of these will go together: faith and hope into one part, and the third, love, into the other. Part I is consultation; Part II, election; or intellect and will; or faith and good works (James 2:22). Innumerable theological compendia were so structured, on good Biblical precedent: "Walk before me and be thou perfect" (Gen. 17:1); "Trust in Jehovah and do good" (Ps. 37:3); "Hear the word of God and keep it" (Luke 11:28); "Believing all things . . ." and "herein do I exercise myself" (Acts 24:14-16); "in faith and in love" (I Tim. 1:13); and "Believe and love" (I John 3:23). Milton divided his *De Doctrina Christiana* into two books: faith or the knowledge of God; and worship or the love of God. First we must inquire into our own salvation and then help our brother, else we overlook the beam in our own eye while worrying about the mote in our neighbor's. The relationship between Browne's two parts is clear.

The structure within each part, however, is more difficult to discern. Browne is obliged, he says, "by the principles of grace and mine own reason" to be a Christian. Thus he begins in the middle, with a dichotomy in the head of that "amphibium," man (I, xxxiv, p. 53), to look from this middle vantage point at God above him and at nature below. Instead of stretching his pia mater to think through all "the wingy mysteries of Divinity" (I, ix), Browne welcomes their impossibilities as a kind of edge to his belief in Grace, conquering the doubts that his reason raises against them by the devotion that impels him to his knees before them. Their reality comes to him not by syllogism but in pictures, ". . . in an easy and Platonick description." Thus he prefers "The soul is man's angel and God's body" to the schoolman's term "entelechia," and "*Lux est umbra Dei*" to the bare abstraction of "*actus perspicui*" (I, x). But such expressions are more than mere images: the word "shadow," for example, implies not only the Platonic concept of the visible world being a reflection of the invisible, but also the Christian typological thesis that each event in history is a shadow of something that went before and a "foreshadow" of something to come from the will of God.

Browne concentrates, in this mode of thinking and expressing, on that "allegorical description" of God of Hermes Trismegistus: God is a circle whose center is everywhere and whose circumference is nowhere.[8] This he may have gotten from his Oxford tutor; Dr. Lushington had made notes on the Christian Neoplatonism of Proclus,[9] that ancient who raised Euclid to divinity.

Though the origins of the definition are unknown, it appears to have been set down first and ascribed to Hermes Trismegistus in the pseudo-Hermetic *Liber XXIV Philosophorum* of the twelfth century. There it is the second of the twenty-four definitions of God: "II. *Deus est sphaera infinita, cuius centrum est ubique, circumferentia nusquam.*"[10] In the thirteenth century this "*definitio per modum imaginandi*" was quoted by St. Thomas Aquinas, Bonaventura, Bartolomaeus Anglicus, Meister Eckhart, and many others. Nicholas of Cusa gave it prominence in the second book of *De Docta Ignorantia* (1462),[11] whose skepticism, paradoxical emphasis on wisdom through ignorance, and Neoplatonic exaltation of mathematics inspired Copernicus and Bruno. Between the twelfth and seventeenth centuries men had perceived in the "soft flexible sense" of this definition God's containment of the Many and the One, the visible and the invisible.

So pervasive is this Hermetic symbol in the first part of *Religio Medici* that I would not be surprised were it vaguely tied in with Browne's leanings toward the old cosmology. The dot in the center is the visible world, which Browne pores over among his books and in his laboratory. The invisible circle swings around it as God's concourse for the heavenly bodies; also, influences descend from the macrocosm to natural and human history and to Browne himself, a smaller dot within the geocentric dot at the center.

With this picture of the circle in his imagination, Browne perceives that God's two main attributes are "Wisdom and Eternity" (I, xi). The wisdom of God is the center of the circle, that dot which is seen everywhere in nature; the eternity of God is the circumference, the circle having no beginning and no end, and eternity existing nowhere in this world. The first attribute, wisdom, re-creates Browne's own mind; the

second, eternity, baffles it. One has to do with space
and time, the other with no-time and no-space. His
own ignorance is the opposite of the first, his mortality
the opposite of the second. As God has both wisdom
and eternity and as Browne is made in His image, he
too partakes in his best moments of that supernal
knowledge which the first can grant and of that intimation of immortality vouchsafed by the second.

But right now he is not much interested in eternity;
he gives it only the rest of section 11 and the short section following. His finite mind cannot really grasp it,
because the circumference of the Hermetic circle is
actually nowhere, it has no *ubi*. Consequently he de-
votes almost all of Part I to God's wisdom, which, as
the center of the circle, is everywhere a picture of the
invisible (I, xii, p. 19). God's wisdom as science he reads
in nature, His wisdom as providence he reads in history,
of which the Biblical story is a *type* or prefiguration.
God is the only first cause, and our knowledge of His
wisdom emerges from our recognition of two secondary
causes: creation and providence (I, xiv), in the "art of
nature" and in the constant guidance of men's lives. If
you want proof of the first, he says, study nature in the
large as well as the small. And if you want proof of the
second, read the Bible. For these are the two manuscripts from which Browne collects his divinity (I, xvi).

At this point another distinction emerges between
God's wisdom in nature and His wisdom in providence,
if we assume (as Browne does at the outset) that God
not only creates but also performs. His created nature
is "a setled and constant course," being the art of God.
But that other aspect of His wisdom, providence, is not
a straight line: it meanders in a labyrinth. God created
this world and everything in it by His art, and He man-
ages the world and everything in it by His providence,
which some persist in calling "Fortune"—as though

any cause could operate in "a loose and stragling way" (I, xviii). The effects of nature and of providence differ in directness. Thus Browne can but wonder at God's wisdom as it appears "straight" in the nature he studies as scientist, and "crooked" in the history he reads as a scholar. He perceives God's hand, not good luck, in the discovery of the Gunpowder Plot and in the defeat of the Spanish Armada (I, xviii). These two events to him are the effect of an unseen cause that works in a secret and winding way.

Either God is irresponsible and human history meaningless, or God is in charge of events and history makes sense. Pre-Christian philosophies of history assert that everything is getting better and better (progress), or worse and worse (decay), or sometimes better and sometimes worse in a blindly repetitive pattern (cycles). But "Christianity is an historical religion in a peculiarly technical sense," writes Herbert Butterfield; "it presents us with religious doctrines which are at the same time historical events or historical interpretations."[12] The Christian believes that history had a beginning and that it must consequently have an end. He believes that at one moment in human history God actually came into it. Since that moment during the reign of Tiberius, the *annus Domini*, the whole duty of man is to reconcile God's time with the world's, to perceive the still point of that nexus between time and eternity, the impact of *chairos* upon *chronos*. Everything Browne wrote is instinct with the Christian view of history, including the view that His own life was "a miracle of thirty years."

Behind Browne is St. Augustine, and behind St. Augustine, the Christian view of time emerged in the Fourth Gospel, of which Browne was extraordinarily fond. St. John's story of Christ differs from the others in the feeling of the author's own contingent relationship to that which he describes: what he describes is Christ's oneness with God and the believer's consequent quarrel with the world. Only in the gospel of St. John is the disciple Thomas actually characterized as the zealous follower of Jesus (John 20:24 ff.) who insisted on seeing and feeling the nail wounds before accepting the Resurrection. His name "Didymus" or "Thomas" means "twin," and his namesake Thomas Browne had the same Janus-polarity of skepticism and faith. Only in St. John is the water turned into wine at the marriage feast in Cana. Only St. John overhears the night-time conversion of Nicodemus at the words: "God so loved the world that he gave his only begotten Son, that whosoever believeth in him should not perish, but have everlasting life." Only in St. John occurs that amazing statement of Christ's on time: "Before Abraham was I am" (John 8:58), a Johannine view of history that appears in Browne's discovery that Eve miscarried of him before she conceived of Cain (I, lix, p. 86). Only in St. John, finally, do we get Christ's most staggering miracle, for a doctor—the raising of Lazarus from the grave (John 11:1-44).

These two "visible hands of God" (I, xix)—one drawing a straight line in nature and the other a winding mark through history—are central to Browne's faith in Part I of *Religio Medici*. He has fought to keep this faith safe from his rebel reason, as he must keep his reason above his passion. These three are at war within him. To allow them to rule as a triumvirate is particularly difficult for an educated man: the devil ". . . takes a hint of infidelity from our Studies, and by demonstrating a naturality in one way" (shall we say the effect of high winds on a body of water?) "makes us mistrust a miracle in another" (the story of the children of Israel crossing the Red Sea?). In spite of this struggle, which Browne temporarily resolves not in a martial posture but on his knees (I, xix), he believes that no reasonable man can be an atheist (I, xx). Almost everyone is willing to believe something, like a bit of gossip, on far less evidence than Browne possesses for thinking of both nature and history, including the miracles in the Bible, as effects of "the little finger of the Almighty" (I, xxi).

As an Anglican Browne is using his human reason to distinguish where possible between central points of faith and peripheral details: he does not take every verse in the Bible as equally "true." Section xxii lists questions that come to his mind as he reads the Bible. Some of these are merely verbal; others, fallible conclusions about nature made by prescientific authors. Despite the plethora of difficulties it presents, the Bible is a great book (I, xxiii-xxiv) because its main thread is the assertion that God is watching over His people. Perhaps He is watching over Browne when he says that he would not be a martyr to a peremptory interpretation of a particular passage. Browne is believing according to his measure, and he hopes he has ". . . a faith acceptable in the eyes of God" (I, xxv). He is trying to attain wisdom, the archetype of which is the very attribute he is describing. From that point of view, of course, no miracle is more miraculous than another. "We doe too narrowly define the power of God, restraining it to our owne capacities" (I, xxvii, pp. 44-45), Browne asserts. That which he cannot understand he has no reason to deny.

Besides miracles and examples of God's providence, the Bible describes spirits and angels. There can be bad spirits (even witches) as well as good, and there can be an oversoul or general spirit hanging over us (I, xxx-xxxii). These are the highest parts of God's creation, as the material world (I, xxxv) is the lowest. We men are the middle creatures (this is where Browne began), those amphibians who by their nature have to live in both worlds at once. There is one world to sense, but two to reason—the visible and the invisible, where his philosophy and theology meet. At the lower end of the chain of being there is a rude mass, then plant life, then animal, then man, and finally spirit. Man is the middle of these five because he partakes of animal on the one hand and of spirit on the other. As an embryologist Browne sees a parallel between this chain and the growth of the fetus in the womb. He perceives causes and effects in the invisible world of spirit. So he continues on man and the theory of traduction or the problem of how and when the soul enters the mass of tissue which we are (I, xxxvi). Our souls are not subject to time but our bodies are. In time we decay, but the crumbling of these walls of flesh releases the soul to eternity.

So Browne ends Part I with a view of death and with eschatology or the endings of things.[13] He is more ashamed of death than afraid of it (I, xl), for living long hardly improves our natures (I, xlii). Thank God no one of us knows exactly when he will die; even this is proof that God is in charge of the "secret glome or bottom of our days" (I, xliii). Thoughts on death conjure up pictures of Judgment Day and the end of the world (I, xlvii), and the mystical philosophy of the resurrection of the body (I, xlviii). For a glimpse into heaven and hell Browne needs a more absolute piece of optics than he owns. He was never scared into being good by thoughts of hell; it is not the vulgar place of torture some say it is (I, li). Whether Browne at death will be sent to heaven or to hell, he is still confident of God's mercy and justice, for both are aspects of His wisdom. The most he can hope for is "to bring up the rere of heaven" (I, lviii). And this is the *tenor* of his belief, what he *holds* to be true in his love of God, that is, his faith and hope.

But the greatest of these is charity. "Now for that other virtue . . . ," he begins his second part, "without which Faith is a meer notion, and of no existence. . . ." This must be the practice of the theory, the means of the salvation he has hoped for. As a doctor and philologist, Browne knows that "salvation" is the word for "health," which is related to "whole." When he looks from his view of the One to the problem of the One in the Many, again he has no other way than that of his own mind and temperament. His loving comes the more easily as he believes that some of God's own love has descended upon him. He likes Jews, Catholics, Hindus, and the Irish. He can eat whatever is served, including snails in southern France. But even this social adjustment must come from God, for charity exercised merely for the sake of proving oneself a good neighbor will soon run out: "I give no Alms only to satisfie the hunger of my brother, but to filfill and accomplish the Will and Command of my God" (II, ii). And as he widens his view from the One to the Many, Browne perceives various ways of carrying out this second great command. Giving alms, clothing the naked, and feeding the hungry are a few, but Browne as a scholar is equally impelled to give of his own mind:

To this (as calling my selfe a Scholler,) I am obliged by the duty of my condition; I make not therefore my head a grave, but a treasure of knowledge; I intend no Monopoly, but a Community of learning; I study not for my owne sake onely, but for theirs that study not for themselves (II, iii, p. 93).

It is useless for brothers to fall out because of differences in religion or on grounds of nationality (II, iv). How can one man judge another's mind and heart when it is all he can do to master the knowledge of his own?

This brings him to friendship and the love he feels

for the friend to whom he appears to be writing all this. When two bodies can thus become one soul, there are in its comtemplation the same enigmas, mysteries, and riddles that there are in divinity (II, vi). Browne the youth acted on moral grounds only, but now he loves for religious reasons and has discovered the paradox that "the truest way to love another is to despise our selves" (II, vii), that is, in utter selflessness. Though I talk of my parts not without loathing, a loving disposition who fails in love can never be accused of pride in the same way that a person who does not admit failure is proud. I know six languages and all the constellations of my horizon, but. . . . This passage (II, viii, p. 104) echoes "Though I speak with the tongues of men or of angels . . . ," or Hamlet's ironic discovery that he is at once the paragon of animals and the quintessence of dust.

As the first part of *Religio* commands a harmony between man and God, so the second commands a harmony among men. Such harmony is in my nature already, Browne says, in my love of painting and of music (II, ix). Thus "no man is alone because every man is a Microcosme" if he perceives his relation to the macrocosm "and carries the whole world about him" (II, x, p. 110). In his own thoughts each man is with God or with the Devil, and what further extremes of society could a man wish for? Some people would call me lucky (or "fortunate"), but actually it is God's providence that has guided me thus far in my thirty years of life. "Nature tells me I am the Image of God as well as Scripture"—my two manuscripts for the study of God I described in Part I: "He that understands not thus much, hath not his introduction or first lesson, and is yet to begin the Alphabet of man" (II, xi, p. 111).

Thus Browne ends where he began, as he completes the circle of his own confession; he ends Part II as he ended Part I with sleep, death, and the love of man in the love of God. Like every truly religious spirit, Browne is in this world and yet not part of it.

Such a paraphrase as this, however, is useful only as it impels us to read Browne's thoughts in Browne's own words, to perceive in prose, as we can perceive in any given poem, the relationship between a particular set of stylistic means and a particular set of conceptual and emotional ends, to which we willingly respond. "For a great prose," Logan Pearsall Smith said of Donne's sermons, "needs a great subject matter, needs great themes and a high spectacular vision, a solemn and steadfast conception of life and meaning."[14] The prose art of *Religio Medici*, like every living piece of music or painting or literature, is symbolically an affirmation of the value of human will and imagination. A sensitive reader comes to *Religio* as he comes to Yeats' "A Dialogue of Self and Soul" or Eliot's "Four Quartets," sensing that all three are struggles to reconcile suffering with faith in the possibility of love and meaning. As literature, all three of these "poems" use the essential methods of art: evocation, incantation, implied and expressed opposition, modulation of one tone set against another, tension, and equilibrium.[15]

Browne's subject matter is religion, and there are only two ways to talk about God: either we cannot speak of the ineffable, or else, recognizing our finitude, we can try. Semanticists often treat language as obfuscation; students of style, on the other hand, are amazed to discover how much words can convey. Language that conveys belief is not merely logical: it becomes larger than true or false, inductive or deductive. If one were to swear "I believe my son is innocent," for example, he is staking his reputation and maybe his life. Such language is exhibitive, for you know what kind of man is saying it. It may also be performative, for a man's life goes beyond grammar, rhetoric, and logic.

Hence the connection between style and certitude and doubt, between style and humility. Professor D. C. Allen, describing the *vida-es-sueno* psychology of the early seventeenth century, notes that whereas early Renaissance prose is the child of blissful man in the full tide of optimistic learning, the Jacobeans strike a chord of spiritual distress.[16] The anti-Ciceronian stylists became the doubters of our living in the best of all possible worlds; or rather, the doubters could not employ in their prose the Ciceronian opulence. Some of them wrote what Professor Morris W. Croll has called "Senecan" style or "baroque." Professor Allen describes Browne's prose as "African." There was an awakened interest in the patristic literature of such fathers as St. Augustine and Tertullian, both of Africa, whose style, filled with adumbrations, is sometimes tentative, sometimes full. Milton, the Ciceronian, complained of the "knotty Africanisms, the pampered metaphors, the intricate and involved sentences of the father" (St. Augustine of Africa).[17] But Sir Henry Wotton, in commenting on the style of Sir Richard Baker's *Meditations* (1636), wrote:

I must necde observe and much admire the very Character of your Stile, which seemeth to mee to have not a little of the African Idea of St. Augustine's Age, full of sweet Rapture, and of researched Conceipts, nothing borrowed; nothing vulgar; and yet all flowing from you (I know not how) with a certaine equal facility. So as I see, your worldly troubles have been but Pressing-yrons to your Heavenly cogitations.[18]

Browne discovered all the prodigies of Africa within himself (I, xv, p. 24). At Winchester he had been imbued with "the Christian Cicero," Lactantius, who was born in Africa; and he was more partial to the Augustinian tradition of Neoplatonism than he was to the Lycian or Roman. Marsilio Ficino said the latter two Neoplatonic academies were "clear," the African academy was "obscure" or "enigmatic."

The paradoxes of Christianity had had a long history in their English expression, from the Biblical translations of Tyndale and Coverdale to the doublets and rhythms of *The Book of Common Prayer*. Note, in the "General Confession," for example, the doublets (sometimes linked by alliteration) and the parallelisms:

Almighty and most merciful Father, we have erred and strayed from thy ways like lost sheep. We have followed too much the devices and desires of our own Hearts. We have offended against thy holy laws. We have left undone those things which we ought to have done, and we have done those things which we ought not to have done; and there is no health in us. But thou, O Lord, have mercy upon us. . . . Spare thou those. . . . Restore thou those. . . . And grant, O most merciful father . . .

Style like this, according to Professor Kemp Malone, explains how the fifty-four scholars who made the King James version of the Bible should have arrived at a style so uniform throughout that vast project:

The 'committee' did not work in a literary vacuum. They had inherited a glorious tradition of literary prose. They had before them the admirable work of Tyndale and Coverdale and other sixteenth-century translators of the Bible. And above all they had the Book of Common Prayer. . . . By virtue of this traditional stylistic unity, the 'committee' which King James appointed were able to speak with one voice, in spite of their fifty-four mouths. They wrote alike because they belonged to the same literary school, they listened to the same literary masters. And the greatest of these masters was Archbishop Cranmer.[19]

Anglican churches had been speaking this language for sixty years when the Anglican clerics started to make the King James Bible.

To the Africanisms of St. Augustine and this common devotional English prose (based partially on Hebraic synonymy), Browne adds the paradoxes of his own mind as he struggles between the faith of his church and the science of Padua. The result is bound to be a series of stylistic devices that exist for the sake of alternate fission and fusion, that throw concepts into antithetical and correlative pairs, or daringly bridge the gaps between. Of the most common traits in *Religio Medici* we shall examine here only three: (a) the doublets, (b) the rising and falling sentences that combine rhetorical and rhythmical pairs of meaning, and (c) the images that both relate the oppositions of his thought and tie together the apparently disparate parts of his discourse.

Doublets

One can start reading anywhere in *Religio Medici* and make a long list of doublets, broken occasionally by triplets:

beget contempt and scorn
improperations and terms of scurrility
name and appellation
in silence and dumb contempt
opposition and prejudice
scorn and laughter
solemnities and ceremonies
allurements and baits of superstition
narrow point and center of virtue
with a reel or stagger to the circumference
in a particular way and method
satires and invectives
confirm and establish our opinions
extravagant and irregular heads like mine

general breach or dichotomy
do subdivide and mince themselves
aenigmas and riddles
an easie and necessary belief
scales and roundles to mount the pinnacles and highest
  pieces of divinity
condemn to the fire those swarms and millions of
  rhapsodies begotten only to distract and abuse the
  weaker judgments of scholars, and to maintain the trade
  and mystery of typographers
to be convulst and tremble
with dread and horror
a constant and settled way of goodness
our primary and predestinate forms
in the causes, nature, and affections of the Eclipses of the
  sun and moon, etc.

Many of the doublets are so close together that one can only surmise that the general wonder Browne brought to the universe and to the contemplation of himself overflowed even to the wonder of language. As Adam first named the objects around him, so Browne seems surprised with words, especially that he can say the same thing in two different ways or even three, which ever so slightly modalize the thing. To him language is a pentecostal experience.

On the other hand, so many of the pairs actually serve a dichotomous function that it is useless to classify them. Some, like the double process of religious faith or doubt, first intellectualize a proposition and then relish it into being. Some exactly prescribe a spatial concept and then, with the second word, give it a psychological qualification. Some combine Latin and Anglo-Saxon, each with a particular effect. Some are different in connotation and similar in denotation; others divide the meaning but produce a single emotional effect. Some are correlatives to reconcile two parts of a concept; others, as antitheses, push two concepts poles apart.

Rising and Falling Sentence Patterns

Another stylistic trait in *Religio Medici* related to the dichotomous mode of procedure but existing in whole periods rather than in phrases is a form of sentence pattern which I shall call the metabolic style. It consists of Browne's taking us in a single sentence from a very low point in subject matter, diction, and rhythm, up to a high point; then, beginning at a high point and bringing us down. First noted, I believe, by Basil Anderton,[20] this stylistic trait gives the effect of building up and breaking down in a series of changes in energy—alternating anabolism and catabolism. The pattern is well suited to the doctor's thoughts on generation and decay, man and God, this world and the next. In a half sentence he swings us up from the trivia of everyday life to the throne of God, often with optimism, concealed pride, and certitude; then the opposite movement takes us down, often with humility and deep irony. Though the word "metabolism" had not been invented, Dr. Browne was aware of the phenomenon in the body of man. Here is one striking expression of it:

Now, for the wals of flesh, wherein the soule doth seeme to be immured before the Resurrection, it is nothing but an elementall composition, and a fabricke that must fall to ashes; *All flesh is grasse*, is not onely metaphorically, but literally true, for all those creatures which we behold are but the hearbs of the field, digested into flesh in them, or more remotely carnified in our selves. Nay, further, we are what we all abhorre, *Anthropophagi* and Cannibals, devourers not onely of men, but of ourselves; and that not in an allegory, but a positive truth; for all this mass of flesh that wee behold, came in at our mouths; this frame wee looke upon, hath beene upon our trenchers; . . . (I, xxxvii, p. 57).

In the Pembroke manuscript we have: ". . . to me that consider things in a naturall and experimental way, man seemes to bee but a digestion . . ." (I, xxxix, p. 61). We shall look at a few rising sentences, then a few falling ones, and finally at a mixed pattern wherein Browne seems to raise us in one manner by dropping us in another, or is apparently letting us down while actually lifting us up.

Here is a simple upward movement: death ". . . though nauseous to queasier stomachs, yet to prepared appetites is Nectar, and a pleasant potion of immortality" (II, ix, p. 109). Again, the famous sentence on music takes us up from a tavern to a mystical mathematics of heaven: ". . . for even that vulgar and Taverne Musicke, which makes one man merry, another mad, strikes mee into a deepe fit of devotion, and a profound contemplation of the first Composer . . ." (II, ix, p. 107). This simple pattern often lifts the reader from the "I" to the "Thou" of Browne's fundamental religious position: ". . . I remember I am not alone, and therefore forget not to contemplate him and his attributes who is ever with mee, especially those two mighty ones, his wisedome and eternitie; . . ." (I, xi, p. 17). As the meaning rises, the grammar becomes more complex, the diction more ponderous, and the rhythm more regular. Once more, Browne takes us from the physical body of man, to angels, and finally to God: ". . . doe but extract from the corpulency of bodies, or resolve things beyond their first matter, and you discover the habitation of Angels, which if I call the ubiquitary and omnipresent essence of God, I hope I shall not offend Divinity; . . ." (I, xxxv, p. 54). A whole paragraph (I, xxviii) starts out with the bones of the dead used as relics and ends with this: "Now one reason I tender so little devotion unto reliques, is, I think, the slender and doubtfull respect I have alwayes held unto Antiquities: for that indeed which I admire is farre before antiquity, that is, Eternity, and that is God himselfe; . . ." (I, xxviii, pp. 45-46). Up to the colon Browne is talking fast and loose, but after the colon he makes us stop at each word.

In the opposite or catabolic type of sentence, Browne almost shockingly tumbles us from a high concept to a low one. To go outside *Religio Medici* for a moment, one of the most remarkable falls in English prose is the final negative Anglo-Saxon verb in this sentence from the dedication of *Urn Burial*: "But remembering the early civility they brought upon their countreys, and forgetting long passed mischiefes; We mercifully preserve their bones, and pisse not upon their ashes." In the following longer sentence, Browne takes us down gently in three successive stages—God, man, beast:

In our study of Anatomy there is a masse of mysterious Philosophy, and such as reduced the very Heathens to Divinitie; yet amongst all those rare discoveries and curious pieces I finde in the fabricke of man, I doe not so much content my selfe as in that I finde not, that is, no Organe or proper instrument for the rationall soule; for in the braine, which wee tearme the seate of reason, there is not anything of moment more than I can discover in the cranie of a beast: . . . (I, xxxvi, pp. 56-57).

Again, Browne deflates himself as well as his reader in a sentence like this: "There are a bundle of curiosities, not onely in Philosophy but in Divinity, proposed and discussed by men of the most supposed abilities, which indeed are not worthy our vacant hours, much lesse our more serious studies; Pieces onely fit to be placed in *Pantagruels* Library, or bound up with *Tartaretus De modo Cacandi*" (I, xxi, p. 36). The hard "c's" of the final word humorously remind us of "curiosity" in the first part of the sentence, particularly as the sound is repeated in "discussed" and "vacant" while the sentence is being lowered conceptually. In a falling sentence, once more, Browne takes us down from the heroic Christian martyrs, through military exploits, to low-brow antics: "For, to speak properly, these are the true and almost onely examples of fortitude: Those that are fetch'd from the field, or drawn from the actions of the Campe, are not oft-times so truely precedents of valour as audacity, and at the best attaine to some bastard piece of fortitude: . . ." (I, xxv, p. 42).

This high-to-low type of sentence has philosophical validity as he contemplates the mysteries of God with his own poor mind:

I know that he is wise in all, wonderfull in that we conceive, but far more in what we comprehend not; for we behold him but asquint, upon reflex or shadow; our understanding is dimmer than *Moses* Eye; we are ignorant of the backparts and lower side of his Divinity; therefore to pry into the maze of his Counsels is not onely folly in Man, but presumption even in Angels (I, xiii, p. 20).

Apropos of attempting to check on the validity of the Bible by means of secular history, Browne writes: "I confesse I have had an unhappy curiosity this way, till I laughed my selfe out of it with a piece of *Justine*, where hee delivers that the children of *Israel* for being scabbed were banished Egypt" (I, xxix, p. 46).

One of the most carefully sustained catabolic passages is that on the Day of Judgment, which starts out like Donne's four imagined corners and ends with one "miserable offender":

This is the day that must make good that great attribute of God, his Justice, that must reconcile those unanswerable doubts which torment the wisest understandings, and reduce those seeming inequalities and respective distributions in this world, to an equality and recompensive Justice in the next. This is that one day, that shall include and comprehend all that went before it, wherein as in the last scene, all the Actors must enter, to compleate and make up the Catastrophe of this great peece. This is the day whose memory hath onely power to make us honest in the darke, and to bee vertuous without a witnesse (I, xlvii, p. 71).

The climax of this kind of falling paradox naturally comes at the end of Part I of *Religio*, a section whose logical intent is to reduce this world to a nonentity before the spaciousness of God, only to begin again, in Part II, with the bustle of this world and of the human beings in it:

Before Abraham was, I am, is the saying of Christ. . . . And in this sense, I say, the world was before the Creation, and at an end before it had a beginning; and thus was I dead before I was alive; though my grave be *England*, my dying place was Paradise, and Eve miscarried of mee before she conceiv'd of Cain (I, lix, p. 86).

The very last sentence of *Religio Medici* in ten words passes from *God* down to *me*, and the *me* is put into a concessive clause: "Thy will bee done, though in my owne undoing." Even the rhythm falls away from the initial spondee and iamb.

Sometimes the rising and falling patterns are mixed in sentences that fall in diction and rhythm while rising conceptually, or vice versa. The ironic result is that Browne gives us an apparent feeling of certitude about things in this world and a real certitude for things not of this world; by being proud in one way, he induces a humility in another. For example: "There are questionlesse, many canonized on earth, that shall never be called Saints in Heaven; and have their names in Histories and Martyrologies, who in the eyes of God are not so perfect Martyrs as was that wise Heathen, Socrates, that suffered on a fundamentall point of Religion, the Unity of God" (I, xxvi, p. 43). The all too human subject of the first part of the sentence is complex in polysyllables and doublets, while the rising from man to God in the last part of the sentence is almost stark in its humanity. In the following sentence disbelief is cast "high" and belief is cast "low," contrary to expectation: "There are a set of heads that can credit the relations of Mariners, yet question the Testimony of Saint Paul" (I, xxi, p. 34).

One sentence begins with the game of bowls (or anticipates Dalton's quincuncial pinball machine) and ends with God's hand guiding the ball: "Surely there are in every man's life certaine rubs, doublings, and wrenches which passe a while under the effects of chance, but at the last, well examined, prove the meere hand of God" (I, xxvii, p. 27). The inclusion of that little word "meere" heightens the paradox of this rising pattern, for as Browne takes us from the low concept to the high he makes the low seem high and the high seem low. The shock comes in the contrast between man's complexity of entanglement and God's clear simple will. The apparently rational answer to the problem of accident-or-design is composed in complex patterns, while the real and therefore the most rational answer is given in plain Anglo-Saxon.

One more example will do: Browne paradoxically links heaven with Homer's chain, and in three stages decreases the apparent means while increasing the achieved end: "There is a neerer way to heaven than *Homers* chaine; an easie Logick may conjoyne heaven and earth in one argument, and with lesse than a Sorites resolve all things unto God" (I, xviii, p. 31). While we are ascending from earth to heaven, we back down from the complex symbol of the chain of being to a fraction of an elliptical syllogism, or not even that.

Metaphors

A third stylistic device in *Religio Medici* which is related to the duality of Browne's mind and the subject matter of his book is the tropes which he so constantly uses. As if this were the most important part of his style, Browne takes special pains in his preface to call our attention to it; and his early critics either admired him for it or discounted his philosophy because of it. We have seen how he prefers the concreteness of an "easie Platonick description" to the abstractions of a logical definition. To the doctor the fabric of man's body with its tissue, nerves, veins, and arteries serves somehow to house an immortal soul. So he seems to be conscious of metaphor as the visible part of his discourse which contains the invisible thought.

For his generation the metaphors constituted "strong" language. Sir Kenelm Digby objected to them, and another early critic, Dr. Alexander Ross, was equally vehement: ". . . as I suspect that friendship," writes this schoolmaster of the small view, "which is set out in too many *Verball Complements*; so doe I that Religion which is trimmed up with too many *Tropicall pigments*, and Rhetoricall dresses. If the gold be pure, why feares it the Touch stone?"[21] Oblivious of his own skill in metaphor just now demonstrated, Ross uses another: "Expect not here from mee *Rhetoricall* flourishes; I study matter, not words: *Good wine needs no bush*."[22] His precedent, he insists, is Aristotle, who ". . . in his *Topicks* will have us to avoid Metaphors, which cast a mist upon the thing desired; every *Metaphor* being more obscure than proper words. But I see you delight in such fancies; for you define light, to be the shadow of God. . . ."[23] Why not, he asks, quote Empedocles on the sea as the sweat of the earth or Plato's poles of the earth as its little feet? "Such definitions are good for women and children, who are delighted with toyes; wise men search into the causes and natures of things." That Browne's language is "strong" is witnessed also by the authors of two early works on microscopy, both of whom knew the style that Browne was master of. Henry Power, his protégé, imitates it with awe and delight. But Hooke apologizes for his inability: ". . . those stronger Works of Wit and Imagination are above my weak Abilities; or if they had not been so, I would have made use of them in this present Subject before me."[24]

At least three different functions of metaphor emerge in *Religio Medici*: metaphors as they simply evoke an idea; metaphors as epistemic means of joining the visible and invisible worlds; and repeated metaphors which serve as symbolic rather than logical links between various parts of Browne's argument.

The first use of metaphor has been well illustrated already. Browne depends upon the concrete representation of ideas, as any poet does. A student of anatomy, he rarely thinks of God without conjuring before our eyes "the hand of God" or "the little finger of the Almighty." It is that part of God which as providence *reaches* down into man's affairs, so well illustrated by Will Marshall in the frontispiece of the book. It is also that part of the human body which Galen made famous in medical literature as proof of the wisdom of the Creator. The danger in this manner of speaking was well recognized, particularly by members of the Royal Society after 1662, and helped make Browne theologically suspect. Images are a source of error when the stupid take them literally: this would be Browne's response. From the habit of deducing rigid interpretations from metaphor ". . . have risen not only popular Errors in Philosophy, but vulgar and sensless Heresies in Divinity. . . ."[25] Thoughts on the right and wrong use of metaphor lead Browne into the nominalist versus realist controversy, and the difference between the Roman Catholic and the Protestant view of the Holy Eucharist.

Another use of metaphor is to make epistemic relations between faith and reason. At a time when Baconian science was making the two worlds more disparate, Browne actually resolved the question of how man can be a part of each. The metaphors of his mind and imagination make him a true "amphibium" that can live in both. Reinhold Niebuhr, in another context, points out that the tropes denoting Christian eschatology, such as "The Second Coming" and "The Last Judgment," *image* forth as future history what are present and permanent spiritual evaluations.[26] In this regard Browne is not an irresponsible stylist, and the best example of metaphor as epistemic link between the known and the hoped-for is the circle image in *Religio*.

These relating metaphors are part of Browne's humility, for definitions and syllogisms teach him nothing that can be immediately apprehended about God: rather they set up new combinations of wordy accidents and qualities which cause man to admire his own rather than God's brainwork. It is sufficient to Browne that God is an artist and not a logician. Twice in his book he discovers that something is not only metaphorically but also literally true: ". . . to call our selves a Microcosm, or little world, I thought it onely a pleasant trope of Rhetorick, till my nearer judgement and second thoughts told me there was a reall truth therein: . . ." (I, xxxiv, p. 53); and "*All flesh is grasse*, is not onely metaphorically, but literally true . . ." (I, xxxvii, p. 57).

Granted that some of his metaphors are stylistic flourishes (I am sure that Browne was pleased with what he wrote), his philosophical metaphors are indispensable for the conceptual complexes they contain. A philosophical metaphor, such as "God *created* matter out of nothing," omits that part of its literal meaning which is not ostensively definable even in principle. Thus "the hand of God" contains the free will, the magnanimity, the potential for artifaction and liberality, the relationship between part and whole, and many other meanings. None of them can be defined ostensively, that is by pointing to the *hand* of God; yet the clash in the comparison to a human hand accomplishes the meaning Browne intends, more economically, more vividly, and more accurately than any other concatenation of words and phrases.

A final use of metaphor is that of repeated symbol to join various parts of Browne's treatise. Throughout its easy and conversational flow and apparent digression, associative images carry us from one part to another. For example, Browne speaks in one section of the rebellion of passion against reason, and of reason against faith. In another, he mentions the religious strife of Jew against Christian and of Mohammedan against both. The link is that the Sadducistic Jews are treated as rationalists, and the Moslems as passionate spreaders of their religion by the sword. A triple struggle in one area of experience is paralleled by a triple struggle in another, and the thoughts joined by an allusion to the triumvirate of ancient Rome. Of this type of metaphorical use is the series that Browne may have first learned as a boy in his father's cloth shop in Cheapside—such metaphors as *thread, glome* (a ball of yarn), *bottom* (for winding thread), *filament,* and *fabric.* Design, Browne believed, characterizes the universe: "There is therefore some other hand that twines the thread of life

than that of nature." Though pages separate the metaphors, they actually act like a thread that twines parts
of his discourse together. Apropos of God's providence,
another series of connecting metaphors consists of
secret walks, circular routes, serpentine paths, and
labyrinthian ways. It was by means of a *thread* that
Theseus found his way out of the maze. Similarly,
providence is linked throughout the book by such metaphors as manuscripts, short characters, stenography,
letters, "two books from which I collect my Divinity,"
"the alphabet of man," and cryptic writing on the wall.
Again, thinking of himself as the microcosm and ad-
miring the works of God in the small rather than the
large, Browne prefers Regiomontanus' fly to his eagle;
in a poem (I, xiii) he calls himself an "industrious fly
buzzing God's praises" (when "fly" was used for any
winged insect, particularly a bee) and uses the phrase
"suck my Divinity from the flower of nature." The
phrase "Regiomontanus his eagle" is linked in his mind
with the Lord Monteagle who received the remarkable
letter that warned of the Gunpowder Plot.

Though hesitant to make stereotypes of national
differences, Browne reads history as an English Protestant in 1634 and perceives "God's hand" in the times
of nations. Spain is throughout a symbol of pride, and
Holland a symbol of humility—one nation Roman
Catholic; the other, Protestant. What men in their
pride will take as accident, others in their humility will
see as God's plan. Hence Browne's use of a Spanish
phrase in this sentence: ". . . nor can I relate the history
of my life . . . with a *Bezo las Manos* to Fortune . . ."
(I, xvii, p. 27). Then from the Gunpowder Plot, sup-
posedly engineered by Roman Catholics from Spain,
Browne goes to the defeat of the Spanish Armada and
finally to King Philip the Second. Near the end of the
long section, he writes:

The successe of that pety Province of Holland (of which the Grand Seigneur proudly said, That if they should trouble him as they did the Spaniard, hee would send his men with shovels and pick-axes, and throw it into the sea,) I cannot altogether ascribe to the ingenuity and industry of the people, but to the mercy of God, that hath disposed them to such a thriving *Genius*; and to the will of providence, that dispenceth her favour to each Countrey in their preordinate season (I, xvii, p. 28).

If the Spaniards ascribed their defeat to bad luck, Browne would remind them that it was the *Romans* who erected a temple to Fortune. Much farther along in his book, when he talks of his lack of national repugnance, he mentions three Roman Catholic countries and one Protestant: ". . . nor do I behold with prejudice the *French*, *Italian*, *Spaniard*, or *Dutch*: but where I find their actions in ballance with my Countrey-mens, I honour, love, and embrace them in the same degree" (II, i, p. 88). But that sentence no longer has the same meaning once we become aware of the already planted symbols. True, *Religio Medici* is impossible to outline, but by means of these allusive metaphors, Browne is connecting part to part.

The analysis of stylistic traits as they function within *Religio Medici* could be long. This will suffice to show that Browne's use of doublets, his dependence upon rising and falling sentences in diction, rhythm, and concept, and his appeal to metaphor are related to the dualism of his mind and to the shape of his account of his religion. These stylistic traits subserve his thought and feeling; they support and stress both idea and tone.

On the flyleaves of Browne's *Vulgar Errors*, Coleridge inscribed a letter to Sara Hutchinson, dated March 10, 1804:

Sir Thomas Brown is among my first favourites. Rich in various *knowledge*; exuberant in conceptions and conceits, contemplative, imaginative; often truly great and magnificent in his style and diction, tho' doubtless, too often big, stiff, and hyperlatinistic—: . . . he is a quiet and sublime Enthusiast with a stronge tinge of the Fantast, the Humorist constantly mingling with & flashing across the Philosopher, as the darting colours in shot silk play upon the main dye. In short, he has brains in his Head, which is all the more interesting for a *little Twist* in the Brains.[27]

Even more importantly, Coleridge confessed of *Religio Medici*: "This book paints certain parts of my moral and intellectual being, (the best parts, no doubt,) better than any other book I have ever met with;—and the style is throughout delicious."[28]

Chapter IX

INTERLUDE:
BROWNE'S
FIRST CRITIC

In spite of "the word of a king" Strafford went to the block in May 1641.[1] With mounting rancor, the rebellion in Ireland turned into the massacre of the English, which Viscount Falkland had feared when young Browne was in Dublin with his stepfather. Parliament's Grand Remonstrance having been tossed aside by Charles on his return from Scotland, the news from Ireland convinced the people of London that Protestantism was being abolished. Mobs shouted, "No Popery! No bishops! No Popish lords!" To anticipate their impeaching the queen (as he feared they would), Charles attempted to impeach the five members of Parliament. The strife, now confused between Parliament and king, Protestant and Roman Catholic, had flared out in actual warfare. The skirmish at Acton had been won by Parliamentary soldiers on November 12, 1642, only nine miles west of St. Paul's Cathedral. Along with the Earl of Dorset's son and the Earl of Middlesex, Sir Kenelm Digby was taken prisoner, and all three placed in comfortable quarters befitting their high rank, in Winchester House in Southwark.[2] The prisoners were allowed great freedom within the house and garden. Meanwhile, King Charles was at Christ Church, Oxford, and his army of Cavaliers had garrisoned the town.

At this juncture in English history, the London bookseller Andrew Crooke released the anonymous book called *Religio Medici*. Within a few days it became the subject of a correspondence between two of the most famous men in England: one, an Anglican earl at the moment counseling King Charles at Oxford to bring the impending war to an immediate end; the other, a handsome Roman Catholic, duelist, amateur theologian, lover, swashbuckling naval hero, and dabbler in science and the occult.

Only two years Browne's senior, Sir Kenelm Digby had already cut a swath through Europe. In 1627, on a privateering expedition with two ships under his own command, he had captured some French and Dutch off Gibraltar and had put to rout a small French and Venetian navy at Scanderoon. In 1625 he had secretly married the well-known beauty (some said too well-known), Venetia Stanley. When she died in 1633, Ben Jonson praised her charms in *Eupheme*, and Owen Feltham, William Habington, and a host of others joined in the poetic mourning. For years the court gossips were identifying the characters in Digby's *Memoirs* and even said that Shirley had derived his plot for *The Wedding* from them. About the time Dr. Browne was beginning his medical practice in Norwich, Sir Kenelm achieved new fame in a duel with Lord Mount le Ros.

Politically, this ultra-Royalist played the Anglicans against the Catholics, and both against Parliament. He collected money from English Catholics at home to help the king force the English prayer book upon the Scots, a move guaranteed to embarrass the English church; and he was constantly crossing the English Channel to round up Roman support for the queen. At Oxford, according to Aubrey, he had been called "the Mirandola of the age,"[3] but others said he was the very Pliny of the age for telling lies. Evelyn thought him "an arrant mountebank."[4] To John Selden, the scholar, he was a "Sir Politick Would-be":

Sir Kenelm Digby was several times taken and let go again, at last imprisoned in Winchester House. I can compare him to nothing but a great Fish that we catch and let go again, but still he will come to the Bait; at last therefore we put him into some Pond for store.[5]

In 1641 Digby had been summoned before Parliament to account for his actions. Accused among other things of seducing the young Earl of Down to the Roman church, he said:

I do not deny, Mr. Speaker, but that I am a Catholique. . . . But withall I must professe that I have ever affected freedom of judgement, and could never yield to fetter up my reason (since I had the use of any) by a blind and implicite fayth.[6]

Four years before, that is in 1638, he had published at Paris a tiny 16mo book of 117 pages entitled A Conference with a Lady about Her Choice of Religion. Such discourses, he wrote, ". . . are deeper looked into when they are pondered by a prudentiall judgement, than when they are examined by scientific speculations."[7] The argument that follows is persuasive, logical, interspersed with happy examples, and yet too proudly sure.

Faith is necessary to men, Digby had argued, because the beatitude we naturally desire for the soul is so immersed in flesh as to render it almost impossible to enjoy. Once the soul is freed from the body, it remains the same for eternity; therefore, it behooves us to give it, while in our earthly bodies, the appropriate bent for felicity. This is where we need the Church. The faith taught by Christ and propagated by the Apostles depends upon the testimony of the Roman Catholic church, which is guarded by the Holy Ghost from allowing any false doctrines to creep into it. The great tradition of the Church is ". . . absolutely more certaine and infallible than any naturall science whatsoever" (p. 55). All this and more Digby wrote to the young lady and published.

While shouts of "No Popery!" filled the streets, Sir Kenelm was momentarily safe. In prison he had pen and ink and an apparently inexhaustible supply of small sheets of paper, approximately six inches by eight, boxed three-quarters of an inch from each edge by thin red lines. His small and beautifully legible handwriting, in perfectly straight lines very close together, filled both sides of the unlined pages.[8] Here in Winchester House, away from wars and duels, chemistry and intrigue, Sir Kenelm had time to work on his *Two Treatises Concerning the Body and Soul of Man*.[9] In his letter to Dorset about *Religio Medici* he refers constantly to this work of his and to the conversations he had had in Paris pertaining to it with his friend the Jesuit Fr. Thomas White.

Sir Kenelm's own mercurial nature as well as his commitment to finish this long theological treatise must account for his reading books and writing about them in prison with such speed. He wrote two such letters about books, recommended by friends, while he was in Winchester House: Spenser's *Faerie Queene* and Browne's *Religio Medici*. On the very next day after receiving the *Faerie Queene*, Sir Kenelm returned it with a letter which, printed in 1643, contained twenty-five pages, limited to the exegesis of a single stanza, the twenty-second stanza of the ninth canto of Book II.[10] This stanza, whose Pythagorean symbols Digby is asked to explain, concerns the abode (i.e., man's body) of Alma (soul) and is worth quoting in full since it forms a link between Digby's most serious theological work and the animadversions he tossed off in a night on *Religio Medici*:

> The frame thereof sed partly circulare,
> And part triangulare: O worke divine!
> These two the first and last proportions are;
> The one imperfect, mortall, feminine,
> Th' other immortal, perfect, masculine;
> And twixt them both a quadrate was the base,
> Proportioned equally by seven and nine:
> Nine was the circle sett in heavens place;
> All which compacted made a good Diapase.

Were there nothing extant but this single stanza, wrote Digby, Spenser could be shown to be ". . . thoroughly verst in the Mathematicall Sciences, in Philosophy, and in Divinity . . ." (p. 4). It is, he continues, a description of the body of man informed with a rational soul. The triangle is the body, least perfect, most angular, containing the least space, and consequently the "lowest" of all geometrical figures. The circle is the mind or soul, and even God. It is the "highest" of the figures because it is made of one substance:

For, as God hath neither beginning nor ending: so, neither of these can be found in a circle, although that being made of the successive motions of a line, it must be supposed to have a beginning somewhere: God is compared to a Circle whose Center is everywhere, but his circumference no where. But mans soul is a Circle, whose Circumference is limited by the true center of it, which is onely God (p. 7).

The whole of man is the "O worke divine," and the quadrate at the base of the figure is the four humours of man's body. Seven and nine are mystical numbers, the superior governing the inferior, as the body (i.e., the seven planets of the sky) are ruled over by the intelligences (i.e., the nine orders of angels). Referring to the second and thirty-second stanzas of Canto 6 of Book III, as well as to the end of Spenser's *Epithalamion*, Digby opines that the soul enters the body at the instant of conception. And now he returns ". . . the book which . . . yesterday you sent me . . ." (p. 24).

On December 21, 1642, after Digby had been in this pleasant prison for five weeks, he received a letter from his friend Edward Sackville, fourth Earl of Dorset, recommending to a man of his interests in letters, religion, and science, a new book that the earl had just read in Oxford. In his reply, Digby "beg[s] leave to ask your Lordship if you now see the cannons, the ensigns, the arms, and other martial preparations at Oxford. . . ." He prays that his friend's "counsels there" will be "happy and successful ones to bring about that peace." He sent a servant out immediately to buy a copy of *Religio Medici*, read it through that very night, and started writing to Dorset about it in the early morning of December 22, 1642. All that winter day he filled sixteen of his small sheets of paper with his "Observations." This, the first criticism of *Religio Medici* that we possess, animadverts upon the man, the style, and the thought. In the first two of these Digby is felicitous, but it is natural that his position, talents, and philosophical bent would lead him astray on Browne's thoughts. It is truer to say that Digby separated religion and poetry than that Browne separated reason and faith, or content and style.

Whoever wrote *Religio Medici*, Digby observes, must be a man of ingenuity and natural evenness of temper (456),[11] but he is obviously not trained as a philosopher (459). Although throughout he shows "strong parts" and a "vigorous brain," he mistakes terms for things and is often not clear (459). The author is a "fine ingenious gentleman" (464) but hardly a scholar.

The "solidity of the judgment" is outweighed by the "airiness of his fancy" and "sudden poetical raptures" (464-65). That the author is more of a poet than a philosopher is shown everywhere in his style. The style is "witty" (454), and this wit detracts from philosophy. A tough matter like the Trinity cannot be dissected by "the dint of wit" (458), which causes the author to proceed by leaps and flashes rather than by orderly discourse (457). How can one deal with the nature of predestination by "short touches" (458)? Like the lines of some divine poets, this style is "strong" (469), and almost everything in it is "handsomely said" (459). The best thing about the book is the "sweetness" of expression and "the sound of the words" (463).

For over three hundred years critics, with Digby, have "been entertained with delights . . . sucked from so noble a conversation" (454), but they have not concurred with Digby's whole judgment. Digby missed the meaning of *Religio Medici*,[12] as the Earl of Dorset must have caught it, because he mistook the author's intention. Of a more scholastic religious temper, Digby was an apologist and tested the persuasive value of Browne's book in the light not only of his little tract of three years before written to persuade a young lady in France to join the church of Rome but also of his treatise on *The Soul and Body of Man*. "What should I say," Digby asks Dorset, "of his making so particular a narration of personal things, and private thoughts of his own?—the knowledge whereof cannot much conduce to any man's betterment; which I make account is the chief end of his writing this discourse" (469). But Browne had explicitly denied that his purpose was to lay down "a rule unto any other." Digby is too vain to understand this author's modesty in the midst of his setting out so many talents for display. What Browne says of his own attainments is used to derogate himself in the praise of his Creator, but this stands between the *Religio Medici* and Digby's grasp of it. Scoffingly he writes that the theology is no deeper than that of an ordinary catechism for vulgar minds (485). Though in reading the *Faerie Queene* Digby is content to take many things "in a soft and flexible sense," in matters theological he proceeds, with his friend Father White, according to strict syllogistic reasoning:

If he [Browne] had well and thoroughly considered all that is required to that strict way of managing our reason, he would not have censured Aristotle for condemning the fourth figure, out of no other motive, but because it was not consonent to his own principles. . . . In a perfect syllogism, the predicate must be identified with the subject, and each extreme with the middle term, and so, consequently, all three with one another (484).

But since Browne is not arguing by syllogism, Digby's animadversions against what Browne says concerning the relationship of matter and form are beside the point. "This language were handsome for a poet, or a rhetorician to speak," Digby says, "but in a philosopher that should ratiocinate strictly and rigorously, I cannot admit it." Throughout, Digby is comparing Browne's leisurely confession with his own argued discourses: "When your lordship pleaseth, I shall show you another more orderly discourse upon that subject, wherein I have sufficiently proved it to be a solid substance and body" (465). He might better have treated *Religio Medici* (whose style he appreciated) as he had treated Spenser's *Faerie Queene*. That poem's "divinity" he found in one stanza expressed by Hermes Trismegistus' metaphor of a circle whose center is everywhere and whose circumference is nowhere—which is the heart of *Religio Medici*.

While engaged in a fast-growing medical practice

in Norwich, Browne saw his confession, written seven years before, in print. He had said that he could not dispute in religion, and was afraid to argue certain points too strongly since he himself might not believe them the next day. Furthermore, the published work was based on "a broken and imperfect copy." What was worse, Browne heard that some "Observations" written by Sir Kenelm Digby were being published by another printer. How would a mind like Sir Kenelm's take those things which he had set down in an "easie and Platonick description"?

So Browne wrote to Digby on March 3, 1643, acknowledging himself to be the author and begging him to withhold publication of his "Observations" on the imperfect copy until he, Browne, could "within a few weeks" deliver a true copy of *Religio Medici*.

On March 20, 1643, Sir Kenelm wrote a reply to Browne so filled with false modesty and blatant praise that its statements of "fact" can hardly be trusted. Sir Kenelm said that when Crooke delivered Browne's letter to him and told him that some printer was publishing the "Observations," he sent out to find that printer but failed. Who was he? (The printer was Daniel Frere at "The Red Bull" in Little Britain, who had brought out Sir Kenelm's letter on the stanza from the *Faerie Queene*.) Then Digby asserts that Browne must be mistaken; these animadversions must be by some other person, for his were hastily set down and their liberty must be attributed "to the security of a private letter." The fact that Dr. Browne had scarcely been heard of and Sir Kenelm prided himself on a European reputation does not keep the knight from writing like this:

If I had the vanity to give myselfe reputation by entring the listes in publike wth so eminent and learned a man as you are, yet I know right well I am no wayes able to do it: It would be a very unaequall congresse. I pretend not to learning. Those slender notions I have, are but disjoynted pieces I have by chance gleaned up here and there. To encounter such a sinnewy opposite, or make animadversions upon so smart a piece as yrs is, requireth a solide stocke, and exercise in schoole learning. My superficiall besprinkling, will serve onely for a private letter, or familiar discourse with lay auditors.[13]

No one can blame Browne for being pleased with this letter from so distinguished a prisoner in Winchester House. He revised the 1642 copy[14] and authorized Crooke to print the first author-corrected edition of 1643. With it appeared the exchange of letters between Dr. Browne and Sir Kenelm Digby.

Crooke's feelings must have been of mixed anguish and delight. That two such men as Sir Kenelm Digby and the Earl of Dorset had been corresponding about *Religio Medici* was a publisher's dream. And yet, how did a competitor, Frere, get hold of Digby's *Observations*? To vent his feelings and at the same time to protect his new author, Crooke, over the initials "A. B.," told the world how far Sir Kenelm had been from assessing the real value of *Religio Medici*: "wherein he would contradict, he mistaketh or traduceth the intention." He goes so far as to hint that Digby only pretended to write to the Earl of Dorset and wrongfully affixed that nobleman's name to his slight "Observations." For sixteen years the books of Browne and of Digby stood side by side; finally, beginning with the fifth edition in 1659, Andrew Crooke, having evidently bought the rights to Digby's *Observations* from Frere, published them with *Religio Medici*.

Roman Catholic readers, ready to perceive heresy, probably read Digby's *Observations* first and the *Religio* second. Anglican readers flew to Browne's defense the more readily because of Digby's strictures. Henry Bates, for example, wrote to Dr. Browne on August 28, 1647:

But it troubles mee like the fall of Phaeton, that Monsieur le Chevalier, who passes both for a wit and a judgement, should attempt to reyne the horses of the sunne, and *Schioppir* on [i.e., "fire upon"] Religio Medici; I wish hee had thought on the motto of that noble family [i.e., the Earl of Dorset's], whence hee took that employment, *aut numquam tentes aut perfice*, or that hee had animadverted better, or had been *aliud agendo*, then soe *nihil agendo* on that piece, sure then he would have crost himselfe, blest him for that undertaking, and gone to bed rather then to have sitt up soe late to soe little purpose, and lose his sleepe, unless hee intended to make an opiate for his readers.[15]

After the execution of his king on January 30, 1649, at ten o'clock in the morning, the culmination of the bitter war which he had failed to stop, Edward Sackville, Earl of Dorset, never left Dorset House in Salisbury Court on Fleet Street. His death there on July 17, 1652, inspired James Howell, the inveterate letter writer who knew everybody, to publish an elegy on him with the strange title *Ah, Ha, Tumulus, Thalamus* in celebration of a simultaneous wedding and his friend's funeral. Of the Earl of Dorset, Howell wrote:

Where e'er he sate he sway'd & Courts did awe,
Gave *Bishops Gospell*, and the *Judges* law
With such exalted Reasons, which did show
So cleer and strong, that made Astrae bow
To his Opinion, for where He did side
Advantag'd more than half the *Bench* beside . . .
For *Brain, Toung, Spirit, Heart*, and *Personnage*
To mould up such a Lord will ask an age.[16]

Dorset most likely had hoped that the quiet irenicism of Browne's book might have affected men like Digby.

Richard Farrar wrote the epitaph for the first critic of *Religio Medici*:

Under this Tomb the Matchless *Digby* lies;
Digby the Great, the Valiant, and the Wise:
This Ages Wonder for His Noble Parts;
Skill'd in Six Tongues, and Learn'd in All the Arts,
Born on the Day He Dy'd, The 'Eleventh of June,
And that Day Bravely Fought at Scanderoun.
'Tis Rare, that one and the same Day should be
His Day of Birth, of Death, and Victory.

R. F.[17]

But such coincidences were not so rare with Browne. He also knew six languages, and he too died on his birthday. His deathday was a victory, too, not with the doctor at the head of his private navy but "content to bring up the rere in heaven."

Thanks to the Latin translation of *Religio* in 1644 by John Merryweather, and to the inevitable linking of the names of Dorset, Digby, and Howell to his own, Dr. Thomas Browne gained a European reputation. But he had long since turned his mind toward science and paid little further attention to the arguments concerning his *Religio Medici*. In moments snatched from his busy practice in Norwich, he was preparing for the press his magnum opus, *Pseudodoxia Epidemica; or an Enquiry into Vulgar Errors*. The chapter on "Electrical Bodies" commends Sir Kenelm Digby's researches into magnetism. Though explained by Cabeus as due to gyrations in the air, magnetism is a continued effluvium as argued by Gilbert; "And this way of attraction," continues Browne, "is best received, embraced by Sir Kenelm Digby in his excellent Treaty *Of bodies*, [and] allowed by Des Cartes in his *Principles of Philosophy. . . .*"[18]

Chapter X

VULGAR ERRORS

Some men dedicate their lives to establishing new truths and announcing them to their colleagues; thus is a profession served. Others study to serve not the profession but the public. Scientists are prone to disparage these as popularizers, although there is really no reason why a Huxley should be a Darwin. Browne was a successful practitioner, scholar, and teacher. He made no scientific discoveries himself, but he studied what others had discovered in order to bring through his writing the light of scientific inquiry to the dark chaos of popular ignorance.[1]

The result was *Pseudodoxia Epidemica, or Enquiries into very many received tenets and commonly presumed truths, which examined prove but vulgar and common errors*—or, as we have come to call it, *Vulgar Errors*, his major work and by far his best seller. He planned it early and kept it by him late, preparing six editions of it between 1646 and 1672, the last one with a new honor to his name—Thomas Browne, KNIGHT. For him the search for truth was a stern and often lone revaluation of the whole history of error. Not even the limitations of the man and of his age can obscure the fact that this book, though partially a hodgepodge of quaint opinion, is a monument to Browne's genius and passion for truth.

From the very title, *Pseudodoxia Epidemica*, his purpose is clear. "Pseudo-" means "false"; "-doxia," "opinions." "Epidemica" is a medical metaphor: "epi-," something laid on, that is, a disease produced by special causes not generally and continually present in the infected locality; "demos," "people."

In his "To the Reader" he wishes that he could be content with Plato that real truth is only remembering; actually it must be bought at the price of forgetting a lot that we "know." He apologizes for the absence in his work of a community of scholars; but he is in Norwich, not London, and in Norwich it was composed amid the credulous and persistent demand of a large clientele for uroscopy. He decided to write it in English rather than Latin, since he owed his service to England, particularly to its gentry. He is aware of his predecessors in the field: Laurent Joubert's *Erreurs Populaires et propos Vulgaires touchant la Médicine et le Régime de Santé* (1579), Girolamo Mercurii's *De gli Errori Popolari d'Italia* (1603), and Jacob Primrose's *De Vulgi Erroribus in Medicina* (1639). But they are all—one originally in French, one in Italian, and the Englishman's in Latin—confined to errors in physic. Browne's subject is larger and more difficult. At the end he abjures dogmatic opinion, humbly submitting his conceptions to all who care to apply, with better success perhaps, the same intellectual instruments for truth that he possesses. Were any succeeding scholars, from John Selden forward (V, xxiii, 157),[2] to correct Browne, that would only advance his design.

To appreciate that design, we shall have to inquire, first, into Browne's epistemological grounds, then into the ordering of his knowledge, and finally into the effect the work can make when it is read as the magnum opus of a seventeenth-century Christian scholar.

Like Milton, Browne assumes truth to be one and error to be multifarious. In the first book or "General Part," he discusses the causes of the disease; and in the following six books, "the particular part," he prescribes for hundreds of cases the three determinators of truth. Hence his epistemological ground is best divided into cause and cure.

Book I can be read without comparing it to Bacon's "Idols." It begins neatly with "the first" cause of error (ch. i) and "the second" (ch. iii). Then "a more immediate cause" comes in ch. iv, whereas ch. v labels *credulity* "a third cause of common errors." In the middle of this chapter he tells us that "the fourth is *supinity*" (p. 39). After that we get two "more immediate causes" (ch. vi and ch. vii), and two chapters (viii and ix) of annotated bibliography. Most appalling, however, for the twentieth-century reader, "the last and greatest promoter of false opinions, the endeavours of Satan" comes at the end. How many causes of errors are there, and why are they arranged like this?

By several devices Browne divides his causes into *three* general classes. In the first place, though he actually numbers four, and only four, that he intends his "third" and "fourth" to be taken together is shown by his combining them into a single chapter. Hence his argument against an obstinate adherence to antiquity in terms of our lending the ancients our belief with "critical and collective reason" and "common and country observation" (I, vi, 44) actually telescopes *supinity* (No. 3) and *credulity* (No. 4), as does a phrase like "credulous supinity" (II, iii, 127). The most explicit hint of the three classes of error—not four, five, or six—comes in the first sentence of ch. x on the devil: "But beside [1] the infirmities of human Nature, [2] the seed of Error within our selves, and [3] the several ways of delusion from each other, there is an invisible Agent, and secret promoter without us, whose activity is undiscerned, and plays in the dark upon us; . . ." Here are three categories of causes,[3] but what of Satan?

Though in each case of numbering Browne uses the key word "cause," he unmistakably denominates Satan a promoter, agent, or instigator.[4] Orthodox Christianity does not hold evil to be a separate power equal with good, or the efficient cause of man's fall. Satan, having deprived himself of good, provokes man into making bad choices. As Browne says in ch. ii, Adam commits an error when he blames Eve as the *cause*, and Eve commits an error when she blithely announces, "The Serpent beguiled me, and I did eat" (I, ii, 21). As a catalyst, Satan only facilitates other causes to bring about a result. Browne does not make Satan a *cause* of error any more than he makes Pliny and a host of bad authorities (in chs. viii and ix) *causes* rather than *promoters* of error.

We should not hold Browne to too tight an outline, for the causes of error existentially and logically overlap, as later do the three determinators of truth. Nevertheless, if we have read the first book on causes with any degree of care, its eleven chapters arrange themselves like this:

I. "Of the first cause of common errors; the common infirmity of human nature"—ch. i. "A further illustration of the same"—ch. ii.

II. "Of the second cause of common errors; the erroneous disposition of the people."

A. Misapprehension among common people—ch. iii.

B. False inference, verbal and logical, among both the uneducated and educated people—ch. iv.

III. "The third cause of error," credulity and supinity—ch. v.

A. Shown in obstinate adherence to antiquity—ch. vi.
B. Shown in obstinate adherence to authority—ch. vii.
    1. "Authorities" who have "most promoted" errors—ch. viii.
    2. "Authorities" who have indirectly "promoted" errors—ch. ix.
Summary: These three causes "promoted" by Satan—ch. x and ch. xi.

Even were we able to find a different numbering of these causes than that given here and a different mode of classifying them, the principles which govern the ordering of the chapters from one to eleven remain. There are at least four of them.

Most apparent is a chronological arrangement from ultimate cause to "more immediate cause": from the initial fall of man to our credulous resort to the latest machination to mislead. This order in time goes from natural to artificial: from the rude heads to those "improved by wisdom." Browne blames wiser heads more than the simple country folk, as he blames Adam more than he does Eve: ". . . strange effects are naturally taken for miracles by weaker heads, and artificially improved to that [false] apprehension by wiser" (II, vi, 169). Thus error is compounded, ironically enough, as history proceeds.

More ironic is the principle that arranges these causes of error obversely in relation to the determinators of truth (which we shall soon examine): authority, reason, and experiment. We surrender, by our initial disobedience, the only real authority, God, and cling at the end to a host of human "authorities" instead of diligently applying ocular proof and reason to God's other manuscript, nature. As reason is the central of the three criteria for truth, so its opposite (the verbal and logical fallacies) is the central of the three causes of error.

Under this lies an order of increasing heinousness and consequently increasing responsibility. Browne begins with the cause we are least responsible for by our innocence. More heinous is our susceptibility for delusion. But "the mortallest enemy unto knowledge" is the obstinate adherence to antiquity and unscientific authority. This implies an increasing area of choice— we have a narrow choice in the first cause, a greater choice in the second, and the widest opportunity to exercise choice among the people we listen to and the authors we read—for our responsibility increases as we pass from that cause which comes from *outside* ourselves, through the causes *within* ourselves, to the causes *among* ourselves; or, to paraphrase Browne's central metaphor, the disease is partially *congenital*, fairly *self-infectious*, and very *contagious*. God may save us from the first condition, but it is up to us to save ourselves from the other two. Years before in the *Religio* Browne had used the same metaphor less optimistically in regard to himself: "But it is the corruption that I fear within me, not the contagion of commerce without me. 'Tis that unruly regiment within me, that will destroy me, 'tis I that do infect my selfe. . . ."[5]

The deepest irony, however, comes as the final principle of arrangement of these three causes of error in the most subtly reasoned segment of Book I, the chapters on Satan. It were "too bold an arithmetic" to count all his wiles; therefore, Browne contents himself with "what most considerably concerneth his popular and practised ways of delusion": deceiving mankind in five main points concerning himself and God, the force for truth which Satan rebels against. These five points are summarized in a single paragraph (pp. 76-77):

And thus how strangely he possesseth us with Errors may clearly be observed, deluding us into contradictory and inconsistent falsities; whilest he would make us believe, That there is no God. That there are many. That he himself is God. That he is less then Angels or Men. That he is nothing at all.

Satan's five propositions are arranged with the arch sin of pride at the very center (No. 3, that he is God). On either side of this, two propositions, one positive and the other negative, lead up to it (No. 1, that there is no God, and No. 2, that there are many gods just as good as the one God); and two similar propositions lead away from it (No. 4, that Satan is less than angels or men, and No. 5, that Satan is nothing at all). By crafty steps Satan overthrows in us the three determinators of truth: at both ends he denies first the *authority* of God and the *authority* of himself; in both intermediate propositions, No. 2 and No. 4, he denies *reason* in denying the hierarchy of values; and in the very center, No. 3, he denies *authority* and *reason* and his own *experiment* in setting himself above God. Thus the Devil's motivations parallel the human causes of error: from the overthrow by our first parents of the *authority* of God to our putting our trust in Pliny and Nicander instead of in ourselves; from the overthrow of *reason* itself to the equally irrational inferences of our own and others' minds; from the demand for experience in tasting the apple to the supinity that leads to the denial of scientifically tested sense data that can lead to truth. So much·for the causes and the climate of the epidemic.

As for the cure, it has often been noticed in Browne's epistemology how chapter after chapter treats a subject first by the authorities for and against a received opinion, then by the application of reason, and finally, where it becomes feasible, by ocular proof. Thus the most famous chapter of all, the one on the badger, begins: ". . . upon enquiry I find [the notion] repugnant unto the three Determinators of Truth, Authority, Sense, and Reason" (III, v, 195). Again, Browne finds the assertion that chameleons feed on air ". . . mainly controvertible, and very much to fail in the three inducements of belief" (III, xxi, 258).

These three determinators of truth shift their ordering and even their names, as they should for the variety of Browne's common errors. For example, they are against the conceit, advanced even by Bacon, that deer live to be a hundred: ". . . since we have not authentick experience for it, since we have reason and common experience against it, since the grounds are false and fabulous which do establish it . . ." (III, ix, 212). For the silly reasons people give for eating and abstaining from certain foods, the criteria change: ". . . necessity, reason and Physick are the best determinators" (III, xxv, 286). Browne concludes his treatment of the fable that swans sing just before they die with this: "When therefore we consider the dissention of Authors, the falsity of relations, the indisposition of the Organs, and the immusical note of all we ever beheld or heard of. . . . Surely he that is bit with a Tarantula, shall never be cured by this Musick; and with the same hopes we expect to hear the harmony of the Spheres" (III, xxvii, 292). There are many other listings of the three in varying order and in a variety of names.

But far more often the three "cures for error" or "determinators of truth" are reduced to two.[6] "Authority" tends to disappear, not because Browne is ambiguous but because in science "reason" and "ocular proof" *are* the authority. There is only one final authority: "In brief, there is nothing infallible but God, who cannot possibly Erre" (I, i, 19). Until we know as we are known, the only authority in this world is sense corrected by reason in ourselves or in those whom we choose as earthly guides. Inured to the Platonic tradition that reality is divided into the visible and invisible realms, Browne is going to use his eyes when he can and his reason all the time to establish his temporary validity. Moreover, as we have become accustomed to reducing a tripartite division to a dichotomy, so here the first cause (original sin) and the first cure (God's authority) are put on one side, and the other two causes (fallacious reasoning and supinity) with their two cures (reason and experiment) are put on the other. There was precedent for this in Galen's *De Sanitate Tuenda* and many Galenical medical treatises: causes and cures of disease are either *outside* or *within* man's power to control. Were Browne not to divide his causes and cures like this, the disease of error in his title would have had to be *endemic* rather than *epidemic*. That God-and-man and reason-and-sense are pairs of dichotomies, opposites yet joined, seems for Browne to have been divinely decreed: ". . . God made all things double, and . . . if we look upon the works of the most High, there are two and two, one against another; . . . one contrary hath another, and poyson is not without a poyson unto it self . . ." (VII, xvii, 320). Thus the first citation of the double rather than the triple criteria for truth comes as early as the very first paragraph of his preface: ". . . proposing not only a large and copious List, but from experience and reason attempting their decisions." *Vulgar Errors* is intended to be a scientific and humane book, not theological or mystical. Its domain is the here and now.

Hence Browne can take "the new and noble doctrine of the circulation of the blood" (IV, iv, 18) as well as "that excellent discourse *of Generation*" as authority because Harvey's validity in these two works is ". . . So strongly erected upon the two great pillars of truth, experience and solid reason" (III, xxviii, 304). That Jews stink has no authority because ". . . the information of reason or sence" is against it (IV, x, 43). In an age when what we call science was called "philosophy," Browne practically shouts: "Now by the decree of reason and Philosophy . . ." (VII, iv, 270). Final authority can no more be forced upon us in science than in religion but only induce itself upon our minds by the co-operation of sense and reason:

For, as it is no reasonable proceeding to compel a religion, or think to enforce our own belief upon another, who cannot without the concurrence of God's spirit, have any indubitable evidence of things that are obtruded: So is it also in matters of common belief; whereunto neither can we indubitably assent, without the co-operation of our sense or reason, wherein consists the principles of perswasion (VII, xviii, 328-29).

In both we give our affirmative not without some fear that we may be wrong, but just as the word of God coupled with a disposition to believe is necessary in the one, so is the actual sensation of our senses and/or the nonopposition of our reasons necessary in the other. Thus the senses for the visible world and the reason for the invisible are interdependent:

For indeed, in matters of belief the understanding assenting unto the relation, either for the authority of the person, or the probability of the object, although there may be a confidence of the one, yet if there be not a satisfaction in the other, there will arise suspensions; nor can we properly believe until some argument of reason, or of our proper sense convince or determine our dubitations (VII, xviii, 329).

Like theory and practice, then, reason and sense can hardly do without each other.

The three determinators of truth are throughout the work applied to the three causes of error. Actual experience brings sharpened sensation to the inherited capacity to misapprehend things. Reason, where possible upheld by sensation, corrects the second cause of error, the disposition we have to indulge in fallacious inference. Untrustworthy authority rather than sense and reason is the result of the third cause of error, credulity and supinity; the plodding character of most of Browne's experiments and the patient application of right reason to everything exemplify the opposite of credulous supinity. As the causes of error increase in the area of our choice, so the means to combat them give little choice in the sensations, since the eyes must see; a wider range of choice in our reasons; and the widest choice among the "authorities" living and dead we give our assent to.

ERRORS AND THE DETERMINATORS OF TRUTH

On this epistemological foundation rest the following six books. After we have seen how Browne orders them, we shall be in a better position to understand how he applies these three kinds of cures to the innumerable cases of disease that arise from any one or any combination of these three causes of error. "To reckon up all" errors ". . . were imployment for Archimedes, who undertook to write the number of the Sands." Once ". . . having a serious and conceded list, we might with more encouragement and safety, attempt their Reasons" (II, vii, 178). The errors that he did choose over the years are arranged in six books in the following order:

(1) Of popular and received tenets concerning mineral and vegetable bodies (Bk. II)

It is difficult to perceive a single principle of unity in this list. We would question No. 4's being in two parts and wonder at the suddenness of "mistakes in pictures" after the first three solid categories. Also, No. 5 and No. 6 overlap, the former ending with "tenets historical" and the latter beginning with "tenets chiefly historical." Perhaps the unity will become apparent as we examine the principles of arrangement.

Except for the ordering of heinousness, the areas of mistakes here are governed by the same principles of order as are the causes of error in Book I. There can be no order of heinousness since truth is truth and falsehood, falsehood; a little lie is no better than a big one (V, xiii, 122). The six books of errors come in this order mainly by chronology and by the three determinators of truth, again not without irony. The books follow the chronological order of the creation—from the earth of minerals and vegetables, through animals, to man—followed by man's works. Thus they go from natural to artificial, from God's clear design to the complex muddles of human history. This is an order from the apparently simple but actually complex to the apparently complex but actually simple. The books pass from that which can be seen and yet misunderstood by the common people to that which has been thought but grossly confounded by the wiser.

Conversely, the really wise heads can apply experiment and ocular proof to the areas at the beginning of the list, whereas even scholars, let alone the uneducated masses, fail to apply reason at the end. Real authority is most easily established in the areas of the first three books and becomes more difficult to establish as we proceed. Browne begins with the greatest confidence in his laboratory experiments, but ends humbly in the last chapter with "some relations whose truths we fear." The six areas of mistakes, like the three causes of error, follow one another with deadly accuracy: the causes from the common infirmity of human nature that God visited upon us to our own supinity; the areas from God's fiat of creation to the credulous accounts of man by man "mainly historical." To understand how the books themselves illustrate the cases and their cures, we must now see how Browne applies here and there in all six books each of the determinators of truth: authority, reason, and experiment.

There is only one absolute *authority*, and that is God. All other authority is dubious: ". . . an argument from Authority . . . is but a topical probation . . . depending upon a naked asseveration: wherein neither declaring the causes, affections or adjuncts of what we believe, it carrieth not with it the reasonable inducements of knowledge" (I, vii, 50). Such authority cannot be used at all in mathematics, only a little in natural philosophy, but ". . . in Morality, Rhetorick, Law and History, there is I confess a frequent and allowable use of testimony; . . ." (I, vii, 52). The kind of authority given to us by ocular proof and reason is always relative: when we say that moles are blind, ". . . if the Eagle were

Judg, we might be blind ourselves" (III, xviii, 253). The worst temporal authorities are those historians who write of events without eyewitnessing them, confuse fact with myth, and in the whole process become magisterial (VI, vi, 206).

Browne would have us examine the grounds of all the "authorities" he cites for or against various propositions. For him, naturally, doctors have the best grounds. A Spanish physician, Franciscus Bustamentinus, won Browne's credence in what he had to say about the animals in Scripture (III, xvi, 239). And a group of doctors, like Sextius, Dioscorides, Galen, Matthiolus, spoke authoritatively about the salamander (III, xiv, 231). But some doctors are guilty of deliberately gulling their patients (I, iii, 29). Other doctors make false deductions arising from ignorance of etymology (II, vii, 175-76); Cardan is caught red-handed (III, xvii, 245), as well as many others. In his massive notebooks Browne tried to elect the "authorities" whose grounds of reason and observation had thus elected them, but he did not always succeed. Yet every "authority" (in the sense of Aristotle, Newton, Einstein) whose "authority" (in the sense of validity) shifts with the advance of science would be measured by Browne in the same way as that authority would be measured by us. Hence, as we have already discovered, authority tends to give way as a criterion of truth to the two major criteria: reason and observation.

Reason as a determinator of truth is applied to popular errors arising from the second cause of error, false inference. A good example is "deuteroscopy" or "the second intention of words" (I, iii, 26). A right rule for distinguishing between literal and poetic statements—for example, in the macrocosm-microcosm conceit— ". . . is beyond the subtlety of sense, and requires the artifice of reason" (IV, iii, 181), which puts it in a different class from the speed of light. Browne insists upon two kinds of truth here, literal and emblematic, in areas of knowledge incapable of determination by experiment.What he has to say about the truth of "an easie and Platonick description" is important for the appraisal of metaphors in his "African style." As a lack of anatomical knowledge through observation gave birth to many an emblem, so the failure to read the emblem aright has compounded the failures of observation into failures of understanding: for example, a pigeon has no gall, therefore it is a symbol of peace; since it is the symbol of peace, it has no gall (III, iii, 190). Many of the Egyptian emblems in chapter xx of Book V are taken by the common people falsely to be literal truth, but as emblems they have a value of their own (V, xx, 138). Noting that the children of Israel had cohabited with the Egyptians for four hundred years, Browne consistently connects Egyptian hieroglyphs with the Orientally metaphorical character of the Bible—in those things which are not necessary to salvation:

And thus . . . it hath fared with the Hieroglyphical Symboles of Scripture: which excellently intended in the species of things sacrificed, in the prohibited meats, in the dreams of Pharoah, Joseph, and many other passages: are oft-times wrackt beyond their symbolizations, and inlarg'd into constructions disparaging their true intentions (V, xx, 138).

So God depicted as an old man "is a dangerous piece" (V, xxii, 147). Egyptian hieroglyphs, in that they were less representational than many a Christian symbol, were actually better in allowing their primary intention to be comprehended. Browne acknowledges the help of Baronius' commentary on Lipellous' *Lives of the Saints* (V, xvi, 128; xvii, 130) in separating literal from poetic truth, and, of course, "the learned Kircherus" (III, xi, 218).

The basilisk emblem has its "allowable" purpose (III, vii, 200), and even a griffin, ". . . countenanced by the Name sometimes found in Scripture and . . . an Hieroglyphick of the Egyptians," had "allowable morality" though no existence in zoology (III, xi, 216). They lack reason who "apprehend a veritable history in an Emblem or piece of Christian poesy" and at the same time fail to see that the emblem is good as emblem (V, xvii, 130). The pelican's slashing her breast to feed her young with blood was ". . . asserted by many holy Writers and was an Hieroglyphick of piety and pitty among the AEgyptians" (V, i, 89); its emblematic meaning is "safe," but its literal meaning, of course, is a vulgar error.

There is still room for poetic license if people understand that poetry is poetry. Martial's famous epigram on the bee in amber is good poetry but bad science (II, iv, 139); and a literal interpretation of Nicander's myth of young vipers at birth tearing through their mother's bowels is an error (III, xvi, 240), though the hieroglyphic meaning based on it of Christ's "generation of vipers" is true (III, xvi, 242). A metaphor is a metaphor and a fact is a fact, and those who fail in the second determinator of truth, reason, wallow in that second cause of error, false inference, by mythologizing fact and factualizing myth, as, for instance, in a story like that of Friar Bacon and Brasenose (VII, xvii, 322).

As there is poetic license, so there is *licentia pictoria* (V, xi, 117), and Browne's devoting half of Book V to mistakes in pictures, many of which he must have seen in Italy, arises from their two kinds of truth. Art which presumes to imitate nature must represent it "true"; otherwise, artists ". . . may delineate old Nestor like Adonis, Hecuba with Helen's face, and Time with Absolom's head" (V, xi, 117). Figures have symbolical

Intent (V, xix, 135): as "we read in Pierius," an apple was the hieroglyph of love with some true meaning, but apples are not thereby aphrodisiacal (VII, i, 264). People misread these pictorial emblems: ". . . Whereas it may be thought that Mandrakes may fecundate, since Poppy hath obtained the Epithite of fruitful, and that fertility was Hieroglyphically described by Venus with an head of Poppy in her hand; the reason hereof was the multitude of seed within it self, and no such multiplying in humane generation" (VII, vii, 281).

A devout reader of the Bible, Browne will not take its face value for history and natural science. To most of its passages he applies the same kind of reasoning[7] that he applies to emblems, poetry, and myth: "And if we shall take it literally what Moses described popularly . . ." (VI, ii, 174), we fall into an error. As for such accounts in secular history as Hannibal's eating his way through the Alps with strong vinegar, ". . . yet may all be salved, if we take it hyperbolically," as wise men interpret certain passages in the book of Job (VII, xviii, 324). He is not one of the "cabalistical heads" who literally read Isaiah 34:4 (VII, iv, 272). Browne knew by deuteroscopy the two kinds of language and brought both to bear upon his religion: to describe nature exactly, ". . . it may be literally said of the wisdom of God, what men will have but figuratively spoken of the works of Christ; that if the wonders thereof were duly described, the whole world, that is, all within the last circumference, would not contain them. For as his Wisdom is infinite, so cannot the due expressions thereof be finite . . ." (VI, v, 189). Thus reason, the central determinator of truth, is shared by being applicable on the one hand to emblem, poetry, and religion, and, on the other, to things of sense.

But the third and last determinator of truth is as limited in its way, to things, as the first, absolute authority, is limited in its way, to God. The third cure for the epidemic of error is ocular proof and demonstration through actual trial.

Dr. Browne, a tireless seeker of specimens in the fens and fields of his native Norfolk, demonstrated a curiosity habitual since his boyhood excursions for "simples" in London's Cheapside. Among the rushes of the northern waterlands he vainly hoped that he would see a bittern "bump," that is, make "that mugient noise," in order to determine whether it "bumped" with its beak in the water or out (III, xxvii, 293-94). Another time he found an eaglestone on the Norfolk beach, a specimen never discovered by his epistolary friend Pastor Jonas in Iceland, where by popular fiction eaglestones were plentiful (II, v, 157). His accurate and beautiful description of the generation of frogs ". . . whereof in ditches and standing plashes we may behold many millions every Spring in England" could come only from hours of careful observation with notebook in hand, to discern ". . . what a long line is run to make a Frog" (III, xiii, 229-30).

Laughingly Browne will admit that one good thing about vulgar errors is that they stir men like himself to experiment (VII, xvii, 330). A far more detailed description of his home laboratory is to be had from Dr. Browne himself than from Evelyn's famous visit.[8] Dogs of various shapes, breeds, and sizes apparently had the run of the house. He fed them finely pulverized glass with no ill effects (II, v, 141) and even small doses of poisons (II, vii, 177). That puppies are blind nine days he finds "not answerable unto experience," for "upon strict observation of many" he discovered that Aristotle was right in seeking here a relationship with the period of gestation (III, xxvii, 295). On his laboratory scales registering one-tenth of a grain (IV, vii, 35), he weighed the brains of a snipe to determine the relationship between the size of the brain and the body (IV, ii, 14); and he strangled a chicken on the scales to discover whether it weighed more dead than alive (IV, vii, 34). He counted over seven hundred stones in the gizzard of a turkey (III, xxii, 270). In various receptacles of water standing around his laboratory he drowned cats, mice, and other animals to discover that their bodies floated to the surface at different times. He loved to float woods, metals, gems, and needles in water, quicksilver, aquafortis, or brine. He dissected every kind of animal from an earthworm (III, xxvii, 297) to a horse (III, ii, 185). He placed spiders and a toad in a jar together and found out that there was no "natural" antipathy but that the toad placidly let the spiders crawl all over its head (III, xxvii, 296). One time a bee settled on the desk and he placed his finger on its diaphragm to feel it hum (III, xvii, 298). He collected deathwatch beetles from the wainscoting of his house and counted and described their ticking sounds made with a proboscis like a tiny woodpecker's—no one in his family died as a result (II, vii, 172). His experiments with electricity and magnetic bodies were ceaseless, even to discrediting (with needless work, it seems) a fancy method of sending written messages by magnetical sympathy (II, iii, 129).

Many of his experiments failed, and when they did he frankly acknowledged the failure (II, vi, 169; vii, 173). But he rarely gave up. Up to 1645 he had failed three times to breed some vipers, so in the third edition of his work in 1654 he had to add some ocular testimony of others that vipers do not tear open their mother's bowels at birth (III, xvi, 238). Browne shot off various weapons to determine the strength of gunpowder, the proper ingredients of noiseless gunpowder, and what happens to bullets of various substances in flight and upon impact (II, v, 147). How Mrs. Browne reacted to the noise and mess issuing from such a laboratory is not recorded. Happily she left her husband alone to experiment and fill his notebooks with jottings like this: ". . . if in two Skiffs of Cork a Loadstone and Steel be placed within the Orb of their activities, the one doth not move, the other standing still, but both hoise sail and steer unto each other" (II, iii, 114).

Browne was a practicing physician and primarily a biologist. Hence he applies most carefully his ocular proof to vulgar errors in those areas closest to his profession and love—generation, metabolism, and death; or sex, growth, and decay. In these matters, at once the least and the greatest experiences of the human lot (VI, viii, 221), there is no hint of the virtuoso.[9] In generation his instinct for Aristotle and for Christian mysticism led him to epigenesis rather than the more modish theory of preformation, and he was scientifically right.

As though he half-remembered that Scorpio, his zodiacal sign, presides over "the secret parts of man," Browne was fascinated by sex as he was aware of the multiplicity of its vulgar errors. Country contraceptives abounded, such as the left testicle of a weasel wrapped in a piece of she-mule hide (I, vii, 55). It was believed that to bring on menstruation a woman should urinate on earth newly cast up by a mole (V, xxiii, 157). Almost every plant in the pharmacopoeia of the day was held by someone to be either a promoter of venery or its opposite. There was the sexual nonsense of the mandrake root (II, vi, 161), and people said that the loadstone was an aphrodisiac (II, iii, 125). As for opium, Browne is inclined to believe those who say its effect ". . . is not so much to invigorate themselves in coition, as to . . . spin out the motions of carnality" (VII, vii, 281).

Living just before the determination of sex in plants,[10] Browne noted that though sex is single in trees, animal generation requires two sexes. He concedes double sex in some creatures and transference from one sex to the other in hares and even in humans (III, xvii, 243). But since God created most living creatures male and female, patiently the doctor watches cocks treading hens (II, vii, 174). From an examination of the genitals he deduced that elephants copulate not like camels (as Pliny said they did) but by supersaliency, like horses (III, i, 183). He lists the size, shape, and position of a variety of pizzles, including one of a deer distended and covered with flies, but not rotting as the natives believed (III, ix, 212). Ignorance of the anatomy of genitalia accounted for the many mistakings of the anal glands for the testicles in beavers, badgers, and hares, giving rise to homespun theories of generation contrary to the laws of nature, reason, and God (III, iv, 194). As part of these laws, he lists every physiologically possible position in coitus (III, xvii, 250).

Perhaps with the play on words of "die" and "die" that Donne knew, he speculated on the possibilities of the overindulgence of the sexual act shortening the life of man. Those carnal acts of man are to be feared which do not have a name. Even a name like necrophilia only partially compensates for the abrogation of sexual law: "Surely, if such depravities there be yet alive, deformity need not despair; nor will the eldest hopes be ever superannuated, since death hath spurs, and carcasses have been courted" (VII, xix, 331).

Sex is to him the means of God's "great benediction": be fruitful and multiply (III, xvi, 237). As the marvelous formation of the young within the womb is more and more impressed upon him, he is the more shocked at "monstrous births" of all sorts, which are ". . . beside the intention of Nature, and the statutes of generation" (III, xv, 235). Even the popular error that bears lick their cubs into shape is "injurious unto

Reason" and casts doubt on the wisdom of the Creator (III, vi, 197). There may well have been inside Browne's etymological head a relationship between "conceit" as a vulgar error and "mistaken conception" in biology. He uses for error the Latin word *mola* (II, vi, 159), which had two meanings: a fleshy mass occurring in the womb, and also a false idea.

From animal and plant generation and growth, Browne turned his observation to the facts of death. He speculates on all the remarkable stories concerning the deaths of famous men. Among them is Plato, for whom the magicians at Athens sacrificed because he died on the day of his nativity, "declaring his death somewhat above humanity" (IV, xii, 65). Throughout *Vulgar Errors* ring solemn words on death, such as these on the conceit of man's immortality on earth, which anticipate *Urn Burial*:

'Twas surely an apprehension very strange; nor usually falling either from absurdities of Melancholy or vanities of ambition. Some indeed have been so affectedly vain, as to counterfeit Immortality, and have stoln their death, in a hope to be esteemed immortal; and others have conceived themselves dead: but surely few or none have fallen upon so bold an errour, as not to think that they could die at all. The reason of those mighty ones, whose ambition could suffer them to be called gods, would never be flattered into immortality; but the proudest thereof have by the daily dictates of corruption convinced the impropriety of that appellation. And surely although delusion may run high, and possible it is that for a while a man may forget his nature, yet cannot this be durable. For the inconcealable inperfections of ourselves, or their daily examples in others, will hourly prompt us our corruption, and loudly tell us we are the sons of earth (VII, x, 290-91).

Thus the application of the last determinator of truth, observation and experiment, is brought full circle to the first great cause of error, our inherited and common in-firmity. Following the familiar hierarchy of sense, mind, and faith, Browne inverts his determinators of truth: experiment and ocular testing come first, reason second, and authority last.

There emerges from Browne's *Pseudodoxia Epidemica* the portrait of a man who is memorable for his writing, a man charitable in his opinions because he is wise in anthropology, a man humorous in his intellectual detachment and devout in his religion.

The man could write, and his writing about science brought science to the people. As Auden said of Yeats:

> Time that is intolerant
> Of the brave and innocent,
> And indifferent in a week
> To a beautiful physique,
> Worships language and forgives
> Everyone by whom it lives; . . .

Browne, among other things, invented English words by the score. Some of these we never use, such as *favaginous* (honeycombed) and *digladiation* (fighting with swords). Other words of his own coinage used to-day are *antediluvian, hallucination, insecurity, incontrovertible, precarious, literary, retrogression, electricity,* and *medical.*

His vocabulary is large because he takes in the whole gamut of knowledge for his province. He is at home in every language, every culture, every clime, and every cuisine. All ages are present to him, though Egypt represents the past, Europe the present, and America the future. Egypt, ". . . which we esteem the ancientest

Nation in the world" (VI, viii, 216), prefigures for him
the Christian era, if the emblems are read aright. Europe
has produced its full quota of mistakes and truths.
America is that "untraveled part of truth" ("To the
Reader"). The beginning of new exploration, commerce, and religion, America, he hopes, will be free from
the old errors of Europe (IV, vi, 33).

The relativity of judgment shown in his insistence
that there is no left or right (IV, v) nor east and west
(VI, vii) except from one's own point of view led him
to reject (IV, v, 28) as anatomical truth such an emblem as Solinus' picture of the microcosm whose religious truth he admired not inconsistently in *Religio
Medici*. The same type of reasoning made him socially
aware of the superficial differences and real identity of
all human beings. The instinct that led him at the age
of thirty to begin the second part of *Religio* with "Now
for that other virtue of charity" had been proved from
1635 to 1645 by his sensible and rational experience;
intellectually he had to assent to Christ's authoritative
second commandment to love thy neighbor as thyself.
Browne is charitable toward Jews and Negroes not out
of sentiment but out of science. That the shape of a
nose or the color of a skin is a deformity is a terrify-
ingly unfounded opinion (cf. VI, xi, 247); and Jews
do not stink "because they crucified Christ," nor are
Negroes black because of the sun or because of a curse
on one of the tribes of Israel. Browne's quiet skepticism
is equally applied to two-headed snakes and the "re-
pugnancy" of rejected nations.

Hence the humor running throughout *Vulgar
Errors* is, like all real humor, a rational detachment from
self which can criticize with love. Being saturnine himself, he confessed to a serious, sometimes melancholy
frame of mind; and yet he could lie awake at night to
think up whole comedies. *Vulgar Errors* is consciously

a vast ironic comedy. Like Shakespeare's of similar title, it compounds error upon error mainly by mistaken identity. Browne felt that Christ could not have lived as a man without smiling: since laughter ". . . stands commended by morality; so is it consistent with Religion, and doth not offend Divinity" (VII, xvi, 312).

His humor ranges from puns to sarcasm. To be governed by the canicular days is ". . . to suffer from the mouth of the Dog above, what others do from the teeth of Dogs below . . ." (IV, xiii, 87). "Curiosity *fruitlessly* enquireth" about the apple Eve is supposed to have plucked (VII, i, 264). In the midst of a serious description of asbestos he includes in a Museum Clausum two other notorious incombustibles, Germanicus' heart and Pyrrhus' big toe (III, xiv, 232). To admit that elephants can walk and yet deny them joints in their legs ". . . were to expect a Race from Hercules his pillars; or hope to behold the effects of Orpheus his Harp, when trees found joints, and danced after his Musick" (III, i, 180). And the story of a woman who got pregnant from taking a bath he calls ". . . a new and unseconded way in History to fornicate at a distance" (VII, xvi, 309).

Browne loves to reduce proverbs to their essential absurdity, especially those which, if taken seriously, violate everyday experience. If Rome were built in a day, this is ". . . an Art quite lost with our Mechanicks" (VII, xviii, 326). Imputing to a plant such as Ethiopian mullein the virtue of opening any lock would ". . . condemn the judgment of Scipio, who having such a picklock, would spend so many years in battering the Gates of Carthage" (II, vi, 170).

By means of humor Browne puts a "chemiatrist" like Paracelsus in his place. At the end of the new chapter on the whale added in 1654, he confesses that the stench of the decomposed leviathan closed his inquiry:

"And yet if, as Paracelsus encourageth, Ordure makes the best Musk, and from the most fetid substances may be drawn the most odoriferous Essences; all that had not Vespasian's Nose, might boldly swear, here was a subject fit for such extractions" (II, xxvi, 290; cf. II, iii, 119). To search for an elixir in the phoenix is even more foolish than ". . . a dependence upon the Philosopher's stone, potable gold, or any of those Arcana's whereby Paracelsus that died himself at forty seven, glorified that he could make other men immortal" (III, xii, 225).

Lightened as it is by humor, *Vulgar Errors* is also the work of a devoutly humble inquirer after truth:

For unto God a thousand years are no more than one moment, and in his sight Methuselah lived no nearer one day than Abel, for all parts of time are alike unto him, unto whom none are referrible; and all things present, unto whom nothing is past or to come. And therefore, although we be measured by the Zone of time, and the flowing and continued instants thereof, do weave at last a line and circle about the eldest: yet can we not thus commensurate the sphere of Trismegistus; or sum up the unsuccessive and stable duration of God (VII, iii, 269).

No longer are we inclined to believe that Satan, having been silenced in the oracles, still speaks in witches and poltergeists, yet if we have substituted new errors for old, it may be as true now as it was in 1645 to say with Browne: ". . . in vain we cry that Oracles are down; Apollo's Altar still doth smoak; nor is the fire of Delphos out unto this day" (VII, xii, 295). Nor will it be out perhaps until the day of judgment when (as Browne anticipates his *Garden of Cyrus*) ". . . men shall rise out of the earth: the graves shall shoot up their concealed seeds, and in that great Autumn, men shall spring up, and awake from their Chaos again" (VI, i, 161).

Chapter XI

INTERLUDE:
A CHOICE OF
PHILOSOPHIES

Browne is a philosopher only as he embraces in his own distinctive language the accumulated and recognizable ideas of Western thought—ideas of God, nature, and man, and the relationship between them. Having formed from youth the habit of collecting *sententiae*, he probably got many philosophical concepts from Diogenes Laertius' *Vitae et sententiae eorum qui in philosophia probati fuerunt*, which he owned[1] in the Stephanus octavo of 1570; from Plutarch's *Lives*, which he had in Cruserius' Latin folio of 1620[2] as well as in Amyot's French of 1594;[3] and from handbooks like Bacon's *De Sapientia Veterum* (1609), translated by Sir Arthur Gorges as *The Wisdom of the Ancients* (1619). His library of individual philosophers was also ample, and his quotations from such works numerous and often recondite.

The new age was almost too much for the men who made it. Inured to seeing Plato corrected by Aristotle, Aristotle tripped by his commentators, and these overthrown by Copernicus and Galileo, many thinkers in the Renaissance took refuge in being skeptical of all philosophies, including skepticism. Browne arrived at this doctrine through Sextus Empiricus and a half-recognition that St. Paul and Calvin were right in describing the Fall in intellectual as well as moral terms. He was led to it also by a feeling that time had come back upon itself, that the century he lived in was like an earlier one when the Christian idea had to engraft the pagan or else perish. Finally, he came upon it through a method of reading texts that had nothing to do with the clash of doctrine between the Middle Ages and the Renaissance, but rather with the Renaissance discovery that the Greek Aristotle was not quite what St. Thomas, or Averroës, or Lombard had said he was. Though the Middle Ages had had a Pauline doctrine and a Mosaic doctrine, it was the Renaissance that perceived the rhetoric in the one and the poetry in the other.[4]

Where is truth? "I have runne through all sects," Browne writes,

yet finde no rest in any: though our first studies and junior endeavors may stile is Peripateticks, Stoicks, or Academicks, yet I perceive the wisest heads prove, at last, almost all Scepticks, and stand like *Janus* in the field of knowledge. I have therefore one common and authentick Philosophy I learned in the Schooles, whereby I discourse and satisfie the reason of other men, another more reserved, and drawn from experience, whereby I content mine owne. *Solomon,* that complained of ignorance in the height of knowledge, hath not onely humbled my conceits, but discouraged my endeavours.[5]

Some said they had *found* truth, like the Peripatetics, the Epicureans, and the Stoics. Browne doubted this, for had the Devil taught himself his own philosophy of Know Thyself at Delphos, he could never have been so sure. On the other hand, the Academic school despaired of the quest for truth, like Carneades, whose law of probability was carried to an extreme by Arcesilaus. If the first group is guilty of human vanity in setting its own reasons so high, the second is equally guilty of another sin, that of debasing reason, which, within us, is most like God's image of wisdom. So, like the Pyrrhonists, Browne would say, let us be skeptical of both, still searching for truth: we do not have it, yet we do not despair of attaining it.

STOICISM

The Stoics were certain that they had grasped it. Steeped in Cicero, Seneca, and Tacitus—as every schoolboy was—only with difficulty could Browne separate the best of Stoic philosophy from Christian humanism. The *contemptus mundi*, the control of the passions by reason, the doctrine of magnanimity—these were claimed by Christian and pagan alike. The English translations of many noble Stoics made it easier to combine Christian and Stoic thought: Holland's Plutarch (1603), Healey's Epictetus (1610), Lodge's Seneca (1614), and Casaubon's Marcus Aurelius (1634), to mention only a few. Browne not only absorbed Stoicism from the original languages and from the English translations; he could also have gotten it from at least these three moderns: Pierre Charron (1541-1603), Justus Lipsius (1547-1606), and Joseph Hall (1574-1656).

One of the books in Browne's library was the English translation of Charron, by Samson Lennard, *Of Wisdom* (London, 1608).[6] Charron lays down the principal rules of wisdom and the proper qualities of the wise man. Here "the first office of Wisdome" is to "studie true Piety," illustrated by the development of various religions from human sacrifices and savage rites to Christianity. Charron defines religion as "the knowledge of God and of our selves (for it is a relative action betweene both)." And that is the best religion

. . . which without great externall and corporall service, draws the soule into itselfe, and raises it by pure contemplation to admire and adore the greatnesse and infinite majestie of the first cause of all things, and the essence of essences, without any great declaration or determination thereof, or prescription of his service; but acknowledging it indefinitely, to be goodness, perfection, and infinitenes, whollie comprehensible & not to be known, as the Pythagoreans, and most famous Philosophers do teach.[7]

Though all religions claim truth, it is not ". . . a matter of labour to know which is the truest, the Christian religion having so many advantages and privileges so high and so authenticall above others."[8]

Roman Catholic modern Stoic that Charron was, he was not nearly so famous as Justus Lipsius, whose Stoicism made it difficult for him to claim any one religion during his life. At Leiden Lipsius had worked on new texts of Seneca and Tacitus, and at Louvain he had taught history. His *Opera* in eight volumes in 1585 introduced a new vogue in Latin "Baroque" style.

Among the most popular of Lipsius' writings was *De Constantia* (1594), translated as *Two Books of Constancie, Written in Latin by Iustus Lipsius . . . Englished by Iohn Stradling, Gentleman* (London, 1595). Lipsius, discontented with Holland, counsels himself not to change countries but rather his mind, which had been ". . . wrongfully subjected to affections, and withdrawn from the naturall obedience of this lawful Ladie, I mean REASON."[9] He defines constancy as ". . . a right and immovable strength of minde, neither lifted up, nor pressed down with externall or casuall accidents." Right reason or "a true sense and judgment of things humane and divine," he continues, ". . . hath her offspring from heaven, yea from God; and Seneca gave it a singular commendation, saying that there was hidden in man parte of the divine

Spirit."[10] He warns the reader against two enemies of constancy of mind, false goods (riches, honors, health, longevity, etc.) and false evils (poverty, lack of promotion, sickness, and death), from which spring the four affections of desire and joy and fear and sorrow. The truly constant mind is unperturbed by such things. This brings Lipsius to the Stoical view of destiny: "I come to the Stoicks my friends (for I professe to hold that sect in estimation and account) who were the authors of VIOLENT FATE." He quotes Seneca to uphold the Stoical doctrine of "A necessitie of all things and actions, which no force can withstand or breake."[11] Lipsius then excuses the Stoics from the impiety they are charged with—that of subjecting God to the whole of destiny. It may well be that from thinkers like Lipsius, Browne got the idea that the "fatall necessitie of the Stoickes is nothing but the immutable Law of . . . [God's] will."[12]

Christian Stoicism and Calvinist doctrine combined in an Anglican bishop like Joseph Hall, "the Christian Seneca," a man who was in controversy with Lipsius as well as Milton. In Kinloch's words, "Like most of the bishops and the vast majority of the laity of his time, [Hall] was an out-and-out Calvinist."[13] Whitefoot said of him in his funeral sermon that all loved the doctor but some loved not the bishop. That Browne loved both the Calvinist Anglican bishop as well as the Neostoical doctor comes from his account of Joseph Hall in *Repertorium*:

My honord freind Bishop Joseph Hall, Deane of Worcester, and Bishop of Excester, was buryed at Heigham, where hee hath his monument, who in the Rebellious times, when the Revennues of the church were alienated, retired unto that suburbian parish, and there ended his dayes: being above forescore yeares of age. A person of singular humility, patience and pietie: his owne works are the best monument, and character of himself, which was also very lively drawne in his excellent funerall sermon preached by my learned and faythfull old freind Mr. John White-foot, Rector of Heigham and very deserving clark of the convocation for Norfolk.[14]

Unlike the Stoics, the Academics tended to under-rate the power of human reason and the values of this world. Beginning with the famous twice-bisected line at the end of the sixth book of the *Republic*, Plato's double view of two worlds, one visible and the other invisible, became the very mold of seventeenth-century thought. The Neoplatonic doctrine was spread by Mar-silio Ficino and his academicians at Florence through their translations of Plato and Plotinus in the *Theo-logica Platonica*, which Browne owned. Plato became almost a god and that mythical Neoplatonist Hermes Trismegistus, the Thrice-great Hermes, his prophet. Milton cited only these two (the Hermetica being, of course, composite writings) for the philosophical read-ing of his thoughtful man, *Il Penseroso*:

> Or let my lamp at midnight hour,
> Be seen in some high lonely Tow'r,
> Where I may oft outwatch the Bear,
> With thrice-great Hermes, or unsphere
> The spirit of Plato to unfold
> What worlds, or what vast regions hold
> The immortal Mind that hath forsook
> Her mansion in this fleshly nook.

Plotinus and the Hermeticists upset the balance of the two worlds—the bright, eternal, invisible world of ideas, and the actual though obscure world of matter and sense—in favor of the "higher truths." Man's business in this life is to rise to a union with the all-pervading, centripetal, and intellectual God. He can afford neither time nor inclination for the dull world of matter. Hence Neoplatonism regarded the world as a system of symbols, and the ascension to truth as requiring an ability to pass from the symbols to the nonsensuous values which they symbolize.

Neoplatonism provides, for Browne as for St. Augustine in *The City of God*, not so much the values themselves as a substructure for the values. A mythopoeic and metaphoric philosophy and analogical view of reality justifies and unifies Browne's "private" faith rather than the public arguments he used to satisfy the "schools." To contemplate a reason why the world was one, as he most deeply felt it to be, is "a sweeter piece of reason, and a diviner point of Philosophy."[15] Neoplatonism lends Browne's complex confession of faith a consistent metaphysical mode, particularly in his doctrine of God and in his concept of man with an immortal soul, midway in the hierarchy between God and nature.

Plotinus' concept of God is the core of the system. God is defined by what Plotinus calls the "Three Principal Hypostases." The lowest level of God is the soul or mind. This is God as the One in the process of combining with the Many. Plotinus sees this part of God as both the World-soul of the *Timaeus* (Brown's "common Spirit of the whole world") and the soul of man (Browne's "common spirit that plays within us"). Thus, the soul of God operates universally as well as individually, seeking causes and effects and the tie between them, subsuming particulars under universals and engaging itself in the process of God-reasoning.

The middle level of Plotinus' God consists of the ideas or forms of the hypostatized values which Plato considered as intelligence or *nous*. This is God as both One and Many at the same time, and can be taken in one sense as the "lure of Faith" to which Browne's reason must stoop, or in another sense as that attribute of God which Browne considered along with His wisdom, i.e., His eternity. The mind experiences this part of God when it returns upon itself; in intense contemplation it blurs the distinction between subject and object. When this happens, the universal and particular merge into one another to become the "real." Such a state is attained after death; hence Browne's preoccupation with death and his desire for its peculiar knowledge.

At the apex of the Plotinian hierarchy stands God as the One, the Good. This is an invisible and superior point from which all is generated, all light emanates. Paradoxically, in mysticism the highest knowledge is something which is not knowledge at all but a point of inner light, a trance. In a psychological sense this hypostasis can be grasped as the state of mind when it withdraws into itself, after the effort of striving outward and of contemplating that effort. The point comes in sleep or in waking moments or when the consciousness is blank. At these times the mind recovers that feeling which is best described as the sense of life, being, or unity. Thus the *Religio* reaches its conclusion with a discussion of dreams and sleep, as do *Hydriotaphia* and *The Garden of Cyrus* also. Browne says: "There is surely a neerer apprehension of any thing that delights us in our dreames, than in our awaked senses . . . we are somewhat more than our selves in our sleepes, and the slumber of the body seemes to bee but the waking of the soule."[16] God as the One is the "dormative" Browne takes bedward: in doing so, he concludes the *Religio* in "a cloud of unknowing," which was the goal of Neoplatonic aspiration—in Nicholas of Cusa, Master Eckhart, and others.

Man's ascent up the Neoplatonic scale of being

from the world of "meer existence" to the world of sense and finally to the world of intelligence proved that man as microcosm embraced all worlds. In his description of man's three states of existence (in the womb, in this world, in the next world), Browne also refers to the womb as that "truest microcosm," perhaps thinking of Plato's doctrine of recollection or of the notion of the "receptacle" in the *Timaeus*.[17] Accordingly,

The severe Schooles [Stoics, Aristotelians] shall never laugh me out of the Philosophy of *Hermes*, that this visible World is but a picture of the invisible, wherein, as in a pourtract, things are not truely, but in equivocall shapes, and as they counterfeit some more reall substance in that invisible fabrick.[18]

SKEPTICISM—"JANUS"

That we owe allegiance to two selves, one in the visible and the other in the invisible realm, which somehow must be rightly ordered one to the other—that is the main problem. And though Browne admired the Stoics, he was wary of their intellectual pride. To be an Aristotelian biologist and at the same time a Neoplatonic Christian was possible, however, though more in a private than in a Schoolman's way. The dilemma could be resolved by Pomponazzi's Latin adjective *anceps, ancipitis* (two-headed, Januslike), almost as familiar to Browne as "St. Paul's sanctuary." It is man's eternal dilemma to be born an amphibium: when you think you have all of this world, you get a glimpse of some other; and as soon as you let yourself fly into that empyrean, you are in danger of forgetting the limitations of a legged, not winged, animal.

Hence Browne discovered that ". . . the wisest heads prove, at last, almost all Skepticks, and stand like *Janus* in the field of knowledge," for most philosophy consists of "Bivious Theorems and Janus-faced Doctrines."[19] "Since I was of understanding to know we know nothing, my reason hath beene more pliable to the will of faith," he confesses;[20] as in many other men, his skepticism leads to fideism. Following Sextus Empiricus, whose works he owned in the 1621 folio,[21] Browne became a wise doubter. How could he do otherwise when at least three noble challenges to human knowledge disclosed deserts of ignorance: in medicine, incurable diseases; in law, indeterminable cases; and in morality, still incorrigible vices?

Skepticism, then, is not, as some think, merely dogmatic disbelief. Rather, in William Mitchell's words:

It would seem . . . to mark that transition stage between the faith of childhood and the faith of manhood. There comes a period, an epoch, a moment in our lives when we have neither one nor the other. The past is gone and with it the faith of the past; the future is not yet here. . . . Truth seems far away and the search for truth involves a struggle. The sceptical moment, therefore, lies in this very struggle of the human soul in its search for truth. It is the feeling of bewilderment and drift, and the discovery that we have lost our moorings, the desolation, emptiness and loneliness which are sure to follow. . . .[22]

Browne's phrase for this skeptical experience was "a wise and pious discretion," which would distinguish it from the jaunty skepticism of Montaigne and the hardboiled skepticism of Hobbes, to neither of whom he was attracted. His own brand of skepticism has been identified with Donne's:

Like Sir Thomas Browne, Donne scorns the desperate search on this earth for a knowledge 'which Death gives every fool *gratis.* . . .' This does not mean that the sceptic abandons the search for truths, tentative and partial though they may be. It means only that because he has seen the extreme difficulty of arriving at any knowledge, he maintains a more casual attitude than other thinkers toward the problem of knowing, especially in view of the contrast between 'man's nothing perfect and God's all complete.'[23]

In the privacy of his study, when the Stoics he had been reading spoke too surely of the capacity of human reason alone to raise man from himself up to God, Browne took leave to doubt. And when the mystic Hermeticists got too far away from this earth in their soul flights, he was not sure that any of them had ever experienced actual ". . . Extasy, Exolution, Transformation, the Kiss of the Spouse, and Ingression into the Divine Shadow. . . ."[24] He was content to live in both worlds at once, as he could in the seventeenth century. The two worlds have always been divided, and man has always yearned to unite them. In religion Browne stored close to his heart the few absolutes of the Apostles' Creed and the double commandment upon which hang all the law and the prophets. For philosophy, in which he could dispute at least two sides of every question, he used the symbol of the classical Janus. To connect the double way of philosophy to his only way of religion, he found Janus Christianized, for example, by Don Sebastian de Covarrubias' *Morales Emblemas* (1610), in a picture of a Janus with one face beautiful, the other a death's head—which will play a part in his *Christian Morals*.

Chapter XII

A LETTER
TO
A FRIEND

A *Letter to a Friend* concerns the death from tuberculosis of a young man intimately known by an absent friend of the author.[1] Thus it performs two distinct functions, which require its two apparently separate parts: the attending physician describes the condition of the young man when he died, and takes this opportunity to give advice to the friend on how best to live—advice which is repeated in the opening sections of *Christian Morals*. The style differs from that of Browne's ordinary correspondence. Combining the clinical facts of a coroner's report with a haunting view of mortality, the main portion of the *Letter* gives evidence of being artistically composed and even polished.

It was not published during the author's life but first given to the world in 1690 by Dr. Edward Browne, Sir Thomas' distinguished son and literary executor. It appeared again in the 1712 *Posthumous Works*.

Its character and the circumstances of its publication pose a problem. Is it a generalized account of death by tuberculosis which Browne has decorated with the literary device of the epistle, or does it describe an actual case? If the latter, who were the people involved? And at what time in the doctor's literary career was it first composed: does it belong with *Christian Morals* (as indeed the parallels between the later portion of it and *Christian Morals* would seem to indicate) or with *Hydriotaphia*?

Though Wilkin was silent on the subject, the date usually given by editors for its composition is 1672, when Browne was sixty-seven years old. Greenhill, for example, wrote that the *Letter* ". . . appears from internal evidence to have been written by Sir T. B. about 1672, ten years before his death, about the same time as the *Christian Morals,* but shortly after."[2] Greenhill's argument for 1672 rests tenuously on a single allusion and a single correction. Browne alludes to Duloir's *Travels* (1654) as being published "yet scarcely twenty years ago" (172),[3] and in a passage first added in 1672 to the sixth edition of *Vulgar Errors* he speaks again of Duloir's description of the Strait of Euripus as having appeared "about twenty years ago."[4] That the *Letter* was written after *Christian Morals* Greenhill argues by the fact that in *Christian Morals* (I, iii) Browne makes a mistake of Darius' "sisters." "Daughters" is historically correct, and the parallel section of advice in *A Letter to a Friend* has been emended. But this merely shows that the *Letter* was better edited.

Despite this argument for late composition, Walter Pater felt that what he calls "this elfin letter" bears a close kinship with *Hydriotaphia*, which was published in 1658:

In its first presentation to the public this letter was connected with Browne's 'Christian Morals'; but its proper and sympathetic collocation would be rather with the 'Urn-Burial,' of which it is a kind of prelude, and strikes the key-note. He is writing in a very complex situation; to a friend, upon occasion of the death of a common friend. The deceased apparently had been little known to Browne himself till his recent visits, while the intimate friend to whom he is writing had been absent at the time; and the leading motive of Browne's letter is the deep impression he has received in his visits of a sort of physical beauty in the coming of death, with which he still surprises and moves his reader. There has been, in this case, a tardiness and reluctancy in the circumstances of dissolution, which had permitted him, in the character of a physician, as it were, to assist at the spiritualizing of the bodily frame by natural process; a wonderful new type of a kind of mortified grace being evolved by the way. The spiritual body had anticipated the formal moment of death; the alert soul, in that tardy decay, changing its vesture gradually, and as if piece by piece.[5]

If this impression is true, then the *Letter* was first drafted in the 1650's rather than in the 1670's.

Obviously, the date of composition cannot be settled until more thought has been given to the occasion which prompted the writing. This requires an examination of all the indications in the *Letter* itself which bear upon the relationship and the particularization of the persons involved: details in the letter concerning the patient, the recipient, and their relationship to each other and to the doctor. The title page of 1690 is: "A Letter to a Friend, Upon the Occasion of the Death of his Intimate Friend." This means that all three persons are connected by friendship in a hierarchy of ascending intimacy. The doctor was called upon in the final stages of the deceased's illness; he and the deceased are on the least intimate level. The recipient is a "friend" of the author, who deserves the favor of knowing through the doctor of the final dissolution of the dying man. The most intimate relationship is that between the recipient and the deceased, which impels the doctor to describe faithfully the symptoms of the patient, the circumstances of his dying, and the meaning which his death may hold for the living friend.

I believe that the patient Browne describes in *A Letter to a Friend* was Robert Loveday, the translator of La Calprenède's *Cléopâtre*; that the friend to whom Browne is writing was Sir John Pettus; and that, since Loveday died in 1656, the *Letter* was first drafted not in 1672 but two years before *Hydriotaphia* was published.

This hypothesis will require a proof in two parts: one for each of the unknown characters, the patient and the recipient—vis-à-vis Browne. For the patient, we shall have to prove that Dr. Browne was called to the bedside of Robert Loveday, who died of consumption in 1656, and that Loveday possessed the traits of age, family, profession, and character indicated in the *Letter*. For the recipient, we shall have to prove that Loveday had an "intimate friend" in Sir John Pettus, who was absent at the time of Loveday's death, that Dr. Browne in 1656 knew Sir John well enough to write this letter to him, and that some of the traits of the letter, particularly the advice at the end of it, are applicable to Sir John Pettus.

Before proceeding to the proof one might ask why no attempt has been made heretofore to identify the patient in the *Letter* and its recipient. A conjectural answer will help to explain the kind of support for these propositions that must be used. There are reasons why care should have been taken by Browne himself during his life and by his son Edward as literary executor to suppress the actual circumstances that may have given the *Letter* its being. If the *Letter* involved Royalists before the Restoration, there may have been political reasons for carefully expunging all easily identifiable signs. Again, within the circle of the famous doctor's acquaintance in the East Anglian counties and in London there might very well be social reasons for concealment, in view of the frankness of the advice at the end. The more distinguished the friends, the greater would be the degree of suppression. The most important reason, however, for deliberate erasure of personal identity is this: to the two doctors responsible for its composition and publication the detailed description of the symptoms of a patient, accompanied by a disquisition on his character, and the results of his autopsy was a violation of the Hippocratic Oath, especially this clause of it: "What I may see or hear in the course of the treatment or even outside of the treatment in regard to the life of men, which on no account one must spread abroad, I will keep to myself, holding such things shameful to be spoken about."[6] Even though Thomas Browne, M.D., may have given the oath an easy Pythagorean interpretation, it seems certain that he would observe the ethics of its final injunction. For these reasons no attempt to identify the patient and the recipient can be an open-and-shut case. It must rest upon probabilities, but individual parallels will be strengthened by the triple relationship demanded by the title page.

THE PATIENT: ROBERT LOVEDAY

The Lovedays were an ancient family at Chediston (sometimes spelled "Cheston") in East Suffolk, two miles west of Halesworth.[7] There was a Robert Loveday living there at the time of Edward I.[8] They were probably the leading citizens in this village of scarcely more than two hundred people, except when Sir John Pettus, that stormy Royalist who had married the daughter of Sir Richard Gurney, lord mayor of London, swept in and out of his mansion, Cheston Hall. The grandfather, Anthony Loveday, had married Ellen, daughter of William Crow of Yarmouth. Their son Henry also married a Yarmouth girl, Alice Skarph. The children of this marriage that we know about were Robert (our subject), Anthony, and two girls—Fenner and Jane.[9] Aunts, uncles, and cousins in profusion dwelt nearby, and brother Anthony appears to have made his home at Barningham, Suffolk, about nine miles southeast of Thetford, a town on the border of the two East Anglian counties. After his education at Peterhouse College, Cambridge, Robert Loveday's regular employment in the early 1650's was that of secretary to Lady Clinton in the family of the Earl of Clare in Nottinghamshire. In their company he traveled up and down England, though suffering from tuberculosis.

At the outset, Browne mentions the well-known *spes phthisca* or inordinate hope, "the common Fallacy of consumptive Persons" (166).[10] Perhaps this false optimism on the part of the patient led his friend not to expect his death. But the doctor on his first visit told the relatives that the patient would probably not live to see the next summer (166). He gives his friend a historical treatise on consumption (168) and a description "in this consumptive Condition" of the victim's remarkable wasting-away of his flesh (170). The emaciation from tuberculosis had been a long drawn-out process, so that the man died very gently—almost as if he had fallen asleep (167). In his extreme thinness he reminded Browne of Dante's grotesque *omo* (170), and when he died his "exuccous corpse" weighed scarcely more than his coffin.

From Loveday's published letters comes the evidence that when he was forced by his illness to return home to Suffolk he was attended by Dr. Thomas Browne of Norwich. The first to mention Loveday's letters with reference to Browne's biography was D. Lloyd Roberts in 1892.[11] Sir Geoffrey Keynes, in his *Bibliography of Sir Thomas Browne*, cites Dr. Roberts' three passages from the 1662 edition and doubts that they refer to Thomas Browne of Norwich. He admits, however, that there was no well-known "Doctor Butler" (who is mentioned on p. 209 of the 1662 edition) then living in Norwich whom the initial "Dr. B-" might intend.[12]

Dr. Keynes did not realize that in Loveday's letters[13] there are two "Doctor B's." The addressee of Letter XXI is obviously the "Dr. B." (Butler?) of Nottingham whom Loveday has been consulting for some time. He gradually loses confidence in this "Dr. B.'s" ability to cure his "hecticall condition." At Bath, with the Clintons, he takes the waters "according to Dr. B.'s prescription, for my head," but it does him little good. Humorously he tells his brother of meeting a notorious character in Nottingham who cures by taking the pulse. This quack calls himself the nephew of "the great Dr. B." and says he has all "the famous doctor's" prescriptions (XXII, p. 40)—obviously not alluding to the inept "Doctor B." of Nottingham. From various places during his travels with the Clintons Robert keeps asking his brother to give his respects to "our friends in Norfolk and Suffolk" (p. 75). In Letter LVI: "If your Affaires shall call you to Norwich . . . I would gladly have the opinion of Dr. B. from whose advice I fancy most hope of all" (p. 100). This could not possibly be the "Dr. B." of Nottingham whose prescriptions he has been using to no avail.

For three years the peripatetic Clintons had taken Loveday from Nottingham to Bath, to London, to Land's End (where they had a married daughter). He wants to come "home to Norfolk" (p. 145), for he has received a prescription from his brother: "I pray present my hearty thanks to the Doctor for bestowing his Receipt upon me" (LXXX, p. 153). Again he writes to his brother: "If you have a Recipe from Dr. B. of some sovereign *lotium*, it will be gratefully welcom. I am invective against cruel interest, and do upbraid my narrow condition that will not suffer me to meet you at

Norwich" (CI, p. 186). At one critical stage he has evidently received a hopeful prognosis by mail, for he writes to Anthony:

I would gladly find Doctor B. not mistaken in the situation of my malady, and I hope my experience will hereafter assure me, as now my observation begins to persuade, that there is no flaw in his judgment. I have a strong fancy that I shall reap much benefit by those lotions he speaks of, and therefore when you go next to Norwich let me intreat you to take note of the ingredients from his dictates. . . . I intend not to straggle the breadth of a hair from what Doctor B. prescribes (CIV, pp. 192-93).

By page 206 he hopes to be allowed to come "home," for "I am resolved to consult Dr. B." By page 222 his condition grows more "hecticall." He knows how serious it is: ". . . this Cough I find has lately fed upon my flesh, & carried away enough from the poor store I had to make me doubt a Consumption; but whatsoever the hand of Heaven sends me I shall endeavour to bid welcome" (CXLIV, p. 267).

One unusual letter (CXLVII, pp. 271-73) deserves special notice. It is the only letter in the entire volume that does not even have initials to identify its recipient. The form of address is merely "Sir." The style is quite different from the other letters: deferential, high-toned, pious, and filled with classical allusion. To this "Sir," Loveday wrote: "How oft I have wisht for a Mercurial *Caduceus* to insomniate the *Argus*-eyes of jealous people, that I might safely steal a visit, & with it the enjoyment of your happy society." In this strain of forced Latinity he continues with allusions to the Remora, Plato's year, and Acheloan shapes. It would appear that this letter was addressed directly to the famous Dr. Browne, author of *Religio Medici*.

But even if Loveday were attended by Browne, he

may not have been the young man of *A Letter to a Friend*. Again from his *Letters* comes the major proof that he possessed the traits of age, family, profession, and moral character indicated in Browne's *Letter to a Friend*.

That Browne's patient was a young man in his early thirties is made explicit. "Consumptive and tabid Roots sprout . . . early" (175), the doctor tells his friend, compared with other diseases: "He conceived his Thred long, in no long course of Years, and when he had scarce out-lived the second Life of Lazarus; esteeming it enough to approach the Years of his Saviour" (177). It is a good time to die, remarks Dr. Browne, "to leave this World about that Age when most Men think they may best enjoy it." He half-congratulates the young man on dying so willingly, leaving no progeny behind him as a vain monument. Browne's young man died in his mid-thirties.

Robert Loveday died of tuberculosis at the age of thirty-five. That he was born in 1621 and died in 1656 can be deduced in the following way. Venn's catalogue of Cambridge matriculations tells us that he was admitted to Peterhouse College.[14] Under his name in Walker's *Admissions to Peterhouse*, as of the date December 20, 1636, there is this: "Eodem die Robertus Loveday Suffolciensis annos natus quindecim educatus in eadem schola admissus est pensionarius ad primum mensam scholarium sub tutela D^{ni} Beaumont."[15] If Robert Loveday was admitted to Peterhouse at the age of fifteen in 1636, he must have been born in 1621.

According to his brother Anthony, he was thirty-five years old when he died. In "An elegy on the decease of his dearly beloved brother, Mr. Robert Loveday," appended to the 1659 *Letters*, signed "A. L.," we learn that Robert, while "in this short life he liv'd," loathed the rude world and aspired to heaven:

But whil'st he lived here seven times five years,
(but half man's age) for time lost no arreares,
His industry did like a River run,
No time allow'd to sin from Sun to Sun.[16]

If Robert Loveday was born in 1621 and died at the age
of thirty-five, he died in 1656. In the parish register of
Chediston Church on May 3, 1953, I found the following entry under "Burials": "Robert Luved [rest of name
illegible] Buryd the one & Twentyeth of December
Anno Dom. 1656." Browne's young man dies in the
middle of May. This detail, with its overtones of astrology, may be a literary flourish added later. December
or May aside, the age at which Robert Loveday died is
close enough to Browne's references to the age of
Christ and of Lazarus' second life[17] to strengthen one's
belief in the identity of Loveday and Browne's young
man.

There are also family references in common.
Browne mentions the "female friends" who asked about
the dying man's dreams (174). Loveday had two sisters,
Jane and Fenner, and female cousins, aunts, and
sisters-in-law, all of whom figure in his letters home. The
reference to his uncle is more apt: ". . . he maintained
not his proper Countenance, but looked like his Uncle,"
Browne writes, "the Lines of whose Face lay deep and
invisible in his healthful visage before" (166). Again,
". . . Age had set no Seal upon his Face, yet a dim Eye
might clearly discover Fifty in his Actions" (179). Loveday had a favorite uncle who appears to have been twice
his age; he addressed Letter XIII (p. 26) "To his Unkle
Mr. W. L.," enclosing "a dull translation out of the
French tongue."

Of more significance than the similarity of death by
tuberculosis at a comparatively young age is that

Browne's patient is a literary man—a fact which the doctor buries in a negative concessive clause:

And this serious Person, *though no minor Wit*,[18] left the poetry of his Epitaph unto others, either unwilling to commend himself, or to be judged by a Distich, and perhaps considering how unhappy great Poets have been in versifying their own Epitaphs; wherein Petrarcha, Dante, and Ariosto have so unhappily failed . . . (176).

Loveday was well-known in literary circles. Thomas Bailey, historian of Nottinghamshire, describes him in these words:

About this time [entry for 1652] there lived, as an upper servant in the family of the Earl of Clare, at Clare Hall, (Thurland House) in Nottingham, Robert Loveday, a very extraordinary person for his station in life; being an excellent scholar, well skilled in the classics, and possessing a very ready pen. He translated the three first parts of *Cleopatra*, and wrote, besides, a volume of letters, both of which performances were in good esteem with the public and *literati* of his time.[19]

Robert Loveday's major work was the translation of La Calprenède's *Cléopâtre*, a twelve-volume romance published in its French original in 1647. Before he died, he had translated the first three parts, calling his romance *Hymen's Praeludia, or, Love's Masterpiece*. These three parts were published separately in octavos beginning in 1652, then bound together and published by R. Lowndes in 1654 with commendatory poems by R. Braithwait, James Howell, John Chapperline, J. Wright, and G. Wharton.

In 1656, under the same title and with the same frontispiece, appeared the fourth part, translated by John Coles. In his dedication to Lady Jane Cheyney, Coles pays his sad respects "to the politer pen of the since deceased Loveday." In his "To the Reader" he explains that the fourth part was begun but—" 'tis my grief"—not completed "by the Elegant pen of the Ingenious Loveday." And among the congratulatory poems by Sir Kenelm Digby and others, "J. W." [John Wright?] asserts in a poem that Loveday before his untimely death had persuaded John Coles to continue the romance. Thus Loveday is alive in a preface dated 1654 and dead in another preface of 1656—the year which coincides with his death at the age of thirty-five. In addition to the translation of only a fourth of this huge French novel which thereafter bore his name, Loveday became well known for a volume of letters which his brother Anthony collected after his death and published, in obvious imitation of James Howell's *Epistolae Ho-Elianae*. That Loveday's *Letters* were in demand for a whole generation is shown by five editions of them listed in the British Museum catalogue: 1659, 1662, 1669, 1673, and 1684. Samuel Johnson mentioned Loveday's *Letters* in his "Life of Pope," in connection with Howell's and other famous collections, but he was mistaken in thinking that Loveday's letters had been printed only once.[20] The frontispiece of the 1659 *Letters* is the portrait of Robert made by the celebrated artist William Faithorne. Under it are these verses:

Wouldst know whose Face this Figure represents;
He was the Muses Darling, in whose Tents
He liv'd and dyde: And on whose Shrine was writ
Here lies the paragon of Art and wit.

Browne's patient was "no minor wit."

More specifically, the patient's literary labors in Browne's *Letter* seem to be connected with the romance languages. French and Italian allusions are more numerous than in Browne's other compositions. Hoping to gain the advantage of a change of air by "imbibing the pure Aerial Nitre of these Parts" (166)—meaning the air of East Anglia—the patient, Dr. Browne notes, was too late. After wandering about, he found "Sardinia in Tivoli," that is, the bad air of the first in the salubrious climate of the second.[21] It was an old Italian, not an Englishman, who long ago had told Dr. Browne that most people die when the moon is leaving its meridian (168). Instead of saying "Great Pan is dead," for some reason Browne Italianizes the Plutarchian phrase to "The great Antonio was dead" (165).[22] We have mentioned Browne's reference to Dante's face and have quoted his allusion to the epitaphs of Petrarch, Dante, and Ariosto.

Loveday's *Letters* tell clearly the story of his acquiring the French and Italian languages and of the translation of La Calprenède that brought him fame so soon before he died. The Clintons used French readily (XVI, p. 30), and Loveday at one point has already acquired French and is learning Italian. "I am very happy in an old *Italian* Gentleman that serveth my Lady Dowager," he writes, "one of the best Linguists in England" (LVI, p. 105). Through hard study he hopes to thrive "in my *French* and *Italian*" (p. 125). He reports to Sir John Pettus such marked progress in these two languages "that I am encouraged to publish" (LXV, p. 128). He ordered the latest edition of Cotgrave's *Dictionary*.[23] The first piece of translation he attempted was "a mad fantastick Dream" out of the French romance of *Françion* (p. 135).[24] He repeated a request of his lord for "some more Italian songs" (p. 191) and offered to compare for "Signior G." an English translation with the Italian original (p. 196). It would appear that the physican and the patient shared an interest in continental tongues, particularly French and Italian.

Finally, the doctor includes explicit details of the patient's character. He was free from avarice: "In this deliberate and creeping progress unto the Grave, he was somewhat too young, and of too noble a mind, to fall upon that stupid Symptom observable in divers persons near their Journey's end" (176). Both his life and death were models of Christian piety. He held the world in sober contempt (177), and he was quite willing to leave it at the time when most men think they may best enjoy it (178). He died unmarried and left no children (175). The most important part of his character was his moral purity, his chastity. In this he seemed early to have attained "the measure of a perfect Stature in Christ" (179).

Chastity was a commonplace theme in the seventeenth century, yet the parallel is striking between the emphasis Browne places on this trait in his patient and the fact of Loveday's dedicating his short life to a French romance that enshrines this particular virtue. In Letter LXXVIII (p. 148) Loveday tells his brother of the plan for the frontispiece, affixed not only to his first three parts of *Hymen's Praeludia* but to those parts, done by friends, which succeeded it. The engraving shows Hymen as the high priest about to light an altar with hearts on it, but Cupid (Robert explains as though writing a masque) stops her with these words issuing from his mouth: "Nondum peracta sunt praeludia" or "It's not time to light your marriage taper, for the wooings are not past." This refers, Robert concludes, to "the unfinished Story, as well by the Author as the Translator." It is clear from the other letters that Loveday was too sick to think of love, marriage, and children. There is no repining the lack of them: "All women have yet appeared so indifferent, as the whole Sex was never able to give me a Passion" (XXXVIII, p. 74). So much for Robert Loveday as the patient in Browne's *Letter*.

We know from the title page that Browne is writing to a friend intimately known to the deceased. The fact of a letter argues that the friend was absent at the time of the death, and we are told: "Altho at this distance you had no early Account or Particular of his Death, yet your Affection may cease to wonder that you had not some secret Sense or Intimation thereof . . ." (165). The friend is well acquainted with the deceased's family and would recognize the allusion to the uncle's face and to the dream interest of the "female friends." He must also be acquainted with the dead man's literary activity and either be especially interested in French and Italian himself or be familiar with the deceased's knowledge of these languages. The recipient is a nonmedical man, for Browne hints that he must be ignorant of "Plautus's sick Complexion" or the famous face of Hippocrates (166). Yet the absent friend is apparently well educated; in spite of his ignorance of physic, he would appreciate the learned and technical account that Browne gives him, as well as the personal details of the patient. He is one who must have understood Browne's strange substitution of "the great Antonio" for the "great Pan is dead." The advice at the end of the letter not only grows out of the *exemplum* given by Browne in his description of the young man but also must have been thought applicable to the absent friend. That Browne presumes to give advice at all may argue that the friend to whom he writes is younger than he is.

Sir John Pettus (1613-90) of Rackheath, four and a half miles northeast of Norwich, could trace his pedigree through some of the most famous families of Norfolk and Suffolk.[25] His grandfather of the same name had bought Overhall Manor in Rackheath in 1606, and the family had given at least three mayors and many aldermen to the city of Norwich.[26] The Sir John Pettus contemporary with Dr. Browne was a wealthy man and, in 1655, was the squire of Cheston Hall in Chediston,[27] the little village which had been the Loveday family seat since Edward I. In 1639 Sir John had married Elizabeth, daughter of Sir Richard Gurney, lord mayor of London. He had been knighted by Charles I on November 25, 1641, as a mark of His Majesty's favor to Gurney. An ardent Royalist, Sir John Pettus sent money to Charles II in France after 1649 and, all in all, contributed over twenty thousand pounds to the Royalist cause. Having depleted his estates, in 1655 he petitioned Cromwell, who made him deputy governor of the royal mines. In the same year Sir John's wife left him, turned Roman Catholic, came back five years later but left again to enter a nunnery; in 1672 she procured her husband's excommunication.[28] Their daughter Elizabeth married Samuel Sandys, and it is in the Sandys family home at Ombersley in Worcestershire that R. White's portrait of Sir John Pettus is hanging today.[29]

Anthony Loveday, in his "To the Reader" of his brother's posthumous *Letters*, boasts of the family acquaintance with this well-known figure.[30] To start the collection off well, he places two letters addressed to "Sir J. P." at the very beginning, and there are innumerable references throughout the book to "Sir J. P." The first item of frontal matter is a letter[31] "To my friend Mr. A. L. [Anthony Loveday]," signed "J. Pettus" and dated May 14, 1657. In this letter Sir John urges Anthony to publish his dead brother's letters, though many of them are written to Sir John himself. As for his letters written to Loveday, Sir John wishes that he had not expressed himself as he had on certain matters of state. Of Robert Loveday, deceased, he says at the end: "I shall onely add this . . . that I well knew your

Brother valiant, faithful, and discreetly industrious in all the concernments of body and mind. I was his Friend."[32] Two sides of a correspondence indicate that he was Robert Loveday's "intimate friend."

It is also true that Dr. Browne knew this Royalist of Rackheath, Norwich, and Chediston. The two had propinquity, politics, and scientific interests to draw them together. The earliest mention of the Pettus family by Browne occurs in his letter to Dugdale of December 6, 1658.[33] Three references to Lady Pettus[34] and one to Sir John are preserved: bits of professional gossip that Dr. Browne often indulged in in his letters to his medical son. The earliest of these is 1679 and the the latest, which is here quoted, is dated May 14, 1681: "Sr. J Pettus sayth hee is well; I have not yet seen his Lady. Sr John is fallen away in his flesh, as it is no wonder."[35]

Was Sir John Pettus away from home when Loveday died? Though his writing career did not begin until the 1670's, by his own account Sir John became interested in geological deposits, metallurgy, and "the spagyrick arts" as a youth during summer vacations from Cambridge spent with Sir Thomas Bendish.[36] During the Civil War, Pettus continues, he knew how helpful the royal mines in Wales were to Charles I, and so in 1650 took some responsibility for their working at the behest of the Society for the Mines Royal and executed his duties faithfully "for ten years."[37] In 1655 he became governor of mines under the Protectorate. From these references to his duties in the mines at Wales and elsewhere, particularly after 1655, we may safely infer that he was absent from the East Anglian counties at the time of Loveday's death in 1656.

It is entirely possible that Dr. Browne, knowing of Loveday's epistolary reputation and of the actual letters that had passed between Loveday and Sir John

Pettus, is doing the dead man and the absent friend a solemn favor in carrying through with one final *Letter to a Friend*, a letter which, like Loveday's epistles, must have some literary merit. The connection with Pettus may explain the puzzling play on the phrase "The Great Pan is dead." In 1887 W. Aldis Wright pointed out[38] that Browne's "the great Antonio was dead" was no mistake but a reference to George Sandys' *Travels* (1615).[39] The Sandys' allusion may thus be a subtle compliment to Sir John Pettus' daughter's marriage into the famous literary Sandys family.

Finally, though parts of the advice with which Browne's *Letter* closes were used in *Christian Morals*, here the *sententiae* must be considered as being of a piece with the rest. That Browne presumes to give advice is not strange. In 1656 he was just fifty, the half-century mark and an appropriate age to give advice to a friend eight years his junior who had shown by his actions that he could use it. The first paragraphs of advice have to do with chastity: a scandal, possibly connected with sex, arose when Sir John's wife left him the year before. Browne's dead man seemed not to care for riches. How wealthy Sir John was after compounding his estates is hard to say. The evidence shows that from 1655 on he was worried about money matters and could use just such advice contained in the next few paragraphs (181-82) on proper attitudes toward wealth. The third group (182) is based on the principle of *noblesse oblige*. Follow the proper ends, Browne says; don't go after applause and worldly fame. Be content to rest "in the soft showers of Providence." After giving generously to the Royalist cause, Sir John accepted from Cromwell the governorship of the mines, and all his life he was a notorious showman ("Rest not in an Ovation," etc., 185).

Browne calls upon his friend, a man of apparently

hot temper, to calm down and know himself: ". . . let not thine own depravity, or the torrent of vitious Times, carry thee into desperate Enormities in Opinions, Manners, or Actions" (183). Did Dr. Browne, while at Loveday's house, read Sir John Pettus' letters to the patient, letters which Sir John himself confessed were politically indiscreet, written by a Royalist during the Interregnum? Finally, Browne concludes, as your intimate friend died young, think of your own chances of longevity; do not act as if you owned the right to live.

These parallels between Browne's *Letter* and Loveday and between the *Letter* and Sir John Pettus cannot be weighed independently, but only within the triple relationship demanded by the *Letter* itself. Let us hope, to use Browne's ending words in our own context, that we have made "an happy Conformity, and close Apprehension of it."

Sir Thomas Browne died in 1682 and left his literary remains with his son Edward. Why didn't Edward publish the *Letter*, which in the Sloan manuscript appears to be in fair shape for publication, any time between his father's death and 1690? Why in 1690? It is possible that Edward Browne took the earliest opportunity to publish *A Letter to a Friend* when no living person could be embarrassed by it. The earliest opportunity was 1690, for that was the year in which Sir John Pettus died.

As for the date of initial composition, the evidence given here must be weighed against that for 1672 given by Greenhill. The presence of parallel passages in the commonplace books suggests that Browne worked the *Letter* over considerably. The Duloir allusion by itself is possible in 1656; the phrase "twenty years ago" could have been added at a later recension. The allusion to the king's evil telling against the king's purse (172) is certainly post-Restoration. But the phrase at the end of the *Letter* concerning "the torrent of vitious times" (183) sounds pre-Restoration. The passage on rickets, the "morbus Anglicus" which in medical history is significant, may coincide far more closely with the first books published on that English disease than Greenhill was aware.[40] On August 29, 1649, young Dr. Henry Power of Halifax had mentioned the new disease to Browne.[41]

A *Letter to a Friend* is not one of Browne's major works, yet it possesses qualities that still cause it to be read. Though highly literary[42] it springs obviously from a particular occasion: the death of one of his patients. It would be dangerous to rule out entirely the possibility that it was not written about Loveday and to Sir John Pettus in the year 1656, but until a better hypothesis explains as many of the traits of the *Letter* as the present one does, I rest the case. I believe it came in time closer to *Urn Burial* than to the end of Browne's life, and thus had formed a kind of directive for that immortal descant on man's mortality which, with its companion piece *The Garden of Cyrus*, marks the apex in the literary development of Sir Thomas Browne.

Chapter XIII

URN BURIAL
AND
THE GARDEN OF CYRUS

Why did Browne publish together in 1658 two essays as different in subject matter as the recent unearthing in Norfolk of a few crematorial remains and Cyrus the Younger's method of planting trees by fives in the shape of the quincunx? And why in that order?[1] Dr. Johnson[2] treated the two essays quite separately, and so did Wilkin.[3] In 1896 Greenhill's annotation was published after his death, unfortunately with no critical introduction.[4] Sir Edmund Gosse fatuously explained the concatenation of these two treatises by typographical utility: "The *Urn Burial* was too short to be published by itself, and therefore there was added to it a treatise on which Browne, apparently at the same time, had been working."[5] The French scholar Leroy saw no connection: "Après un silence de douze ans, Browne publia deux opuscules arbitrairement réunis."[6] Although Cline has explained the paradox of *Hydriotaphia*,[7] only three or four critics have insisted that *Urn Burial* is not complete without *The Garden of Cyrus*.[8]

TWIN ESSAYS AND THE NUMBER FIVE

That they stand together[9] by design rather than by accident is suggested in the fact that their author gave each five chapters. For the caption under the engraving of urns that preceded *Hydriotaphia,* moreover, Browne chose from Propertius' imagined funeral speech of Cornelia a quotation which, in its use of the number *five,* contains the merest hint of the quincunx of the second essay: *En sum quod digitis quinque legatur, onus.*[10] In the dedication of the second essay to Nicholas Bacon of Gillingham, he not only challenges his readers to discover the concinnity of the whole, but hints at their main relationship: "That we conjoin these Parts of different Subjects your Judgment will admit without impute of Incongruity; since the delightful World comes after Death, and Paradise succeeds the Grave."

This sentence implies that to Browne the second essay was the more important, though few modern readers, baffled by the number *five,* would agree. This number is not, as other numbers are in many numerological writings, haphazardly arrived at: ". . . not only seven and nine, but all the rest have had their eulogies," Browne had complained in *Vulgar Errors.*[11] Five is the number of beads in the Roman abacist's column; it is the number which follows the tetrad, 1, 2, 3, and 4, which add up to 10. The 10 itself in Roman numeral is X, or two V's (five's) joined at their apices. The Latin *uncia,* from which we get our words "inch" and "ounce," is 1/12; *quinc-unx* or 5/12 is related to the ancient method of planting trees in a mathematical pattern of fives which allows the roots the greatest amount of earth for nourishment and the branches the greatest amount of space for sunshine. Though the design could be square, Browne prefers the rectangle; a planted orchard is shown on the following page.

The shaded portion of this design indicates a repeated pattern of lozenges, with a central point and four points about it, making five; the diagonals form a chiasma

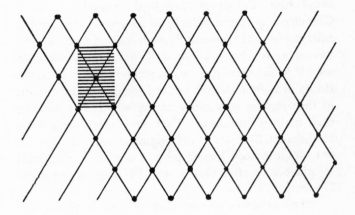

or Roman ten or Greek chi. In such a plantation, continues Browne, ". . . every enclosure makes a *Rhombus* . . . , the intervals bounded with parallel lines, and each intersection built upon a square, affording two Triangles or Pyramids vertically conjoyned; which in the strict Quincunxial order do oppositely make acute and blunt Angles" (*Garden of Cyrus*, IV, 110).[12]

But the reticulations of these man-made gardens (as also of fish nets and tennis rackets) are, like Plato's objects of art, thrice removed from reality or the IDEA: architects and latticemakers imitate the quincuncial design from nature, and nature imitates the archetype in the mind of God. Thus *The Garden of Cyrus* is a Platonic progression rising from the lowest to the highest and is itself a quincunx: Chapters I and II are the *artificial* considerations; Chapter III contains the quinary estivation in botany and other instances of five in *nature*; Chapters IV and V ascend to the *mystical* considerations. The long chapter on nature, in this arrangement, is the center or decussation. So much is clear from Browne's title page and the transitional sentences at the beginnings of his chapters.

The mystical perusal of the number five is related to Plato, particularly to the *Timaeus*, and ultimately to Pythagoras. Not only is the very first allusion in *The Garden* (I, par. 1) to Plato's *Timaeus*, but Browne finds his central emblem in that source.[13] In the next to the last paragraph of Chapter IV of *The Garden*, he writes:

Of this Figure Plato made choice to illustrate the motion of the soul, both of the world and man; while he delivered that God divided the whole conjunction length-wise, according to figure of a Greek χ, and then turning it about reflected it into a circle; By the circle implying the uniform motion of the first Orb, and by the right lines, the planetical and various motions within it. And this also with application unto the soul of man, which hath a double aspect, one right, whereby it beholdeth the body, and objects without; another circular and reciprocal, whereby it beholdeth it self. The circle declaring the motion of the indivisible soul, simple, according to the divinity of its nature, and returning into it self; the right lines respecting the motion pertaining unto sense, and vegetation, and the central decussation, the wondrous connexion of the severall faculties conjointly in one substance. And so conjoyned the unity and duality of the soul, and made out the three substances so much considered by him; That is, the indivisible or divine, the divisible or corporeal, and that third, which was the *Systasis* or harmony of those two, in the mystical decussation.

And if that were clearly made out which Justin Martyr took for granted, this figure hath had the honour to characterize and notifie our blessed Saviour, as he delivereth in that borrowed expression from Plato: *Decussavit eum in universo*, . . . (IV, 117).

Plato and Browne tell us to make two strips of

paper into two circles, then place one circle within the other so that each bisects the other as the equator bisects the meridian at zero and 180. Now we can easily perceive the two familiar adjuncts of the Greek theta, θ, which is *thanatos* or death: the circle is God, perfection, immortality; the horizontal represents the corporal, divisible, death. At the end of *Urn Burial* Browne says: "Circles and right lines limit and close all bodies, and the mortal right-lined circle must conclude and shut up all. There is no antidote against the Opium of time, which temporally considereth all things"(V, 45). At the beginning of *The Garden of Cyrus*, the Egyptians (he says) ". . . expressed the processe and motion of the spirit of the world, and the diffusion thereof upon the Celestial and elemental nature; implyed by a circle and right-lined intersection" (I, 73). Again: "Right lines and circles make out the bulk of plants . . ." (III, 102). But constructing the Greek theta out of two strips of paper in solid rather than in plane geometry allows us to see a third adjunct: the quincunx, the chiasma, the cross, the only antidote (in Browne's Christian mind) to the opium of time.

Despite the fact that some readers see little to choose between the two essays in their antiquarianism, Browne's scientific central chapter in *The Garden* is the heart of the whole matter. One-third longer than *Urn Burial*, *The Garden of Cyrus* grew out of his first and last study: botany, biology, God's other manuscript—nature.[14] The design of *The Garden*, therefore, is primary, leading up to the very mind of the Infinite Geometrician. The number of its chapters, five, illustrates the quincunx they describe, whereas *Urn Burial* has five chapters more by sympathy than by organic necessity. Dr. Johnson, a kindred spirit in many ways, was impressed by the research in *The Garden of Cyrus* but said of *Urn Burial*: "It is scarcely to be imagined, how many particulars he has amassed together, in a treatise which seems to have been occasionally written; and for which, therefore, no materials could have been previously collected."[15] The funeral urns broke in upon the more serious inquiry: "We were hinted by the occasion," Browne apologized in his dedication, "not catched the opportunity to write of old things, or intrude upon the Antiquary. We are coldly drawn unto discourses of Antiquities, who have scarce time before us to comprehend new things or make out learned Novelties."

Nevertheless, Browne could perceive how useful his archaeological interruption would be to his quincuncial design. The two essays form a Platonic dichotomy: two parts opposed yet conjoined, with a rising from the lower or elemental *Urn Burial* (death) to the higher or celestial *Garden of Cyrus*, the "numerical character" of reality (life).

More particularly, the two discourses are related in at least these three ways: (1) in their subject matters, as death is to life; (2) in their epistemologies, as ignorance is to knowledge; and (3) in their images, which play upon darkness and light, on womblike urns and new birth, on the sleep of death and drowsiness when "the quincunx of heaven runs low."

SUBJECT MATTER

That Browne intended us to read the two essays together and in the order he gave them is seen most obviously in the deliberateness of their opposition in subject matter. One concerns death, the other, life; one the body, the other the soul; one passions, the other reason; one accident, the other design; one substance, the other form. Together and only together they become a subject "not impertinent unto our profession, whose study is life and death" (dedication of *Urn Burial*). The first essay treats of time; the second, space. And together these two concepts delineate the character of God, in that time is an image of His Eternity, whereas number and geometrical figures in space are a key to His Wisdom.

The main subject of *Urn Burial* is momentary and local. It is a few bones and fragments of cinder, and even these will rejoin the dust in time. After an introduction of "This way of burial" or "the Roman practise of burning," Browne lays the subject before us at the beginning of Chapter II:

In a field of old Walsingham, not many months past, were digged up between fourty and fifty Urnes, deposited in a dry and sandy soile, not a yard deep, not far from one another: Not all strictly of one figure [the quincunx is most strictly of one figure], but most answering these described; some containing two pounds of bones, distinguishable in skulls, ribs, jawes, thighbones, and teeth, with fresh impressions of their combustion. Besides the extraneous substances, like peeces of small boxes, or combs handsomely wrought, handles of small brasse instruments, brazen nippers, and in one some kinde of Opale (II, 14).

From this point on Browne takes us into every corner of antiquity in order to bring our minds back to this occasion and to these bones. He does not know when "*these* Urnes" were deposited (II, 17), but "*these* Urnes may challenge above thirteen hundred years" (II, 18). A discourse on Roman cremation sharpens the abruptness with which he returns us to "the contents of *these* Urnes" (II, 19). "The *present* Urnes" are of varying capacities. He has seen many red urns, but "*these*" are black, though some of "*these* Urnes" seem to have been silvered over (III, 23-24). He could not be sure of the coverings "among *these* Urnes" because "*these* Ossuaries" were well burnt (III, 26). The skulls of "*these*

Urnes" (III, 30) were no less burnt than the other bones despite the humidity of the brain. It is useless to look for urns in the ruins of a temple: "*these*" (III, 31) were found in a field. Severe contemplators of "*these* lasting reliques*" (III, 33) may well think of a resurrection, and yet "*these*" were not the bones of persons struck with fire from heaven (IV, 38).

After such concentration upon the demonstrative adjective, no one can be surprised that the final chapter begins: "Now since *these* dead bones. . . ." For that is what *Urn Burial* is about. Its subject is small, temporal, local, *sui generis*, mutable, pathetic, nameless. The subject of *The Garden of Cyrus* is the diametric and complementary opposite: it is large, universal, immutable, everlasting, and as far from being unidentifiable as experimental botany and the propositions of Euclid can give exact names to things.

Urn Burial emphasizes dryness and even sandy soil, whereas *The Garden* flourishes amid rivers. *Urn Burial* is distraught with the passions of human beings who see those who were once perfect in form now a handful of ashes. *The Garden*, however, takes us from "crude pubescency unto perfection" (III, 91) in plants, and in the whole treatise from man's imperfect imitation of the quincunx in bedsprings and fish nets to the perfect figure of "the ordainer of order and mystical Mathematics of the City of Heaven" (V, 125). In the first essay the large bulk of a man has shrunken to a few pounds (III, 30). In the second essay a minute seed expands into an immense frond (III, 93), not only botanically but in Browne's very design.

The moral grows out of this kind of opposition. *Urn Burial* exposes the vanity of human wishes; *The Garden of Cyrus* exhorts to humility. When the poor mortals in the first essay mistakenly attempt to "participate" in God's eternity, they fail. In the sequel, where human work imitates nature and nature imitates God, there can be nothing but triumph. The first is Ecclesiastes; the second, the Wisdom of Solomon.

EPISTEMOLOGY

This inescapable nexus through contrast in subject matter is maintained, just below the surface, in the epistemology of the two treatises: in the mode of their knowledge, the kinds of questions each can raise and answer. In the *Religio Medici* Browne had heightened his paradox by setting side by side expressions of rationalistic doubt and assertions of intuitive certitude. Both kinds of statements exist in these twin works. But, as though to give the impression that he was a professional botanist and only an amateur antiquarian, Browne made *The Garden of Cyrus* a volume of exact knowledge and the first four chapters of *Urn Burial* a tissue of doubt. In the second and longer discourse he knows particulars through universals, whereas the best knowledge anyone can attain of "these dead bones" is that of particulars through other particulars. Truth is at stake here. And Browne's two essays argue (as does *Vulgar Errors*) that it is better to seek truth in nature than in the authority of the past.

Urn Burial, therefore, presents no more pattern and regularity of knowing than does the subject matter known. The very lack of uniformity in customs of disposing of the dead, in monuments that are raised to the dead, and especially in the poor fragments of evidence before him purposefully contrasts with the procedures of "regularity" and "rule" and "order" in *The Garden of Cyrus*. The first chapter of *Urn Burial* should lay before us a universal norm by which Browne can evaluate these urns; he finds only a wide variety of methods of disposing of the dead. Of the two main ways, however, the Roman way of cremation too quickly reduces the body (Egyptian embalming keeps the body too long). Christian sepulture in the ground, on the other hand, "God himself, that buried but one, was pleased to make choice of" (I, 8). Again, "Christians abhorred" cremation and preferred "depositure" to an "absumption," "properly submitting unto the sentence of God, to return not unto ashes but unto dust again, conformable unto the practice of the Patriarches, the interrment of our Saviour, of Peter, Paul, and the ancient Martyrs" (I, 11). Even under subjection to Rome they refused cremation, thereby bringing about the prophecy "concerning the body of Christ, that it should not see corruption, or a bone shall not be broken" (I, 12). Here, in the customs of mankind, is a norm—God's and nature's way of gentle return to the elements of which the body is made. But "these Urnes" do not represent that way, and consequently there is a lack of anything certain. For though, quite apart from religion, burial has some disadvantages, at least it allows one to know more about the dead: it leaves a bony form from which an anatomist can reconstruct the appearance of the flesh (*Urn*, III, 33; *Garden*, II, 84).

Hence the questions asked in *Urn Burial* are mostly impossible to answer, like "What song the Sirens sang, or what name Achilles assumed when he hid himself among women?" Who were these people? What did their friends think? Was this opal burnt on the finger of the dead person's hand, or was it cast into the fire as a gesture of affectionate grief? We will never know (III, 25). The Socratic tradition decrees that confession of ignorance alone can lead to knowledge; and before we can assent in Chapter V to the proposition that "nothing is strictly immortal but immortality," Browne must first overwhelm us with the necessity of guesswork. "We have no Authentick conjecture" (I,

10) of this; only a "wavering conjecture" (I, 13) of that; and "no obscure conjecture" (II, 14) of something else. One historian says this, another that (II, 20). For the cessation of urn burial in England, "we can discern no assured period" (II, 21). The fact that these fragments are black and dull-sounding "begat some doubt" (III, 23) as to whether they were actually burned or merely oven-baked. Such an admission would be shattering in an essay purporting only to exhaust the human methods of disposing of the dead that history can furnish us. The final court of appeal which science can give, experimental observation and reason, is absent from the first of these twin treatises, absent on purpose.

All that Browne is sure of at this stage is that these bones were calcined and were dug up in Norfolk. His ambling through the labyrinths of antiquity accentuates this bleak fact. And though Sir John Evans quite rightly pointed out[16] that a glance at Browne's engraving of the urns shows their origin to be not Roman but Saxon and much later than Browne supposed, does not Browne actually convey that *as far as he can tell* they are Roman? The Romans cremated their dead. The Romans came as far north as East Anglia. These urns were discovered near Brancaster, not far from the seven Burnham villages (II, 14)—etymological straws which in the absence of real evidence he must grasp at to answer his question. The fact is "A great obscurity herein, because, no medall or Emperour's coyne enclosed, which might denote the dates of their interrments" (II, 17; cf. IV, 38). After inclining for pages toward the Roman theory (no obscure conjecture), he suddenly confesses:

Some men considering the contents of these Urnes, lasting peeces and toyes included in them, and the custome of burning with many other Nations, might somewhat doubt whether all Urnes, found among us, were properly Romane

Reliques, or some not belonging unto our Brittish, Saxon or Danish Forefathers (II, 19).

Then he gives a detailed account of non-Roman cremations. His qualified conclusion is that ". . . the most assured account will fall upon the Romanes, or Brittains Romanized" (II, 21), which anyone might have guessed. Though these bones were unmixed, there can be no exact knowledge when

The ashes of Domitian were mingled with those of Julia, of Achilles with those of Patroclus: All Urnes contained not single ashes; Without confused burnings they affectionately compounded their bones; passionately endeavouring to continue their living Unions (III, 27).

Personally Browne prefers burial to cremation, but he skeptically ends his discourse with Lucan's "Tabesne cadavera solvat . . ."—"it makes little difference whether earth or the funeral fire dissolves these bodies."

The epistemology of *The Garden of Cyrus* is a direct contrast. Browne dedicated it to the kinsman of Sir Francis Bacon, warning him not to expect "mathematical Truths" and generalities in nature without exemption. And yet, as Cyrus "brought about the treasures of the field into rule and circumscription" (I, 71), so Browne employs the possibilities of exactitude which an advancement of learning can furnish him. The process of knowing is sure, and even the adumbrations lead toward significant, rather than vain, knowledge.[17] His "augmenting glasses" disclose the quinary arrangement in plants which he brings forward into the art of man and takes back into the mystery of intelligent creation. Where there is ignorance in the second essay, almost invariably it comes with the assumption that some day man will have a better instrument to lead him to the truth: "He that would exactly discern the shape of a Bees mouth," Browne writes, "needs observing eyes, and good augmenting glasses" (III, 97). Other impossibilities of knowing are due not to the inadequacy of the evidence or of the instruments but only of time and the occasion. Had not the examination of the famous whale of 1652 been so necessarily swift amid its stench, "we might have perhaps discovered some handsome order in those Net-like seases and sockets, made like Honey-combs, containing that medicall matter" (III, 100).

In *Urn Burial* knowledge is soon exhausted, and the favorite word is "conjecture" rather than "discern" or "discover." But in *The Garden* knowledge keeps opening like an ever-budding flower for further investigation in directions which Browne can merely suggest to a universal forum of inquiry. "The elegancy of this order" will be "discerned" by anyone who "more nearly considereth" (I, 74). "Studious Observators," again, "may discover more analogies in the orderly book of nature, and cannot escape the Elegancy of her hand in other correspondencies" (III, 101). Browne's knowing as well as his knowledge are of "well-contrived order" (I, 74). It partakes of "the generality and antiquity of this order" (I, 75), and the scientist is like the wise Solomon, "that eminent Botanologer and orderly disposer" (I, 75). The process of cognition in *The Garden of Cyrus* is one of "regular ordination" (I, 71), like the quincunx itself.

Hence Browne's main questions in *Cyrus* lead us to first causes in a Mind as far behind nature as nature lies behind the human artificer. Again and again in the second discourse, a series of *why's*, even though they are not always answered, serves to enlarge the inquiry: "Why the form of the germe doth not answer the figure of the enclosing pulp," "why" we rarely see two nebs in a single seed, "why" in the infinite reaches of plenitude trees give forth so many times their own weight in fruit (III, 93)—these cannot be answered yet, but they are laboratory notes for future investigation, whereas the notes in *Urn Burial* look backward. It is only lack of room and not of science that prevents Browne from answering chained paragraphs of sentences that all begin with "whether" (IV, 108 ff.).

Something has been made of the pity of Browne's "single contribution to science"[18] appearing in the "quaint" pages of *Urn Burial*: his discovery of *adipocère*, the fatty substance like "Castle soap" that clings to certain cadavers (II, 32). And yet in the contrasting and complementary epistemologies of these two essays, this is ironically appropriate. It is a single, accidental, unimportant discovery, like much of the antiquarian knowledge in *Urn Burial*. But knowledge in *The Garden of Cyrus* challenges the science of the future in this peroration for "acuter enquirers":

A large field is yet left unto sharper discerners to enlarge upon this order, to search out the *quaternio's* and figured draughts of this nature, and moderating the study of names, and meer nomenclature of plants, to erect generalities, disclose unobserved proprieties, not only in the vegetable shop, but the whole volume of nature; affording delightful Truths, confirmable by sense and ocular Observation, which seems to me the surest path, to trace the Labyrinth of truth (V, 124).

Browne perceived a parallel between optics and the psychology of comprehension. In vision, objects from without form a V̇ to converge upon the eye; thence, another V, with its apex in the retina, carries the image to the convolutions of the brain. So in *The Garden* the myriad forms of the number five in human arts pyramid themselves into nature; thence, from that nature by another pyramid into the multifarious mind of God

(IV, 116). But there is no such form in *Urn Burial,*
nor such means of knowing. Browne meant what he
had said long before in *Religio Medici*: "Now one
reason I tender so little devotion unto reliques, is, I
think, the slender and doubtfull respect I have alwayes
held unto Antiquities: for that indeed which I admire is
farre before antiquity, that is, Eternity, and that is God
himselfe; . . . ."[19]

STYLE

Finally, as in all good prose, the stylistic traits of
these two essays are inseparable from the philosophy
they convey. All the rhetorical devices at Browne's command are employed to underscore this relationship of
opposition and conjunction between *Urn Burial* and
The Garden of Cyrus. The first essay in languid sentences plays upon death and the endings of things; the
second nervously speaks of life, conjugal numbers, and
seminal activity. The famous "organ peal" in the final
chapter of *Urn Burial* adumbrates the "rising" into the
"mystical" considerations of *The Garden of Cyrus.*
Space will permit us here to examine only one aspect of
style: that is, two basic groups of images whose subtle
contrivance opposes and unites Browne's twin treatises.
The first of these is the *womb-generation-birth-death*
cluster. The other, practically inseparable from it, is a
series of evocations of *darkness-light-depth-surface.* Both
of these image groups convey the Christian and Neoplatonic thought in the form of a metaphor in mathematical proportion: our mortal birth is to our mortal
life what our mortal death is to a new life beyond the
grave. The womb is the truest microcosm and God's
infinitude the only macrocosm, which we enter by dying. Thus the images accurately embody the central
idea of the emblem: God's infinity is the circle which

our lives, in the horizontal line that crosses, touch at two points, birth and death. The concept was familiar to readers of Donne's "Second Anniversary," lines 435-38:

> Then, Soule, to thy first pitch worke up againe;
> Know that all lines which circles doe containe,
> For once that they the Center touch, doe touch
> Twice the circumference; and be thou such; . . . .

The very shape of the urns discovered at Walsingham reminded Browne of the womb: ". . . the common form with necks was a proper figure, making our last bed like our first; nor much unlike the Urnes of our Nativity, while we lay in the nether part of the Earth, and inward vault of our Microcosme" (*Urn*, III, 23). This made Browne wonder at urns being placed in the earth with their mouths downward (II, 22). Some people even buried their dead in crouched positions, not unlike ". . . our pendulous posture, in the doubtful state of the womb" (IV, 37). Hence the image of the two unborn infants discussing their imminent expulsion from their narrow world of experience, which so often has been taken out of context as one of Browne's *jeux d'esprit*, becomes part of the construction in the whole of Browne's thought in these *twin* essays: "A Dialogue between two Infants in the womb concerning the state of this world, might handsomely illustrate our ignorance of the next, whereof methinks we yet discourse in Plato's den, and are but Embryon Philosophers" (*Urn*, IV, 40).[20] The image accurately summarizes the ignorance and backward glance of the first essay while anticipating the clarity and hope of the second. In the following sentence, again, the *Urn Burial* and *The Garden of Cyrus* are stylistically linked to the unifying emblem, the theta:

And since death must be the Lucina of life, and even Pagans could doubt whether thus to live, were to die; Since our longest Sun sets at right descensions, and makes but winter arches, and therefore it cannot be long before we lie down in darknesse, and have our light in ashes; Since the brother of death daily haunts us with dying *memento's*, and time that grows old it self, bids us hope no long duration: Diuturnity is a dream and folly of expectation (*Urn*, V, 47).

The continuation of this passage draws us into the second image cluster—that of shadow and light to express ignorance and knowledge. In *Hydriotaphia* the bones that have been invisible in their womblike urns for three conquests are suddenly and shockingly exposed to the prying eyes of day. In *The Garden* the visible effects of man's ingenuity and nature's law receive their life from the invisible seeds in the mind of God. Those things which are God's lie deep; the urns were only a yard underground. "Nature hath furnished one part of Earth," Browne reminds us on the first page, "and man another. The treasures of time lie high, in Urnes, Coynes, and Monuments, scarce below the roots of some Vegetables."

The darkness of *Urn Burial* ("the dark habitations of the dead" mentioned in Chapter IV of *Cyrus*) is occasionally lit with great funeral pyres or sometimes more dimly with sepulchral lamps. Bright fires analyze that which has been created, whereas the sun synthesizes (*Urn*, III, 31). Fire reduces us to the formlessness of our precreation, to the chaos of black night before the great First Command. Thus "Life is a pure flame, and we live by an invisible Sun within us" (*Urn*, V, 48). The light in the generally dark *Urn Burial* is balanced with the darkness in the generally light *Garden of Cyrus*, and in that darkness seeds begin to sprout according to God's idea for them. Then they bend as plants toward the sun until they die (*Cyrus*, IV, 107).

Urn Burial is night: ". . . we lie down in darkness, and have our light in ashes" (V, 47). This "uncomfortable night of nothing" is the time of opium and sleep, the simulacrum of death, when "the iniquity of oblivion blindely scattereth her poppy" (V, 46). *The Garden* opens with "shooting rayes" and "luminaries"; it closes with the famous passage on night and sleep to bring Browne's whole thought to a complete circle: "But who can be drowsie at that hour which freed us from everlasting sleepe? or have slumbering thoughts at that time, when sleep itself must end, and as some conjecture all shall wake again?" The urns are chaos; the quincunx, design. And "Night which Pagan Theology could make the daughter of Chaos, affords no advantage to the description of order" (*Garden*, V, 125).

The shadow of *Urn Burial* and the sunlight of *The Garden* unite to form this paradox:

The greatest mystery of Religion is expressed by adumbration, and in the noblest parts of Jewish Types, we finde the Cherubims shadowing the Mercy-Seat: life it self is but the shadow of death, and souls departed but the shadows of the living: all things fall under this name. The Sun it self is but the dark *simulachrum*, and light but the shadow of God (*Garden*, IV, 115).

Christ looks through the latticework,[21] that is, "partly seen and unseen, according to the visible and invisible sides of his nature" (II, 79)—Christ, Who as the seed of God had to pass from the womb of Mary into death in order to achieve immortal life. Christ is the cross, the chiasma that brings heaven to earth, the central decussation in the quincuncial emblem. His incarnation stamped the whole universe with the sign of the X, and (Browne believed) our world has not been the same since He received on that cross the five wounds that "killed" Him. Browne, then, conceived these two essays as one, for their double dialectic carries us upward from mutability to deiformity.

CONCLUSION

To make Browne's scheme part of the seventeenth century, it is appropriate to quote Marjorie Nicolson on the relationship between Donne's two *Anniversaries*:

The first [Anniversary] is a lament over the body—the body of man and the body of the world—a meditation upon death and mortality. The second [Anniversary] is a vision of the release of the soul from its prison. The whole, with antitheses of doubt and faith, despair and hope, death and the triumph of immortality, is a great symphony in which the harmony is more profound because of the cacophony.[22]

Of Browne's twin essays, readers will continue to prefer *Urn Burial*, as they do Dante's *Inferno* to the *Paradiso*. Although it is possible that Browne fell short in the latter and main half of his design, the first essay can be grasped by all of us at home in the "flux." The eternal mind requires a flight few of us are willing to make. This Platonic conclusion is nicely expressed by St. Augustine:

Owing to that very order of our nature, whereby we are made mortal and carnal, we handle visible things more easily than things intelligible; since the former are perceived by bodily senses; the latter are understood by the mind.[23]

To grant their basic design is not to rob the discourses of their perennial delight. Browne apologizes for "the extraneous things": we accompany him through the surprising turns of funeral custom and cry out with Coleridge's surprise, ". . . Quincunxes in Heaven above,

Quincunxes in Earth below, & Quincunxes in the water beneath the Earth; Quincunxes in Deity, Quincunxes in the mind of man; Quincunxes in bones, in optic nerves, in Roots of Trees, in leaves, in petals, in everything!"[24] If from Plato and his followers Browne inherited a sense of opposition as being a law of life, then the opposition between seriousness and playfulness[25] must also be present in these works, as it is in *Religio Medici* and *Vulgar Errors*. To be able to play in the face of eternity marks that type of mind which we meet in the puns of metaphysical poetry, in Hamlet's wry jokes on sex, in the fantastic horseplay of the Zen Buddhist on the verge of *satori*, and in T. S. Eliot's mixing of Martinis with the price of redemption.

Long before, Browne had defined God (in Hermes Trismegistus' "circle whose center is everywhere and whose circumference is nowhere") as Wisdom and Eternity.[26] A religious view that conceives God alone as never-ending must unmask all human pretensions to immortality without Him (*Urn Burial*); and one that defines God as all-wise must insist that man's final knowledge of reality is to be found only in the mind of God as it is reflected in nature and in art (*The Garden of Cyrus*).

Chapter XIV

CHRISTIAN MORALS

The manuscript of *Christian Morals* was lost for more than thirty years in the clutter of an archbishop's study. When Dr. Edward Browne became his late father's literary executor in 1682, he took some of the leftover manuscripts back to London with him. The following year the Reverend Thomas Tenison, rector of London's St. Martin-in-the-Fields, edited the *Miscellany Tracts*. Once of Norwich and a dear friend of Sir Thomas Browne's, he was a good man to help Edward in the literary work that lay before him. "There still remain other brief discourses written by this most learned and ingenious author," Tenison wrote in his preface to this 1683 work. "Those, also, may come forth, when some of his friends shall have sufficient leisure; and at such due distance from these Tracts, that they may follow rather than stifle them."

In what to Edward was a "due distance" in time, that is, "during the reign of James II" (1685-88), another box of manuscripts was sent to the Reverend Thomas Tenison. After some time had elapsed without result, at her brother's insistence Browne's daughter Mrs. Elizabeth Lyttleton fetched the box back from Dr. Tenison. But Edward did not find in it ". . . the choicest of the papers, which were a continuation of . . . my father's Religio Medici, drawn up in his elder years."[1]

In 1690, as we have seen, Edward published A *Letter to a Friend* without Dr. Tenison's aid. By 1694 Tenison had been elevated to succeed Tillotson as archbishop of Canterbury, and the manuscript had not yet been returned. Edward died in 1708.

In 1712 a volume of Browne's writings was published in London by Curll, who acknowledged the help of Mr. Owen Brigstock, the late Dr. Edward Browne's son-in-law, in the securing of the manuscripts. *Christian Morals* was not among them, although Mrs. Lyttleton remembered being at her father's house when he was preparing it, and the Reverend John Jeffery of Norwich recalled having seen the manuscript shortly after Sir Thomas Browne died.[2] Elizabeth Lyttleton hoped that the lost manuscript could still be recovered among the archbishop's papers or in the possession of Edward's only daughter, Mrs. Brigstock.[3] The gross omission of *Christian Morals* from the 1712 posthumous volume may have prompted Elizabeth in November 1712 to tell her story of the missing manuscript to the Reverend White Kennett in Windsor. We can believe that this genial and whiggish Anglican priest—wearing the black patch over one eye injured in a shooting accident—asked Archbishop Tenison for the manuscript. The two had been friends, for in 1701 Tenison had appointed Kennett to the original Society for the Propagation of Christian Knowledge. But no manuscript turned up.

At last, in his preface to the published volume of *Christian Morals* in 1716, Reverend John Jeffery wrote:

The reason why it was not published sooner is, because it was unhappily lost, by being mislaid among other manuscripts, for which search was lately made in the presence of the Lord Archbishop of Canterbury, of which his Grace, by letter, informed Mrs. Lyttleton when he sent the manuscript to her.

The choice of Jeffery of Norwich for the editor of *Christian Morals*, probably made by Mrs. Lyttleton, was a natural one. Jeffery in 1678 had been unanimously chosen rector by the parishioners of St. Peter Mancroft, of whom Sir Thomas Browne was at the time the most distinguished. And although the Reverend John Whitefoot of Heigham, having been Browne's friend for a longer period, was asked to gather materials for a biography, Jeffery probably presided over Browne's interment in the chancel of his church (where he himself was put to rest in 1720). Jeffery must have been beloved by Browne for his piety, learning, and detestation of religious controversy; and Jeffery, after Browne's death, had been among those most anxious about the lost manuscript. In 1694 Archbishop Tillotson had appointed him archdeacon of Norwich. Jeffery therefore edited the volume called *Christian Morals*, which first appeared in 1716 at the Cambridge University Press. It contains a dedication by Mrs. Lyttleton to David Earl of Buchan, who, as the husband of the illustrious author's granddaughter, had sired the only descendants capable of keeping the line alive.

The original manuscript which thus survived Archbishop Tenison's long safekeeping is now irretrievably lost, so that we must trust Jeffery's word that "there is nothing printed in this discourse, or in the short notes, but what is found in the original manuscript of the author, except only where an oversight had made the addition or transposition of some words necessary."[4] The editor is not so specific about the title. Had it been Browne's, it seems that his two children who had cared most about the long-lost piece would have referred to it as "Christian Morals." The Reverend White Kennett in 1712, too, it seems likely, would have used this appropriate and convenient title in retelling Mrs. Lyttleton's story of how it got lost. It would appear, then, that either Tenison or Jeffery gave it the title *Christian Morals.*

In view of its character, it is impossible to assign a definite date for its composition; the loosely gathered together *sententiae* could have been written at various periods in the author's life. That the first part is a re-writing of the last part of *A Letter to a Friend* points toward its having been a repository of moral maxims that came to Browne at odd moments in a long and busy career. If my argument for the composition of *A Letter to a Friend* in 1656 rather than in 1672 holds true, then these parts of *Christian Morals* at least are not the thoughts of a man nearing three score years and ten, and other paragraphs may well have been drafted even earlier. In 1642 Browne had confessed in his preface to the pirated work of his young manhood that he had written *Religio Medici* ". . . about seven yeares past, with some others of affinitie thereto. . . ." Though the whole manuscript from which *Christian Morals* was printed is no longer extant, passages from it are found in other manuscripts[5]—a fact that lends weight to the theory of desultory composition and careful polishing over a period of years. Some of the many papers left by Browne at his death, Whitefoot said, ". . . designed for the press, were often transcribed and corrected by his own hand, after the fashion of great and curious writers."[6]

Certainly, a more seasoned wisdom, a greater humility, a more vivid eschatology, and a more patterned style set off most of *Christian Morals* from the youthful *Religio Medici* of which Edward had remarked it was a continuation.

In the early work the very absence of a clear outline is part of the art and charm. The last work has no logical or poetic link to its purposely separated paragraphs, nor is there any apparent reason for its being divided as it is. A careful reading of it, however, hardly confirms the whole of Edmund Gosse's conclusion that "The first of these [parts] is nothing more nor less than the closing pages of A *Letter to a Friend,* much expanded and adorned. The second is concerned with the criticism of opinion; the third collects a series of principles for the conduct of life."[7] Part I is far more than Browne's advice to his friend, by Gosse's own admission; the central portion is only partially concerned with intellectual conduct; and the whole, not just Part III, is "a series of principles for the conduct of life." In fact, the last half of the last part does evolve into a series of rules not for living but, perhaps echoing Jeremy Taylor, for dying. Thus the work is not completely devoid of form.

It illustrates once more Browne's preoccupation with the two worlds in which he was so amphibiously at home. "'Tis therefore happy that we have two Worlds to hold on," he concludes in *Christian Morals.* "To enjoy true happiness we must travel into a very far Countrey, and even out of our selves; for the Pearl we seek for is not to be found in the Indian, but in the Empyrean Ocean" (III, xi, p. 141).[8] Again, "Reconcile the events of things unto both beings, that is, of this World and the next; so will there not seem so many Riddles in Providence, nor various inequalities in the dispensation of things below" (III, v, p. 136). The noun, "Morals," of its title describes the historical, classical, humanely reasoned half of it, and the adjective, "Christian," describes the other half: where something not ourselves has raised the morals of the greatest pagans to a point beyond *recta ratio.* Its form thus stems from the aphoristic method of both Marcus Aurelius and Lombard, of Epictetus' *Enchiridion* as well as of Pascal's *Pensées.*

Many of the allusions evoke the classical figures of

the two centuries before and after the birth of Christ--
historians such as Livy, Suetonius, and Plutarch; em-
perors and generals such as Julius Caesar, Pompey,
Tiberius, Nero, and Commodus the son of Marcus
Aurelius; poets and playwrights such as Plautus, Terence, Horace, Ovid, Seneca, Lucan, and Juvenal;
philosophers such as Zeno the founder of the Stoics,
Cato the Younger, and Cicero. Behind these lies Aristotle's *Nicomachean Ethics.*

On the other hand, there are constant echoes of
the Bible, and allusions to Adam, Ahab, Belshazzar's
feast; David, Elias; Job and Jonathan; Mary Magdalene,
Methuselah, Moses, and Noah; St. Peter, St. James, St.
John, and St. Paul; and Jesus Christ.

The key to Browne's total meaning, however, lies
in such double allusions as those to Socrates *and* Job
(I, xiv, p. 106), Horace *and* St. Luke (I, xxxiv, p. 118),
Hercules *and* God (I, xiii, p. 106), Phocylides *and*
Solomon (III, xxi, p. 149), Socrates *and* Cardan (I,
xxix, p. 115), God's book *as well as* "the Censor's"
(I, xxvii, p. 114). In *A Letter to a Friend* Browne had
advised his recipient against those narrow-minded vices
that fall ". . . not only short of S. Paul's noble Christian,
but Aristotle's true Gentleman" (Keynes, I, 184). In
Christian Morals, again, by joining the two (I, xvi, p.
107), Browne anticipated Cardinal Newman's definition
of the "gentleman" as forming only part of the ideal
product of a Christian university. No more than Newman is Browne against the virtues of the gentleman:
". . . bright Thoughts, clear Deeds, Constancy, Fidelity,
Bounty and generous Honesty are the Gems of noble
Minds; wherein, to derogate from none, the true He-
roick English Gentleman hath no Peer" (I, xxvi, p.
119). But this is not enough: the central passage of
Browne's *sententiae* is section xxi of Part III:

Rest not in the high-strain'd Paradoxes of old Philosophy supported by naked Reason, and the reward of mortal Felicity, but labour in the Ethicks of Faith, built upon Heavenly assistance, and the happiness of both beings. Understand the Rules, but swear not unto the Doctrines of Zeno or Epicurus. Look beyond Antoninus, and terminate not thy Morals in Seneca or Epictetus. Let not the twelve, but the two Tables be thy Law. Let Pythagoras be thy Remembrancer, not thy textuary and final Instructor; and learn the Vanity of the World rather from Solomon than Phocylides. Sleep not in the Dogma's of the Peripatus, Academy, or Porticus. Be a moralist of the Mount, an Epictetus in the Faith, and christianize thy Notions.

This rubric seems to have informed the work as we have it from the beginning, for in the opening section of Part I, Browne rewrote the advice to his friend of several years before by modifying the classical pattern for conduct while emphasizing the Christian. In *A Letter to a Friend* he had written:

Sit not down in the popular Seats and common Level of Virtues, but endeavour to make them Heroical. Offer not only Peace-Offerings but Holocausts unto God. To serve Him singly to serve our selves, were too partial a piece of Piety, nor likely to place us in the highest Mansions of Glory (Keynes, I, 180-81).

This became, while Browne was growing older:

Sit not down in the popular Forms and common Level of Virtues. Offer not only Peace-Offerings but Holocausts unto God: *where all is due make no reserve, and cut not a Cummin Seed with the Almighty*. To serve him singly to serve our selves, were too partial a piece of Piety, not likely to place us in the illustrious Mansions of Glory (III, i, pp. 101-2, my italics).

Browne believes that despite their stars "men at some time are masters of their fates": "Whatever Influences,

Impulsions, or Inclinations there be from the Lights above, it were a piece of wisdom to make one of those Wise men who overrule their Stars, and with their own Militia contend with the Host of Heaven" (III, vii, p. 138). Some ancient Romans did just this—*sapiens dominabitur Astris*.[9] Without pausing, Browne adds: "Unto which attempt there want not Auxiliaries from the whole strength of Morality, supplies from Christian Ethicks, influences also and illuminations from above, more powerful than the Lights of Heaven."

Noble though the Stoics were and difficult though it was for Browne and many another Christian to separate classical ethics from those of Christianity, there were and are basic differences. For one thing, no Stoic ever warned his followers against practicing the good for the purpose of self-advancement, as Jesus scorned those who made honesty the best policy (I, iv). Again, the Stoics tended to view all evils equally, whereas for the Christian there is a hierarchy of sins as there is of virtues (III, xii). Further, the Stoics (and some Christians, it must be admitted), in subscribing to *contemptus mundi*, so longed for the quietus of this world's ills that they sought death by violence upon themselves. But even while insisting that the next life must be better, the Christian does not hold contempt for this life, since he believes that God did send into it His only begotten Son. Finally, Stoics believe in chance, Christians in providence (I, xxv; III, xii). Providence works more often circuitously than in a straight line. "What a labyrinth is there in the story of Joseph," Browne had remarked in *Religio Medici* (I, xvii), "able to convert a Stoick!" In *Christian Morals* he continues the theme:

When Cato intended to kill himself, from a blow which he gave his servant, who would not reach his Sword unto him, his Hand so swell'd that he had much ado to effect his design. Hereby any one but a resolved Stoick might have taken a fair hint of consideration, and that some mercifull Genius would have contrived his preservation. To be sagacious in such intercurrences is not Superstition, but wary and pious Discretion; and to contemn such hints were to be deaf unto the speaking hand of God, wherein Socrates and Cardan would hardly have been mistaken (I, xxix, p. 115).

To know ourselves is good classical doctrine, but to know ourselves as made in God's image and therefore constantly in God's mind is to look upon this life, this world, and this world's history in a far different light from that of any of the most "virtuous heathen." This is why Browne turned the peculiarly Roman symbol of Janus, the two-faced God, into a Christian one. "In Bivious Theorems and Janus-faced doctrines," he writes at one point, "let virtuous considerations state the determination. Look upon Opinions as thou dost upon the Moon, and chuse not the dark hemisphere for thy contemplation" (III, iii, p. 135). At another point: "Let the mortifying Janus of Covarrubias be in thy daily Thoughts, not only on thy Hand and Signets" (III, x, p. 140). Here Browne notes in the margin: "Don Sebastian de Covarrubias writ 3 Centuries of moral Emblems in Spanish. In the 88th of the second Century he sets down two Faces averse and conjoined Janus-like, the one a Gallant Beautiful Face, the other a Death's Head Face, with this Motto out of Ovid's *Metamorphoses, Quid fuerim quid simque vide.*" The Spanish "Christian Morals" from which he is quoting belonged to him in the quarto edition published at Madrid in 1610.[10] Thus Janus becomes a symbol of the Christian who faces two worlds of time: "What is Prophetical in one Age proves Historical in another, and so must hold on unto the last of time; when there will be no room for Prediction, when Janus shall loose one Face . . ." (III, xiii, p. 143). Again, "He is like to be the best judge of Time who hath lived to see about the sixtieth part thereof. Persons of short times may Know what 'tis to live, but not the life of Man, who, having little behind them, are but Januses of one Face, and Know not singularities enough to raise Axioms of this World: . . ." (III, xxii, p. 149). In 1658 Browne had employed the emblem of Janus in the fifth chapter of *Urn Burial:* "We cannot hope to live so long in our names as some have done in their persons, one face of Janus holds no proportion to the other" (Keynes,· IV, 45).

As these references to the Christian Janus show, the variety and plenitude of classical allusions is not out of place in *Christian Morals:* they lend the work a wisdom seasoned with a far wider reading and a far deeper contemplation than appear in *Religio Medici*. The space given to pagan and Christian authors whose thoughts are so similar to Browne's, moreover, leaves less room for the weeds and tares of his own brain to grow in; the result is a humility sans irony which differs from the charming egocentrism of his earlier work.

It differs from *Religio* in another way. Though Browne ended the first part of *Religio Medici* with a view of the end of the world, the eschatology of the last part of the final section of *Christian Morals* is far more deeply interfused. Just after Part 11, section xxi, which I hold tó be the key to the Stoic-Christian thought, Browne expands his view of the end of things which he, as a Christian about to outlive his allotted three score years and ten, has arrived at. The passage can be paraphrased like the following paragraph.

To live thus by God's time is to know time in epitome (sec. xxii). Put more thought on eternity than on pleasure, for since we live forever think on the capital end (sec. xxiii). Stars are unequal in magnitude and so are men; hence live expecting that perhaps the first shall be last, and the last first (sec. xxiv). Stoics undervalue this life, but Christians believe that the greatest underweening of this life is to hold of little worth that for which this life is but an exordium (sec. xxv). How long the world will last no man knows, though some of us are surprised that God has put up with it for as long as He has; pray for the accomplishment of His word (sec. xxvi). It is not bad to wish to die during good times in this world, rather than in evil days (sec. xxvii). How many saints there are already in heaven we do not know, yet happy are they who hasten here on earth to enroll themselves among their number when they die (sec. xxviii). Our life is really not such a brief moment in proportion to the promised duration of the world; study the past in order to realize that you've already lived through time (sec. xxix). Lastly, don't count on a long life; approximate your last days by apprehending them as present; mystical theology has anticipated heaven for you (sec. xxx).

A comparison of my paraphrase with Browne's own words will reveal, finally, the characteristics of the style of *Christian Morals*. Austin Warren calls some of the style here decadent: "Hostile criticism has often taken as typical the style of *Christian Morals*, written at the end of his life . . . , a work showing signs of decadence, in its exaggeration and stiffening of Brunonian traits."[11] The two traits Warren emphasizes are the Latinate diction and the curt balanced period. It does contain sentences like "Move circumspectly, not meticulously, and rather carefully sollicitous than anxiously sollicitudinous" (I, xxxiii, p. 117), and the more famous, "Festination may prove Precipitation; deliberating delay may be wise cunctation, and slowness not slothfulness" (I, xxxiii, p. 118). And yet a Latinate vocabulary is conspicuously relieved by sentences like "Guide not the Hand of God, nor order the Finger of the Almighty, unto thy will and pleasure; but sit quiet in the soft showers of Providence . . ." (III, v, p. 136).

The curt period in *Christian Morals* is not a sign of decadence but a part of Browne's stylistic method for a work which is frankly aphoristic and actually Senecan. In contrast to the "Ciceronian Hooker," Warren quotes Francis Thompson as saying that Browne is ". . . steeped in classic models more compact and pregnant than Cicero." Hence, Warren concludes, though Browne can express himself in long sentences, ". . . there is another Browne who is a Stoic and a pragmatist, aphoristic of utterance: . . . ."[12] This is true, and the *style coupé* or serried style has to be more common in *Christian Morals,* a partial imitation of Epictetus, than in *Religio Medici.* But that is not decadence.

Just as characteristic of the style of *Christian Morals* is the metabolic balance between "high" and "low" which we find in the earlier work. In a well-tested philosophy which does not include the shades of doubt that *Religio Medici* does, the three levels of conduct are continued from the observations of an earlier day: a man can live on the level of the passions, like an animal; he can live by his unaided reason, as the Stoics did; and he can live like a Christian, by God's grace, within the realm of the spirit. In *Christian Morals* the subject matter and the very rhythm of the sentences and paragraphs travel, as it were, up and down this scale. The result is that Brown's three styles—low, middle, and high[13]—are present not only in his *Vulgar Errors* (low), in his *Religio Medici* and "decadently" in *Christian Morals* (middle), and in the fifth chapter of *Hydriotaphia* (high), but all three are artfully disposed for the ideas they carry within *Christian Morals*.

The lowest world one can live in is that of the seven deadly sins: covetousness, for example,

> . . . cracks the sinews of Faith; numbs the apprehension of any thing above sense, and only affected with the certainty of things present, makes a peradventure of things to come; lives but unto one World, nor hopes but fears another; makes their own death sweet unto others, bitter unto themselves; brings formal sadness, scenical mourning, and no wet eyes at the grave (I, viii, p. 104).

Another passion is hatred:

> *Let not the Sun* in Capricorn *go down upon thy wrath,* but write thy wrongs in Ashes. Draw the Curtain of night upon injuries, shut them up in the Tower of Oblivion, and let them be as though they had not been. To forgive our Enemies, yet hope that God will punish them, is not to forgive enough; to forgive them our selves, and not to pray God to forgive them, is a partial piece of Charity: forgive thine enemies totally, and without any reserve, that however God will revenge thee (I, xv, pp. 106-7).

In these, as in many other passages of advice against living by passion, there is no excessively Latinate diction. On the contrary, the vocabulary and the rhythm are as low as the matter. The clauses are independent and advance with little complexity in one's and two's, occasionally co-ordinated with conjunctions.

As the passions can be corrected by reason, which the noble Romans used so wisely, so the world of the mind is more often described in Latinate words. The two extremely inkhorn examples already cited illustrate this function, which is faintly adumbrated in the single word "ambulatory" in the following:

Live by old Ethicks and the classical Rules of Honesty. Put no new names or notions upon Authentick Virtues and Vices. Think not that Morality is Ambulatory; that Vices in one age are not Vices in another; or that Virtues, which are under the everlasting Seal of right Reason, may be stamped by Opinion (I, xii, p. 105).

The Latinate diction may occupy, then, the middle world, that of human reason; and no one can escape the impact of the subordinate clause in the element that follows the final semicolon.

The high style is most often given to us with the low and the middle style in rising and falling successions of rhythm and mainly English diction. The antitheses are those of heaven and earth, God and man, the trivial and the sublime. Sometimes Browne moves us from the large, unknown, and perhaps fearful concept down to the small, familiar, and comfortable. Here his Christian morality in its essential paradox of the "first shall be last and the last, first" is inseparable from the stylistic trait:

The Divine Eye looks upon high and low differently from that of Man. They who seem to stand upon Olympus, and high mounted unto our eyes, may be but in the Valleys and low Ground unto his; for he looks upon those as highest who nearest approach his Divinity, and upon those as lowest who are farthest from it (I, xxvii, p. 114).

Following are two consecutive sentences which, without excessive Latinity, between them again illustrate the opposition and conjunction, and the tension. The first sentence goes down from the vague unknown to a specific event in the distant future; the second moves upward from present "things" to "the chaos of futurity":

Leave future occurrences to their uncertainties, think that which is present thy own: and since 'tis easier to foretell an Eclipse, than a foul day at some distance, look for little regular below. Attend with patience the uncertainty of Things, and what lieth yet unexerted in the Chaos of Futurity (I, xxv, p. 112).

Again, in one short sentence Browne takes us from the view we get here on earth up to the idea of providence, and then descends to a middle height in the single italicized Latin word: "Carry no careless Eye upon the unexpected scenes of things; but ponder the acts of Providence in the publick ends of great and notable Men, set out unto the view of all for no common *memorandums*" (II, xi, p. 128). In the end passage of *A Letter to a Friend*, now slightly rephrased and again placed last in *Christian Morals*, the descent from this life into the grave is unexpectedly turned into a rise from the Latinisms of one concept to the simple but profound Anglo-Saxon of the other, to come back again to the present "happy conformity" and "close apprehension" of the truth thus expressed:

Approximate thy latter times by present apprehensions of them: be like a neighbour unto the Grave, and think there is but little to come. And since there is something of us that will still live on, join both lives together, and live in one but for the other. He who thus ordereth the purposes of this Life will never be far from the next, and is in some manner already in it, by a happy conformity, and close apprehension of it (III, xxx, p. 156).

Samuel Johnson prefixed his 1756 edition of *Christian Morals* with a life of Browne written partially in order to discover ". . . what influence learning has had on its possessors, or virtue on its teachers." Throughout he was impressed by Browne's scholarship:

But it is not on the praises of others, but on his own writings, that he is to depend for the esteem of posterity;

of which he will not easily be deprived, while learning shall have any reverence among men: for there is no science, in which he does not discover some skill; and scarce any kind of knowledge, profane or sacred, abstruse or elegant, which he does not appear to have cultivated with success.

Johnson was even more attracted to Browne by the zealousness of his Christianity:

. . . there is scarcely a writer to be found, whose profession was not divinity, that has so frequently testified his belief of the sacred writings, has appealed to them with such unlimited submission, or mentioned them with such un-varied reverence.

This is very similar to what a present-day critic and scholar finds in Browne: Douglas Bush notes that we read Donne's sermons ". . . without much religious quickening, and . . . without a sense of intimacy; we get both from almost any page of the layman Sir Thomas Browne."[14] All the testimonies Samuel Johnson's rummaging mind could discover ". . . prove that Browne was a zealous adherent to the faith of Christ, that he lived in obedience to his laws, and died in confidence of his mercy."[15] *Christian Morals* is a sententious anticlimax, to be sure; and yet its ideas and the dress Browne gave them deserve more study than most critics since Dr. Johnson have been willing to give.

Browne knew that there are two kinds of "nature": the phenomena he studied in his laboratory and the "nature" of man's greatest potentiality. He knew, therefore, that there are two sets of laws governing them. The Stoics he consistently quotes lived as successfully as anyone can according to the laws that govern the moral nature of man. The laws of right reason and virtuous action have to be constantly urged by our best minds, but even when they are pleaded for by the most eloquent (Cicero, for example, in *De Legibus*), man constitutionally fails to live up to them.

Christianity realistically asserts that man cannot live even by his own best formulations of right reason —without the gift of Grace. What Browne would call "the vulgus" do not use reason at all. And reason is not helped when even rationalists repudiate its laws. Montaigne, for example, found the law of nature to be merely the law of custom, substituting mores for morals. And Hobbes did not trust the law of reason: when law disappears, might must take its place, and a man obeys a law not because it is just but because a "sovereign" makes him obey it.[16] Browne subscribed to the universal laws of human reason that came from Greece and Rome, and sought aid in prayer to keep them. On the other hand, merely to pray is not enough. His withdrawal from the Civil War may well have resulted from the uneasiness (expressed for many by Marvell's ode) at seeing a Cromwell and the sword take the place in England of a Sir Edward Coke and common law. That the Parliamentary armies prayed before battle perhaps marked them as Christian, but they had upset the great consensus of Cicero.

In *Christian Morals* Browne reaffirms the ancient pagan doctrine, and, finding the cause of its failure not in it but in man, insists on "Christianizing" its "notions."

Chapter XV

LIVING
IN
TWO WORLDS

Browne's last years were very tranquil, except for two events.[1] One, the witch trial in 1664 at Bury St. Edmunds, has been blown up out of all proportion to its actual significance. Presided over by Sir Matthew Hale, the trial took evidence on the bewitching of certain children by two women, Amy Duny and Rose Cullender. The women were indicted on the usual charges. Forty crooked pins and a two-penny lath nail had been vomited up by their victims. A frog found in one of the children's blankets exploded like a pistol when it was thrown into the fire. A farmer by the name of Soams accidentally scraped his cart against Rose Cullender's house; soon afterwards a wheel, apparently possessed, fell off and he was thrown into the ditch. Dr. Thomas Browne, fifty-nine years old and at the height of his reputation, was in the courtroom and was asked to speak. He said nothing about the two defendants, but pointed out to the court that two years before in Denmark a trial of witches had showed similar evidence.

The two women were hanged protesting their innocence. Sir Edmund Gosse calls this ". . . the most culpable and the most stupid action of his life . . . their blood, poor creatures, was on the head of the author of *Religio Medici*."[2]

It is true that Browne and hundreds of his educated contemporaries did not apply their skepticism to the whole subject of witchcraft as Sir Kenelm Digby did. Digby wrote: "Neither do I deny there are witches. I only reserve my assent till I meet with stronger motives to carry it."[3] Even Browne, however, made a distinction between possession and its application: "Wee are no way doubtfull that there are witches, butt have not been alwayes satisfied in the application of their witchcrafts or whether the parties accused or suffering have been guiltie of that abomination, or persons under such afflictions suffered from such hands."[4]

Actually Brown's testimony in 1664 weighed very little with the jury and the judge.[5] Gosse and others who have enlarged Browne's culpability took their material from the Reverend Francis Hutchinson's diatribe against witch trials published in 1718,[6] quite overlooking the 1682 reportorial account of the Bury St. Edmunds trial.[7] The earlier and more factual report was easily accessible. Cotton Mather used it in his *Wonders of the Invisible World* (London, 1693), and William Turner copied Mather's version word for word in his *Compleat History of the Most Remarkable Providences* . . . (London, 1697), ch. 92. In none of these earlier accounts is Browne's testimony interpreted as being very important.

The other event of his last years, happier by far, was his being knighted by His Majesty Charles II in September 1671. For the royal progress, which had begun that day at Newmarket, the City of Norwich had voted the sum of nine hundred pounds. Lord Henry Howard met the entourage at the edge of the city and conducted it to the Ducal Palace. After a long service in Norwich Cathedral, the guests assembled for the banquet in New Hall. Toward the end of the toasts, the king, as was his custom, proposed to knight the mayor of the city, one Mr. Henry Herne. But the mayor "earnestly begged to be·excused" and suggested in his stead Norwich's most famous citizen, Dr. Thomas Browne. We can imagine Browne blushing more than usual (he blushed to the end of his days) as he knelt and rose—Sir Thomas Browne.

One more story should be told, that of the loss, recovery, and reburial of Browne's skull. During some reconstruction of the chancel of the church of St. Peter Mancroft in 1840, the coffin containing the remains of Sir Thomas Browne was accidentally broken into. The coffin plate, a lock of Browne's hair, and his skull were removed, apparently by the sexton, and sold for what they were worth. The coffin plate turned up later in the desk drawer of one of the wardens of the church, a Mr. Fitch. A plaster cast of the skull was presented to Norwich Castle Museum in 1841 by a Mr. Muskett, also a warden. Four years later a skull exactly corresponding to the plaster cast was presented to the Norfolk and Norwich Hospital by a Dr. Lubbock, who never told how it came into his possession. Having become available at the time when people were interested in the possible relationship between the size and shape of a cranium and the mind it housed, Browne's skull is certainly the most measured, most photographed, and most charted skull of any literary man.[8] It had a disappointingly sloping forehead, however: a man of Browne's imagination and erudition should have been high-domed, to please the phrenologists. For over fifty years the skull lay for the curious in a glass case at the hospital.

On July 4, 1922, Sir William Osler, who had determined to wipe out the desecration, finally succeeded after his own death in having the skull reinterred. Within the polished oak casket, one cubic foot in size, were placed the skull and a parchment giving its history. The prayer of recommittal was read by the Reverend Canon Meyrick, and the additional stone of Browne's grave reads: "O caput Augustum, Petro custode sepulchri sit tibi pax: nomen vivat in urbe, vale, M. D. CCCCXXII."[9]

Taking a cue from Browne's own wonder at the processes of human thought, we can say that it is not only metaphorically but literally true that Browne lived in two worlds at once. The dichotomies that crowd this book are not mine but those of the age he lived in, of the life he personally achieved, and of the major works he left us. If Milton justified the ways of God to man, Browne, a humbler Christian, sought only to justify the ways of man to God. He appeals to many readers today largely because of his ability, in language that startles while it informs, to reconcile science and religion.

On the relationship of these two worlds in his thinking, one view, represented by Basil Willey, extends to Browne that "unified sensibility" which Eliot found in the metaphysical poets:

It meant the capacity [Willey writes] to live in divided and distinguished worlds, and to pass freely to and fro between one and another, to be capable of many and varied responses to experience, instead of being confined to a few stereotyped ones. . . . [The worlds of the mind] were divided and distinguished, perhaps, but not, as later, by such high barriers that a man was shut up for life in one or another of them. . . . The point about these different worlds was not that they were divided, but that they were simultaneously available. . . . Something of the peculiar quality of the "metaphysical" mind is due to this fact of its not being *finally committed* to any one world. Instead, it could hold them all in a loose synthesis together, yielding itself, as only a mind in free poise can, to the passion of detecting analogies and correspondencies between them.[10]

But D. K. Ziegler holds that Sir Thomas divorced reason and faith through his use of rational faculties in the one world and a rhetorical display of metaphor and paradox in the other. Ziegler accuses Browne of merely playing with religion:

The result is that the analogical and anthropomorphic thinking which he rejects as a scientist delights him as the religious man. As a scientist he tries to clarify and enlarge the field of knowledge, as a religious man he says "I love to lose myself in a mystery."[11]

To separate and join, at once, science and religion, the Middle Ages made theology queen of the sciences, differing not in kind but degree. Even with the limited advance of empirical science up to Browne's time, this method was questioned; yet Browne does not deviate from the hierarchy. He places divinity above philosophy as a higher or ultimate truth. But they are not held together (as Willey suggests) in a "loose synthesis." The two terms, divinity and philosophy, are strictly complementary. Together they make a complete whole only as Browne can make the vital connections between them, which lift him, as in a Platonic dialogue, from the visible to the invisible world. More the poet than the philosopher, more the devotional writer than the theologian, and more the scholar than the scientist, Browne puts his metaphors to work not only to express the reality but also the immediately apprehended attributes of that reality. Metaphors mark the necessary correspondencies.

Despite Ziegler, then, Browne does not separate his two worlds by metaphor but actually joins them through metaphor. His style is not a toy but an epistemological instrument: "There is a neerer way to heaven than *Homers* chaine; an easie Logick may conjoyne heaven and earth in one argument, and with lesse than a Sorites resolve all things into God."[12]

There is nothing new in our discovery that man is born to dilemma. What perhaps is new is that man thinks he can resolve a dilemma by grasping only one of its horns. Browne calls on us to fight once more the battle of Origen and of Jerome to conjoin the pagan and the Christian worlds, the university and the church, the museum and the cathedral.[13] In single sentences, in paragraphs, in whole works, he takes us from earth to heaven and from heaven to earth. He is a psychologist with a sense of humor; a botanist, embryologist, archaeologist, and physician; a guest at the banquet of beauty, knowledge, work, and religion. He is an amateur professional, forced by his humanity gladly to embrace a position that is at once hierarchical and ecumenical.

He reconciled his love of learning and his medical practice by making them both issue in the love of God. From that single oblation, part returned to him in the gift of charity and part returned to him in his inspired love of truth in the created order. Such disruptive forces as his biology and botany, his civic responsibilities, his family life, his coin collection, and his hundreds of importunate patients were integrated by his Christian belief and his liturgical actions. After living outwardly in that busy world for awhile, he could withdraw into his study. From the conflicts among his books, he could withdraw again, this time to the altar of St. Peter Mancroft. From there he received the power to go out once more into the market place of ideas and action. The altar of his church linked his practice to his library and both of these to God.

NOTES

NOTES TO CHAPTER I

1. *Stow's Survey of London* [1603], ed. Kingsford (London, 1908), I, 341-42.
2. The story is told by Browne's daughter, Mrs. Elizabeth Lyttleton, in her letter to Bishop Kennett published in *The European Magazine*, XL (1801), 89; the letter is in the bishop's handwriting and was contributed by one "C. D."
3. *Religio Medici*, ed. J.-J. Denonain (Cambridge, 1953), II, i, p. 87.
4. *Ibid.*, I, xlviii, p. 72.
5. These details appear in a typescript paper by Mr. H. Gordon Ward of Liverpool, read before the English Association there on Oct. 26, 1934, and lent to me by Sir Geoffrey Keynes.
6. *The Works of Sir Thomas Browne*, ed. Geoffrey Keynes (London, 1931), VI, 233-34 (Jan. 9, 1681/2).
7. Sir Edward Bysshe, *A Visitation of the County of Suffolk*, ed. W. Harry Rylands, Harleian Soc., 1910; *Le Neve's Pedigrees of the Knights Made by Charles II, King James II, and Queen Mary, King William Alone, and Queen Anne*, ed. George W. Marshall, Harleian Soc., 1873, p. 267; Francis Blomefield, *An Essay Towards a Topographical History of the County of Norfolk, Containing the History of the City of Norwich* (Norwich, 1745), II, 291.
8. *The Cheshire Sheaf*, 3d series, III (Oct., 1899), 107.
9. "The Pedigree of Sir Thomas Browne, Drawn Up by Simon Wilkin, 1836, with Additions and Corrections by Charles Williams, 1902," *Norfolk and Norwich Archaeological Soc.*, XV (1902-4), 110.
10. Miriam M. Tildesley, *Sir Thomas Browne: His Skull, Portraits, and Ancestry* (Cambridge, 1923), pp. 54-57.
11. M. Gaidoz, *Le Dieu Gaulois du Soleil et le Symbolisme de la Roue*, quoted by William Simpson, *The Buddhist Praying-Wheel* (London, 1896), p. 242.
12. Liselotte Dieckmann, "Renaissance Hieroglyphics," *Comparative Literature*, IX (1957), 309.

13. *Religio Medici*, II, ii, pp. 112-13.
14. *Ibid.*, I, xviii, pp. 30-31.
15. Quoted by Simon Wilkin, ed., *Sir Thomas Browne's Works* (London, 1836), Vol. I, "Supplementary Memoir."
16. Anthony à Wood, *Annals*, ed. Gutch (Oxford, 1798), II, 368.
17. *Religio Medici*, I, vii, p. 13.
18. *A Letter to a Friend, Works*, ed. Keynes, I, 169-70.
19. *Religio Medici*, II, xiii, pp. 115-16.
20. Charles Williams, "The Will of Thomas Browne, Mercer, Cheapside, London," *Norfolk and Norwich Archaeological Soc.*, XVI (1905-7), 132-46; reprinted as a pamphlet (n.d.), p. 2. The will is in Somerset House; indexed in Vol. V of "Index of Wills" [*British Record Society* (1912), p. 80]: "1613 Browne, Thomas, citizen and mercer of London (P.A.B. St. Michael le Querne), 123 Capell."
21. N. J. Endicott, "Sir Thomas Browne as 'Orphan', with Some Account of His Stepfather, Sir Thomas Dutton," *University of Toronto Quarterly*, XXX (1961), 180-210.
22. *Repertory* 31 (2), fol. 356, as cited by Endicott, p. 184.
23. *Posthumous Works of the Learned Sir Thomas Browne*, etc. (London, 1712), pp. i-ii.
24. Andrew Kippis, *Biographia Britannica* (2d ed.; London, 1730), pp. 627-37.
25. J. Torbuck, ed., *Religio Medici*, etc. (London, 1736), p. xxviii.
26. Samuel Johnson, "The Life of Sir Thomas Browne," Simon Wilkin, ed., *Sir Thomas Browne's Works* (London, 1836), I, xviii.
27. Further evidence of Sir Thomas Dutton's dubious character will emerge in ch. IV.
28. Olivier Leroy, *Le Chevalier Thomas Browne* . . . (Paris, 1931), p. 5; Tildesley, p. 76.
29. *Letters, Works*, ed. Keynes, VI, 179 (August, 1680).
30. Walton's *The Lives*, ed. S. B. Carter (London, 1951), p. 71.
31. John Rodgers, *The Old Public Schools of England* (London, 1938), p. 34.
32. I am particularly indebted for this part of my chapter to Samuel Ernest Sprott's unpublished Columbia University dissertation, "Tom Browne's Schooldays" (1954).
33. *Religio Medici*, I, xlvi, p. 71.
34. Rodgers, p. 33.
35. Sprott, p. 17, quoting *Preces*, pp. 1-2.
36. The curricula and life of the seventeenth-century public school have been well reconstructed by T. W. Baldwin, *William Shakespeare's Small Latine & Lesse Greek*, 2 vols.

(Urbana, Illinois, 1944); Donald I. Clark, *John Milton at St. Paul's School* (New York, 1948); Foster Watson, "The Curriculum and Text-books of English Schools," *Trans. of the Bibliog. Soc.,* VI (1900-1902), 159-267; the history of Winchester College by A. F. Leach in *A History of Hampshire and the Isle of Wight,* Vol. II of *The Victoria History* (Westminster, 1903), etc. Two seventeenth-century works which most of these scholars use are John Brinsley's *Ludus Literarius, or the Grammar School* (1612, 1627) and Charles Hoole's *New Discovery of the Old Art of Teaching School,* published in 1660 but based on twenty years of experience.

37. Foster Watson, p. 177.
38. *The Sale Catalogue of Sir Thomas Browne's Library* (London, 1711), p. 48, No. 72, English quarto.
39. Sprott, p. 88.
40. *Ibid.,* p. 46.
41. *Religio Medici,* II, iii, p. 94.
42. Sprott, p. 54.
43. *Library Catalogue,* p. 14, No. 46.
44. *Letters,* VI, 27.
45. Sprott, pp. 102-3.
46. *Ibid.,* p. 86.
47. *Ibid.,* pp. 140 ff.; cf. William P. Sandford, "English Rhetoric Reverts to Classicism, 1600-1650," *Quarterly Journal of Speech,* XV (1929), 503-25.
48. *Rhetorica Brevis,* pp. 45-46, quoted by Sprott, p. 175.
49. Erasmus' dedication of *Ciceronianus* in *Opera,* I, col. 1026, quoted by Sprott, p. 251.
50. *Letters,* VI, 179.
51. *Ibid.,* VI, 307.
52. *Religio Medici,* II, viii, p. 104.
53. *Letters,* VI, 22 (Jan. 1, 1664/5).

NOTES TO CHAPTER II

1. James Froude, *Short Studies on Great Subjects,* 2d series, "Calvinism" (New York, 1877), p. 12.
2. Edward Dowden, *Puritan and Anglican* (London, 1910), pp. 79-80.
3. Modernized from the facsimile ed. of 1896 by G. Moreton.
4. *Religio Medici,* I, i, p. 5.
5. *The Worthies of England,* ed. John Freeman (London, 1952), p. 133.
6. *Vulgar Errors, Works,* ed. Keynes, II, 53 (V.E., I, vii).
7. Tr. Barkedale (London, 1653), pp. 2-3.
8. *Ibid.,* pp. 7-8.
9. Daniel Neal, *History of the Puritans* (London, 1822), III, 308.

10. Ed. 1653, p. 412.
11. *Religio Medici*, I, lvi, p. 84.
12. *Ibid.*, I, vii, p. 14.
13. *Ibid.*, I, viii, pp. 14-15.
14. The list could be extended from J. H. Blunt's *Dictionary of Sects, Heresies*, etc. (London, 1874).
15. *A Relation of Several Heresies*, ed. 1646, p. 7; cf. Alexander Ross, ed. 1653, pp. 4-5.
16. Wilhelm Fraenger, *The Millennium of Hieronymous Bosch* (Chicago, 1951).
17. *A Relation*, pp. 9-10.
18. Quotations from Robert Barclay, *The Inner Life of the Religious Societies of the Commonwealth* (3d ed.; London, 1879), p. 29.
19. *Familiar Letters*, ed. Jacobs (London, 1892), II, 337 (Bk. i, sec. 6).
20. Ed. 1641, Sig. 2 r.
21. *Ibid.*, p. 7.
22. "Bishop Hall's Account of the Sacrilegious Prophanation of This Church in the Time of the Civil Wars," *Posthumous Works of the Learned Sir Thomas Browne*, etc. (London, 1712), Sig. A 1 r.
23. Ed. 1646, Sig. A 2 r.
24. *Ibid.*, p. 15.

NOTES TO CHAPTER III

1. The original Latin speech is in Henry Savage, *Balliofergus, or a Commentary upon the Founders, and Affairs of Balliol College* (Oxford, 1668), p. 92; tr. by E. Bensley in Charles Williams' documents relating to Browne in *Norfolk and Norwich Archaeological Soc.*, XVI (1907), 132-45.
2. *The Diary of Thomas Crosfield*, ed. F. S. Boas (London, 1935), p. 12.
3. *Ibid.*, Mar. 20-21, 1626; p. 2.
4. *Ibid.*, p. 54.
5. R. T. Gunther, *Early Science in Oxford* (Oxford, 1923-45), III, 155.
6. *Ibid.*, III, 264-79.
7. *Diary*, July 7, 1634; p. 71.
8. Gunther, III, 200; the reference to Cheapside is found in *Religio Medici*, II, viii, p. 104.
9. *Diary*, p. 12.
10. *Ibid.*, July 14, 1626; p. 5.
11. *Letters, Works*, ed. Keynes, VI, 96.
12. *A Register and Chronicle Ecclesiastical and Civil . . . Faithfully Taken from the Manuscript Collections of the Lord Bishop of Peterborough* (London, 1728), p. 761.

13. *Diary*, p. 13.
14. *Ibid.*, June 1, 1630; p. 43.
15. *Religio Medici*, I, vi, p. 12.
16. Arnold Chaplin, "The History of Medical Education in the Universities of Oxford and Cambridge, 1500-1800," *Proceedings of the Royal Society of Medicine*, XIII (Sect. Hist. Med., 1920), 85.
17. Cf. D. MacLeane, *A History of Pembroke College* (Oxford, 1897), pp. 185-88. The required lecture in theology was probably given by the Reverend Thomas Jackson, learned divine of Corpus Christi who taught once a week at Pembroke until 1625 (*ibid.*, p. 220).
18. *Ibid.*, p. 189.
19. Anthony à Wood, *Fasti*, ed. Bliss (London, 1815), I, 426.
20. Chaplin, p. 87.
21. *Works*, ed. Keynes, V, 231.
22. *Vulgar Errors*, IV, xiii (ed. Keynes, III, 77).
23. *Ibid.*, II, ii (ed. Keynes, II, 107).
24. *Ibid.*, II, iii (ed. Keynes, II, 114).
25. In 1638 the *Tractatus de Globis* by Robert Hues was translated into English by John Chilmead of Christ Church. Edited by Clements R. Markham, it is No. 79 in the Hakluyt Society Publications (1889).
26. *Vulgar Errors*, VI, xiv (ed. Keynes, III, 258).
27. Letter to Edward Browne, June 13 [1678] (*Works*, ed. Keynes, VI, 95-96).
28. H. M. Sinclair and A. H. T. Robb-Smith, *A Short History of Anatomical Teaching in Oxford* (Oxford, 1950), p. 11.
29. *The Anatomy of Melancholy*, ed. A. R. Shilleto (London, 1893), I, 36.
30. Sinclair and Robb-Smith, p. 12; cf. *Oxford University Statutes*, I, 289-90.
31. Quoted by Sinclair and Robb-Smith, p. 13.
32. Gunther, III, 45-46.
33. Quoted by Phyllis Allen, "Medical Education in 17th Century England," *Journal of the History of Medicine*, I (1946), 140-41.
34. There have been six printed editions, usually of the pair of sermons as follows: (1) 1659; (2) 1659; (3) 1707, *The Phoenix*, II; (4) 1711; (5) 1741 by T. Davies; (6) 1741 by T. Warner. Four mss. of the sermons are at the Bodleian; one in the British Museum and one in Corpus Christi College. As for fame, the entry for the year 1624 in Wood's *Annals* (II, 352-53) is largely given over to the two sermons; Falconer Madan in *Oxford Books* (Oxford, 1912), II, 96, for the year 1624 has merely: "On Easter Monday Thomas

Lushington delivered a University sermon which was supposed to reflect on the King's dignity, and had to recant it."

35. Cf. Sir C. E. Mallet, A *History of the University of Oxford* (London, 1924), II, 246-47.

36. Ms. Bodl. Eng. Th. f. 14, Fol. 11 r; besides this ms. three other mss. of the sermon are in the Bodleian: Rawlinson E 95; Rawlinson E 21; and Additional B 82.

37. *Annals*, ed. Gutch (Oxford, 1798), II, 353; *Athenae*, II, 71-72.

38. Ms. Bodl. Addit. B 82, sermon on Romans 7:11.

NOTES TO CHAPTER IV

1. *European Magazine*, XL (1801), 89.

2. *Vulgar Errors, Works*, ed. Keynes, III, 308, my ital. (Bk. vii, ch. xv).

3. *Letters, Works*, ed. Keynes, VI, 351, my ital.

4. Sir Edmund Gosse, *Sir Thomas Browne*, English Men of Letters Series (London, 1905), p. 6.

5. Jeremiah S. Finch, *Sir Thomas Browne* (New York, 1950), p. 51.

6. "The Life of Sir Thomas Browne," Simon Wilkin, *Sir Thomas Browne's Works* (London, 1836), Vol. I, "Supplementary Memoir."

7. *Ibid.*, I, lvii.

8. Olivier Leroy, *Le Chevalier Thomas Browne* (Paris, 1931), p. 8.

9. *Letters*, ed. Keynes, VI, 231.

10. Charles Williams, "The Will of Thomas Browne, Mercer, Cheapside, London, father of Sir Thomas Browne of Norwich," *Proceedings of the Norfolk and Norwich Archaeological Soc.*, XVI (1905), 132-36.

11. *Calendar of State Papers Relating to Ireland, 1615-1625* (London, 1880), # 135, p. 72. The originals are preserved in the Public Record Office.

12. *Ibid.*, # 545, p. 250.

13. *Ibid.*, # 633, p. 283.

14. *Calendar of State Papers Relating to Ireland, 1625-1632* (London, 1900), # 880, p. 295.

15. *Ibid.*, p. 296.

16. *Ibid.*, # 693, pp. 239-40.

17. For generally known facts like these, I have depended on Richard Bagwell, *Ireland under the Stuarts* (London, 1909), Vol. I; and W. D. Killin, *The Ecclesiastical History of Ireland* (London, 1875), Vol. II.

18. *Calendar*, 1625-1632, # 1553, pp. 498-99.

19. *Ibid.*, # 1562, pp. 500-501. Part of the "restoring of order"

consisted of razing the Carmelite friary in Cook Street in the presence of the recusant aldermen (Bagwell, I, 187).

20. *Calendar, 1625-1632,* # 1640, p. 528.
21. *Ibid.,* # 1243, p. 411.
22. Somewhere in *The Anatomy of Melancholy* Burton wrote: "Our life is an Irish Sea, wherein there is naught to be expected but tempestuous storms, and troublesome waves, and those infinite."
23. *Calendar, 1625-1632,* # 1684, p. 541.
24. *Ibid.,* # 1050, p. 422, July 10, 1623.
25. *Ibid.,* # 1299, p. 541.
26. *European Magazine,* XL (1801), 89.
27. Begun guardedly by Wilkin but carried to an extreme by Gosse.
28. The twelve-line fragment of dueling ends:
    o let mee never know the cruell
    & heedless villany of duell,
    or if I must that fate sustayne
    Let mee bee Abel & not Cain (*Works,* ed. Keynes, V, 191).
29. Thomas Birch, *The Life of Henry, Prince of Wales* (London, 1760), pp. 199-200.
30. *Calendar, 1625-1632,* # 1868, p. 593.
31. *Religio Medici,* I, iii, pp. 6-7.
32. *Letters,* ed. Keynes, VI, 231.
33. *Ibid.,* VI, 227.
34. *Miscellaneous Writings, Works,* ed. Keynes, V, 192.
35. *Religio Medici,* II, i, p. 88.
36. *Ibid.,* I, xl, p. 62.

NOTES TO CHAPTER V

1. Arnold Chaplin, "The History of Medical Education in the Universities of Oxford and Cambridge, 1500-1850," *Proceedings of the Royal Society of Medicine,* XIII, Sect. Hist. Med. (1920), 83-107; cf. Phyllis Allen, "Medical Education in 17th Century England," *Journal of the History of Medicine,* I (1946), 115-43.
2. *Letters, Works,* ed. Keynes, VI, 17; cf. *ibid.,* p. 13.
3. *Miscellaneous Writings, Works,* ed. Keynes, V, 302.
4. *Sale Catalogue of Sir Thomas Browne's Library* (London, 1710), p. 57, No. 28.
5. *Ibid.,* p. 34, No. 62.
6. *Religio Medici,* II, viii, p. 104: "For my owne part, beside the *Jargon* and *Patois* of severall Provinces, I understand no lesse than six Languages. . . ." Cf. A. C. Howell, "A Note on Sir Thomas Browne's Knowledge of Languages," *Studies in Philology,* XXII (1925), 412-17.

7. The Florio is listed in the *Library Catalogue* at p. 39, No. 19; the Minsheu at p. 46, No. 93.
8. *Ibid.*, p. 34, No. 66.
9. *Letters, Works*, ed. Keynes, VI, 232.
10. *Religio Medici*, II, viii, p. 104.
11. *Ibid.*, II, i, pp. 87-88.
12. *Ibid.*, II, iv, p. 95.
13. *Ibid.*, I, xxii, p. 104.
14. Letter to Tom, Nov. 1, 1661, *Letters*, VI, 16-17.
15. *A Letter to a Friend*, sec. x, *Works*, ed. Keynes, I, 171.
16. *Vulgar Errors*, IV, i (ed. Keynes, III, 10).
17. Olivier Leroy, *Le Chevalier Thomas Browne* (Paris, 1931), pp. 9-10.
18. Sir William Osler, *An Alabama Student and Other Biographical Essays* (London, New York, and Toronto, 1908), p. 251.
19. *Letters*, VI, 278.
20. Cf. especially J. H. Randall, Jr., "The Development of Scientific Method in the School of Padua," *Journal of the History of Ideas*, I (1940), 177 ff. Gosse first added to the Browne biography a careful reconstruction of Padua's medical faculty, a work continued by Sir William Osler.
21. *Coryat's Crudities*, 2 vols. (Glasgow, 1905), I, 297-98.
22. *Religio Medici*, I, xxi p. 34.
23. *Ibid.*, pp. 38-39, but surely Denonain's emendation of *famulus* for *family's* is gratuitous.
24. *Ibid.*, p. 37.
25. *Ibid.*, II, ix, p. 107.
26. *The Complete Poems of Sir John Davies*, ed. A. B. Grosart (London, 1876), I, 66-67.
27. Erwin Panofsky, *The Life and Art of Albrecht Dürer* (Princeton, 1955), pp. 260-70.
28. *Religio Medici*, II, ix, p. 106.
29. Leonardo dissected horses to make the equestrian statue of Sforza. A horse anatomy was published in Bologna in 1598 by Ruini, probably pirated from Leonardo. The great artist's cartoon for "The Defeat of Niccolo Piccinino in Tuscany in the Battle of Anghiari, 1439, A.D." is cited by Vasari especially for the horses; also by Jean Richter in his biography of Da Vinci.
30. Galen, *On the Passions*, in *Greek Medicine . . . from Hippocrates to Galen*, ed. Arthur J. Brock (London and Toronto, 1929), p. 173.
31. *Letters*, ed. Keynes, VI, 156.
32. *Ibid.*, VI, 63.
33. *Religio Medici*, I, xii, p. 19.
34. Edward Bulwer-Lytton, "Sir Thomas Browne's Work," a

review of Wilkin in *Quarterly Essays by the Right Hon. Lord Lytton* (London, 1875), p. 174.

35. Cf. Rosalie M. Colie, "Sir Thomas Browne's 'Entertainment' in xviith Century Holland," *Neophilogus*, xxxvi (1952), 162: "Actually, Browne's period of study at Leiden was something less than three weeks:. . . ."

36. *Album Studiosorum Academiae Lugdano-Bataviae, 1575-1875* ('s Gravenhage, 1875), p. 259.

37. P. C. Molhuysen, *Bronnen tot de Geschiedenis der Leihdsch Universiteit* ('s Gravenhage, 1916), p. 181.

38. *The Diary of John Evelyn*, ed. E. S. deBeer (Oxford, 1955), II, 52.

39. R. W. Innes Smith, *English Speaking Students of Medicine at the University of Leyden* (London, 1932), Introd., pp. ix-x.

40. *Letters*, VI, 86; cf. *ibid.*, p. 98.

41. *Library Catalogue*, p. 20, # 29, 30; p. 23, # 29.

42. Charles Singer, *The Evolution of Anatomy* (London, 1925).

43. *Library Catalogue*, p. 23, # 10.

44. *Letters*, VI, 87.

45. *Vulgar Errors*, ed. Keynes, II, ii, 126.

46. *The Diary of the Rev. John Ward, A.M.* (London, 1839); quoted by Osler, *An Alabama Student*, p. 251.

47. *Epistolae Ho-elianae: The Familiar Letters of James Howell*, ed. Joseph Jacobs (London, 1892), I, 31.

48. *Lettres de Gui Patin* . . . (Paris, 1846), I, 354.

49. Jean Astruc, *Mémoires pour servir à l'histoire de la Faculté de Médicine à Montpellier* (Paris, 1767), I, 354.

50. John Keevil, M.D., *The Stranger's Son* (London, 1953), p. 69.

51. F. L. Huntley, "Sir Thomas Browne's Leyden Thesis," *TLS*, May 8, 1953.

52. *Miscellaneous Writings*, V, 193-94.

53. *Letters*, VI, 278.

NOTES TO CHAPTER VI

1. As in Gosse's theory that Browne's letters to Oldenburg show a petulancy in his hope to become a member, Lytton Strachey's [*Books and Characters* (London, 1922), pp. 31-44] that he was more of an artist than a scientist; C. H. Herford's [Everyman ed. of Browne (London, 1903), Introd., pp. xiv-xv] that his style blackballed him, a view augmented by R. F. Jones [*PMLA*, XIV (1930), 991]. Cf. A. C. Howell, "Sir Thomas Browne and Seventeenth Century Scientific Thought," *Studies in Philology*, XXII (1925), 61-80; and Gordon K. Chalmers, "Sir Thomas Browne, True Scientist," *Osiris*, II (1936), 28-79.

2. Three helpful books for this chapter have been: Edwin A. Burtt, *The Metaphysical Foundations of Modern Physical Science* (London and New York, 1925); Herbert Butterfield, *The Origins of Modern Science* (London, 1949); and A. R. Hall, *The Scientific Revolution, 1500-1800; the Formation of the Modern Scientific Attitude* (London, 1954).

3. Dorothy Stimson, *The Gradual Acceptance of the Copernican Theory of the Universe* (New York, 1915). Cf. Francis R. Johnson, *Astronomical Thought in Renaissance England* (Baltimore, Md., 1937).

4. *Religio Medici*, I, xv, p. 23.

5. Galileo, *Dialogues*, tr. Thomas Salisbury, *Mathematical Collections and Translations* (London, 1661), p. 301; quoted by Burtt, pp. 68-69.

6. Translated by Crew and De Salvo (New York, 1914), p. 194; quoted by Burtt, pp. 94-95.

7. Egon Stephen Merton, "Sir Thomas Browne on Astronomy," *The History of Ideas News Letter*, IV (Autumn, 1958), 86.

8. Cf. "The Archidoxis of Paracelsus," *The Hermetic and Alchemical Writings of . . . Paracelsus*, tr. and ed. Arthur E. Waite, 2 vols. (London, 1894), Vol. II.

9. Donne's *Letters to Several Persons of Honour* (London, 1654), p. 15.

10. *Christian Morals*, II, v (*Works*, ed. Keynes, I, 124).

11. *The Advancement of Learning*, I, ii, 3, ed. Wright (Oxford, 1876), p. 12.

12. *The Anatomy of Melancholy*, ed. Shilleto (London, 1893), II, 16.

13. For this part of the survey I have leaned on Arturo Castiglione, *The Renaissance of Medicine in Italy* (Baltimore, Md., 1934).

14. Arthur J. Brock, tr. and ed., *Greek Medicine . . . from Hippocrates to Galen* (London and Toronto, 1929), p. 29; cf. Lynn Thorndike, "Galen: The Man and His Times," *Scientific Monthly*, XIV (1922), 83-93.

15. In chapter x of Book III of *De Usu Partium*.

16. *Religio Medici*, I, xxvi, p. 56.

17. *Ibid.*, I, xiv, p. 23.

18. Simon Wilkin, ed., *Sir Thomas Browne's Works* (London, 1836), II, 25.

19. Cf. Introd. by A. J. Brock to Galen, *On the Natural Faculties*, Loeb Classics (London, 1916).

20. Brock, *Greek Medicine*, p. 160.

21. Castiglione, p. 47.

22. *Letters*, *Works*, ed. Keynes, VI, 72.

23. *On the Natural Faculties*, ed. Brock, III, xv, p. 321.

24. J. F. Fulton, M.D., *Selected Readings in the History of Physiology* (Springfield, Illinois, 1930), pp. 41 ff.

25. K. J. Franklin, M.D., "Valves in Veins: An Historical Survey," *Proceedings of the Royal Soc. of Medicine*, XXI (Sect. Hist. Med., 1927), 1-33.

26. The story has been told often. Perhaps the best account for the layman is H. P. Bayon, "William Harvey, Physician and Biologist," *Annals of Science*, III, IV (1938-39). Cf. Sir William Osler, *The Growth of Truth as Illustrated by the Discovery of the Circulation of the Blood*, "Harveian Oration" (London, 1906). Cf. Walter Pagel, "A Background Study to Harvey," *Medical Bookman and Historian* (Oct.– Nov., 1948); and Richard S. Westfall, *Science and Religion in 17th Century England* (Yale, 1958).

27. Cf. Charles Singer, *The Evolution of Anatomy* (London, 1925); Michael Foster, *Lectures on the History of Physiology during the 16th, 17th, and 18th Centuries* (Cambridge, 1901); A. C. Crombie, *Augustine to Galileo: The History of Science, A.D. 400-1650* (Cambridge, Mass., 1953), pp. 328-342.

28. F. L. Huntley, "Sir Thomas Browne and the Metaphor of the Circle," *The Journal of the History of Ideas*, XIV (1953), 353-64.

29. From the translation of *De Motu Cordis* by Chauncey D. Leake, "The Tercentennial Edition, 1928" (Springfield, Ill., 1958), p. 71.

30. Quoted by Dr. Norman Moore, *The History of the Study of Medicine in the British Isles* (Oxford, 1908), pp. 2-3.

31. *Letters*, VI, 277. It is interesting that Browne's use of the popular name anticipated by three years the title of Harvey's book, which beginning in 1649 added "De Circulatione Sanguinis" to "De Motu Cordis." Cf. Keynes, *Bibliography of Harvey* (London, 1928), No. 8.

32. Columbus the voyager seems to be a more likely candidate than Columbus Realdus, in view of the metaphorical bent of Browne's mind. This type of mind led Fludd the Rosicrucian to accept Harvey's thesis while many a more rationalistic mind repudiated it.

33. Ed. 1601, pp. 5-6; here I depend upon Paul H. Kocher, *Science and Religion in Elizabethan England* (San Marino, Calif., 1953).

34. Book II, ch. vii.

35. *Sales Catalogue of Sir Thomas Browne's Library* (London, 1710), p. 17, No. 14.

36. *Ibid.*, p. 31, No. 11.

37. *Ibid.*, p. 17, No. 13.

38. *The Old Man's Dietarie*, ed. 1586, Sig. D 2 r (Kocher, p. 246).
39. *Vulgar Errors* (ed. Keynes, II, 17, 261, 268; III, 298).
40. Kocher, p. 247, note 21.
41. *Ibid.*
42. *Ibid.*, pp. 247-48.
43. *Ibid.*, p. 272.
44. *The Great Amphibium: Four Lectures on the Position of Religion in a World Dominated by Science* (London, 1931), pp. 21-22. Professor Evelyn Hutchinson of Yale, reviewing Needham's *A History of Embryology* (Cambridge, 1934), calls Needham ". . . one of the very few authors who have done justice to Browne as a biochemist and an experimental biologist" [*American Scientist* (Jan., 1951), p. 181.]
45. Bacon, "Descriptio Globi Intellectualis," *Philosophical Works* (London, 1905), p. 685; quoted by Chalmers, p. 62.
46. *Religio Medici*, II, xiii, p. 116.
47. *Ibid.*, III, xv, p. 119.
48. *Vulgar Errors*, I, v (*Works*, ed. Keynes, II, 39).
49. Cf. Robert P. Adams, "The Social Responsibility of Science in *Utopia, New Atlantis*, and After," *Journal of the History of Ideas*, x (1949), 374-98; cf. Ernest Tuveson, *Millennium and Utopia* (Berkeley and Los Angeles, Calif., 1949), p. 85; cf. Victor Harris, *All Coherence Gone* (Chicago, 1949).
50. *Religio Medici*, I, xiii, p. 21.
51. Cf. Harcourt Brown, "The Renaissance and Historians of Science," *Studies in the Renaissance*, VII (1960), 27-42.

NOTES TO CHAPTER VII

1. H. E. Sigerist, "The History of Medical Licensure," *Journal of the American Medical Association*, CIV (1935), 1058.
2. *Letters, Works*, ed. Keynes, VI, 198-99: "It was kindly done of old Dr. Denton to call you in. Hee must be a man of great yeares, for hee is much my senior & I remember him in Oxford." This may be another indication of Browne's delayed maturity as a young man: his contemporaries seemed older.
3. *DNB*, XIV, 381; thanks to my colleague Professor William Willcox for looking up Dr. Ashworth in and around Oxford, albeit the results were negative.
4. Cf. the well-known allusions to his age at the time of writing *Religio Medici*: II, xi, and I, xli.
5. *Religio Medici*, II, vi, p. 101.
6. *Ibid.*, II, ix, p. 108.
7. *Athenae Oxonienses*, ed. Bliss (London, 1820), IV, 56-59.
8. Sir Edmund Gosse, *Sir Thomas Browne*, English Men of Letters Series (London, 1905), p. 19; Olivier Leroy, *Le*

Chevalier Thomas Browne, etc. (Paris, 1931), pp. 7 and 21; Jeremiah S. Finch, Sir Thomas Browne (New York, 1950), pp. 51 and 89.

9. Halifax and Its Gibbet-Law Placed in a True Light (Halifax, 1708), p. 89.

10. Simon Wilkin, Sir Thomas Browne's Works (London, 1836), I, lviii.

11. The Reverend Thomas Wright, The Antiquities of the Town of Halifax in Yorkshire (Leeds, 1738), p. 152.

12. J. S. Fletcher, Halifax (London, 1923), p. 3.

13. John Watson, History of Antiquities of the Parish of Halifax in Yorkshire (London, 1775), p. 459.

14. One beheading took place in 1636 (Fletcher, pp. 46-53) during Browne's supposed residence there.

15. Letters, VI, 48.

16. I am grateful to Miss Phyllis Bentley, the distinguished novelist, for putting me in touch with these men and their publications.

17. N & Q, IV, 155; cf. "The late Mr. James Crossley," Palatine Notebook, III (Oct., 1883), 221-29.

18. Chaplin, p. 89.

19. Religio Medici, II, v, p. 99.

20. Ibid., II, vi. This is the reading in all the mss. and in 1642 (Denonain, p. 100).

21. Ibid., II, v, p. 99.

22. Ibid. II, xv, p. 119.

23. Ibid., line 2862, note; the quotation of the Pembroke ms. comes from J. J. Denonain, Une Version Primitive de Religio Medici (Paris, 1958), p. 91.

24. Religio Medici, II, vi, p. 100.

25. Ibid., II, xi, p. 112.

26. The Bradford Antiquary (July, 1896), p. 51.

27. The letter was first noticed by Wilkin.

28. Letters, VI, 280.

29. Henry Power's book on microscopy was the first in its field in England, preceding Robert Hooke's Micrographia (1665) by a few months.

30. Transactions of the Halifax Antiquarian Society, 1917, p. 1; 1935, p. 5.

31. Letters, VI, 289.

32. Ibid., pp. 294-95.

33. N. B., Oxfordshire antiquaries!

34. Dame Dorothy Browne's pedigree in the Mileham family is found on pp. 154-55 of East Anglian Pedigrees, The Publications of the Harleian Society, XCI (1939), part. i.

35. Cf. Sir Geoffrey Keynes' account of Simon Wilkin's conscientious effort to get information on the Browne children,

A *Bibliography of Sir Thomas Browne* (Cambridge, 1924), Appendix IV, pp. 234-35.

36. This part of Browne's story condenses my article "The Publication and Immediate Reception of *Religio Medici*," *Library Quarterly*, XXV (1955), 203-18.

37. Cf. Elizabeth Cook, "The First Edition of *Religio Medici*," *Harvard Library Bulletin*, II, No. 1 (1948), 22-31; Miss Cook's argument that the longer of the two 1642 editions is really the first edition (as Wilkin and Greenhill had maintained) persuaded Sir Geoffrey Keynes to reverse the order he had given the two editions in his *Bibliography* (1924). Keynes' decision, announced in *TLS*, April 18, 1952, p. 265, caused some consternation among the dealers who had these two editions to sell.

38. Fredson Bowers, "The Headline in Early Books," *English Institute Annual* (New York, 1941), pp. 90 ff.

39. John Nichols, *The Literary Anecdotes of the 18th Century* (London, 1812-15), III, 597.

40. Samuel A. Tannenbaum, *Ben Jonson: A Concise Bibliography* (New York, 1938), No. 672. This edition, retaining the portrait of Jonson, was edited by Sir Kenelm Digby.

41. Douglas Bush, *English Literature in the Earlier Seventeenth Century* (Oxford, 1946), p. 294.

42. Twenty-five editions had been published before Crooke bought it. In 1665 it was translated by John Eliot into an American Indian language at Cambridge, Mass.; and in 1675 into Welsh by R. Vaughn. By 1735 it was in its fifty-ninth edition. Bunyan said that this was one of the two books, brought to him by his bride, that helped to awaken him to religious zeal [cf. J. E. Bailey, "Bishop Lewis Bayly and His Practice of Piety," *Manchester Quarterly Review*, July 1883; and John Brown, *John Bunyan: His Life, Time, and Work* (London, 1828), pp. 53-55]. As late as 1842 Grace Webster re-edited *The Practice of Piety* with a new biographical preface.

43. Nichols' *Literary Anecdotes*, V, 73; Dunton's work was published in 1691 as *Religio Bibliopolae* (Keynes, *A Bibliography of Sir Thomas Browne*, No. 407), later (1704) with Bayly's title (Keynes, No. 418).

44. Joseph Strutt, *A Biographical Dictionary of Engravers* (London, 1786), II, 125-26.

45. *Early English Engravers* (London, 1905), pp. 154-59.

46. A book Browne owned, *Library Catalogue* (London, 1710), p. 45, No. 49. Similarly Marshall had engraved the title page for Philemon Holland's translation of Xenophon, the *Cyrupaedia* (1632).

47. Sir Geoffrey Keynes, *A Bibliography of John Donne* (2d ed.;

Cambridge, 1932). The young Donne as courtier, grasping his sword, with the eight lines by Walton and the Spanish motto "Antes muerto que mudado" is Keynes' No. 79, *Poems* (1635). The winding sheet portrait is in Keynes' No. 39 (1634); it appeared again in Keynes' No. 40 (1638).

48. After the engraving for the 1642 *Religio Medici*, Marshall's work helped sell Beaumont and Fletcher's *Comedies and Tragedies* (1647) and several of the Shirley plays published by Crooke.

49. Browne's original notion occurs in *Religio Medici*, II, ix, p. 106. Howell made the joke in a letter to Thomas Young, April 28, 1645 (*Letters*, ed. Jacobs, I, 308).

50. Masson's *Life of Milton* (London, 1873), III, 456-59. Cf. J. F. Marsh, *Engraved and Pretended Portraits of Milton* (Liverpool, 1860).

NOTES TO CHAPTER VIII

1. In my treatment of *Religio* (as indeed throughout my thinking on Browne) I have tried with difficulty to remain independent of the two most incisive books written on Browne: William P. Dunn, *Sir Thomas Browne: A Study in Religious Philosophy* (2d. ed.; Minneapolis, Minn., 1950); and Egon Stephen Merton, *Science and Imagination in Sir Thomas Browne* (New York, 1949). To Jeremiah S. Finch go my thanks for his rich bibliography in *Sir Thomas Browne: A Doctor's Life of Science & Faith* (New York, 1950). A nice introduction to Browne is Mr. Peter Green's little volume in the Writers and Their Work Series, No. 108, published by Longmans Green (London, 1959).

2. Cf. Joan Bennett, "A Note on *Religio Medici* and Some of Its Critics," *Studies in the Renaissance*, III (1956), 175-84.

3. Quoted by Mrs. Emma Marshall, *In the East Country with Sir Thomas Browne, Kt., Physician and Philosopher of the City of Norwich* (London, 1886), p. xiii.

4. Charles Whibley, *Essays in Biography* (London, 1913), pp. 288-89.

5. Hardin Craig, C. K. Anderson, L. I. Bredvold, and J. W. Beach, *A History of English Literature* (Oxford, 1950), p. 314.

6. Austin Warren has collected a "litany" of expressions of doubt and certitude in "The Style of Sir Thomas Browne," *Kenyon Review*, XIII (1951), 685-86.

7. The fact that Browne was not being didactic or purposely "humorous" hardly needs to be emphasized. The serious contribution of *Religio Medici* to the literature of autobiography has been defined by Margaret Bottrall, *Every Man a Phoenix* (London, 1958), pp. 30-56.

8. Cf. my article "Thomas Browne and the Metaphor of the Circle," *Journal of the History of Ideas*, XIV (1953), 361-62. Emerson, in his essay on "Circles," assigns this definition to St. Augustine [*Essays*, 1st series (Boston, 1876), p. 281].

9. The ten folios of neatly written ms. in British Museum Sloan 1838, entitled *Procli Elementa & Prologica*.

10. Clemens Baeumker, "Das pseudo-hermetische Büch der vierundzwanzig Meister (Liber XXIV Philosophorum)," in *Studien und Charakteristiken z, Geschichte der Philosophie insbesondere des Mittelalters* (Münster, 1928), 208 (re-edited from his 1913 study). Cf. Marie-Thérèse d'Alverny, "Un Témoin muet des luttes doctrinales du xiii° siecle," *Archives d'histoire doctrinale et littéraire du Moyen Age*, XXIV (1949), 223-48. Cf. D. Mahnke, *Unendliche Sphäre und Allmittelpunkt* . . . (Halle, 1937), 148 ff. and 174 ff. Cf. Le P. Vicaire, *Revue des sciences philosophiques et théologiques*, XXVI (1937), 449-82.

11. Ernest Hoffman and Raymond Klibansky, Nicolai de Cusa, *Opera Omnia*, Vol. I, *De Docta Ignorantia* (Leipzig, 1932), p. 104.

12. *Christianity and History* (London, 1957), p. 12.

13. Cf. C. A. Patrides, "Renaissance and Modern Thought on the Last Things: A Study in Changing Conceptions," *Harvard Theological Review*, LI (1958), 169-85.

14. Ed., *Donne's Sermons: Selected Passages* (Oxford, 1920), pref.

15. Suggested by M. L. Rosenthal and A. J. M. Smith, *Exploring Poetry* (New York, 1955), p. 703. Cf. on Browne's style Edwin Morgan, " 'Strong Lines' and Strong Minds; Reflections on the Prose of Browne and Johnson," *Cambridge Journal*, IV (1951), 481-91; and F. P. Wilson, *Seventeenth Century Prose: Five Lectures* (Berkeley, Calif., 1960), No. 4.

16. "Style and Certitude," *English Literary History*, XV (1948), 168.

17. Quoted by Allen, *ibid.*, p. 174.

18. "Of Reformation," *Works*, ed. Ayres (New York, 1931), III, 34; quoted by Allen.

19. "Our Literary Heritage and the Book of Common Prayer," *The Maryland Churchman*, May 1950, from an address delivered Nov. 27, 1949, in the Cathedral of the Incarnation, Baltimore, on the occasion of the 400th anniversary of *The Book of Common Prayer*.

20. *Sketches from a Library Window* (Cambridge, 1922), pp. 152-53.

21. *Medicus Medicatus: or the physicians religion cured, by a lenitive or gentle potion:* . . . (London, 1645), Sig. A 3 v–4 r.

22. *Ibid.*, Sig. A 3 r.

23. *Ibid.*, pp. 20-21.
24. Robert Hooke, *Micrographia* (London, 1665), pref., Sig. B r.
25. *Vulgar Errors*, I, iv (ed. Keynes, II, 34).
26. "The Truth Value of Myths," *The Nature of Religious Experience* (New York, 1937).
27. Quoted from *Coleridge on the Seventeenth Century*, ed. Roberta F. Brinkley (Durham, N.C., 1955), pp. 447-48.
28. *The Literary Remains of Samuel Taylor Coleridge*, ed. H. N. Coleridge (London, 1836-39), I, 248; quoted by Brinkley, p. 447.

NOTES TO CHAPTER IX

1. This chapter appeared in part in my article "The Occasion and Immediate Reception of Sir Thomas Browne's *Religio Medici*," *The Library Quarterly*, XXV (1955), 203-18.
2. Winchester House is described in detail by William Maitland, *London* (London, 1756), II, 840.
3. *Aubrey's Brief Lives*, ed. Clark (Oxford, 1898), I, 224-29.
4. John Evelyn, *Diary*, ed. Bray (New York, 1870), Nov. 7, 1651, p. 216.
5. *Table-Talk*, ed. S. H. Reynolds (Oxford, 1892), pp. 82-83.
6. Quoted by E. W. Bligh, *Sir Kenelm Digby and His Venetia* (London, 1932), p. 232.
7. *A Conference with a Lady* . . . (Paris, 1638), p. 5.
8. Such are the sheets of the ms. of his "Observations" on *Religio Medici*, Br. Mus. MS 904, fol. 223-39.
9. After eight months in prison Digby was released in July 1643; the work was published in Paris in 1644.
10. *Observations on the 22. Stanza in the 9th Canto of the 2nd Book of Spencers Faery Queen. Full of excellent Notions concerning the Frame of Man, and his rational Soul. Written by the Right Noble and Illustrious Knight Sir Kenelm Digby, at the request of a Friend.* London: printed for Daniel Frere Bookseller, at the Red-Bull in Little Britain, 1643.
11. The incorporated references to Digby's "Observations" are to Wilkin's text in the Bohn reprint of *The Works* (London, 1852), III, 433-87.
12. How far he missed it has been nicely argued by Joan Bennett, "A Note on *Religio Medici* and Some of Its Critics," *Studies in the Renaissance*, III (1956), 175-84.
13. *Works*, ed. Keynes, VI, 273.
14. One would assume the second 1642 edition, whose readings are nearer Browne's authorized edition of 1643.
15. *Works*, ed. Wilkin (London, 1836), I, 353.

16. *Ah, Ha, Tumulus, Thalamus* (London: printed for Humphrey Moseley, 1654).
17. (London: H. Harringman, 1665), quoted by John F. Fulton, M.D., *Sir Kenelm Digby* (New York, 1937), p. 29.
18. *Vulgar Errors*, II, iv (ed. Keynes, II, 136).

NOTES TO CHAPTER X

1. Portions of this chapter were read before the University of Michigan Research Club on May 18, 1960.
2. References, incorporated in the text, are to the edition of *Vulgar Errors* by Keynes, Volumes II and III of Browne's *Works*. The first number is the number of Browne's "book," the second is the chapter within that book, and the third number is the page in Keynes, regardless of the volume.
3. In 1661 Joseph Glanvill seems to have followed Browne somewhat in his catalogue of the causes of error in *The Vanity of Dogmatizing*, whose subtitle is "A Discourse of the Shortness and Uncertainty of Our Knowledge and Its Causes." Glanvill's first cause is the Fall; then follow the difficulty of attaining truth, the way we deceive our imaginations, and the precipitancy of our understanding; finally come our "affections," i.e., love, custom, interest, and reverence for antiquity and authority.
4. Cf. Egon S. Merton, "Sir Thomas Browne's Scientific Quest," *Journal of the History of Medicine*, III (1948), 214-28. This is the best study so far of *Vulgar Errors*, but I disagree with Mr. Merton's statement (p. 218): "Browne's last cause of error [Merton sees six causes] is the *endeavors* of Satan."
5. *Religio Medici*, II, x, p. 110.
6. Merton, *ibid.*, p. 220, notes the reduction of the three determinators of truth to two: reason and experiment.
7. Interesting material on Renaissance reading of the Bible is found in D. C. Allen, "The Legend of Noah: Renaissance Rationalism in Art, Science, and Letters," *University of Illinois Studies in Language and Literature*, XXXIII (1949), 3-4. Cf. G. K. Chalmers, "Hieroglyphs and Sir Thomas Browne," *Virginia Quarterly Review*, XXI (1935), 547-60; and Arnold Williams, *The Common Expositor: An Account of the Commentaries on Genesis*, 1527-1633 (Chapel Hill, N.C., 1948).
8. *The Diary of John Evelyn*, ed. Austin Dobson (London, 1905), Oct. 17, 1671, II, 333-35.
9. Cf. W. E. Houghton, "The English Virtuoso in the Seventeenth Century," *Journal of the History of Ideas*, III (1942), 51-73 and 190-219.

10. Egon S. Merton, "The Botany of Sir Thomas Browne," *Isis*, XLVII (June, 1956), 170.

NOTES TO CHAPTER XI

1. *Sale Catalogue of Sir Thomas Browne's Library* (London, 1710), p. 14, No. 59. Professors J. S. Finch and T. J. Westfall are working on a much-needed edition of this catalogue. The fullest study of Browne's use of his own books has been made by Professor R. R. Cawley, "Sir Thomas Browne and His Reading," *PMLA*, XLVIII (1933), 426-70. Cf. W. J. Bishop, "Some Medical Bibliophiles and Their Libraries," *Journal of the History of Medicine*, III (1948), 229-62, esp. pp. 255-58.
2. *Library Catalogue*, p. 7, No. 64.
3. *Ibid.*, p. 31, No. 9.
4. I am grateful to Professor McKeon of Chicago for some of these ideas heard long ago, which of course he will scarcely recognize, much less claim.
5. *Religio Medici*, II, viii, p. 105.
6. *Library Catalogue*, p. 48, No. 82.
7. *Of Wisdom* (London, 1608), II, v, 283.
8. *Ibid.*, II, v, 276-77.
9. *Two Books of Constancie* (London, 1595), p. 3.
10. *Ibid.*, pp. 9-10.
11. *Ibid.*, p. 45.
12. *Religio Medici*, I, xx, p. 33.
13. T. F. Kinloch, *The Life and Works of Joseph Hall, 1574-1655* (New York, 1951), p. 32.
14. *Repertorium, Works*, ed. Keynes, V, 159.
15. *Religio Medici*, I, xiv, p. 23.
16. *Ibid.*, II, xi, p. 112.
17. *Timaeus*, 41d.
18. *Religio Medici*, I, xii, p. 19.
19. *Christian Morals, Works*, ed. Keynes, I, 135 (Bk. III, sec. 3).
20. *Religio Medici*, I, x, p. 16.
21. *Library Catalogue*, p. 7, No. 62.
22. Quoted by Margaret L. Wiley, *The Subtle Knot* (London, 1952), p. 19, from William Mitchell, "The Meaning of Skepticism," *The Arena*, XL (1908), 396.
23. "John Donne and the Poetry of Scepticism," *Hibbert Journal*, XLVIII (1950), 165; *The Subtle Knot*, p. 123.
24. Ending of *Christian Morals*.

NOTES TO CHAPTER XII

1. This chapter is rewritten from my article, "The Occasion and Date of Sir Thomas Browne's *A Letter to a Friend*," *Modern Philology*, XLVII (1951), 157-71.

2. W. A. Greenhill, ed., *Sir Thomas Browne's Religio Medici, Letter to a Friend, &c. and Christian Morals* (London, 1881), Introd., pp. x-xi.

3. The incorporated references to Browne's *Letter* are to the page in the text of it provided by Sir Geoffrey Keynes, ed., *The Works of Sir Thomas Browne*, I (London, 1928), 165 ff.

4. *Vulgar Errors*, VII, xiii (ed. Keynes, III, 300). Greenhill's argument for dating appears in his notes, p. 298.

5. "Sir Thomas Browne," *Macmillan's Magazine*, LIV (London, May 1886), 15. "In its first presentation" the *Letter* actually was not "connected with 'Christian Morals.'"

6. Ludwig Edelstein, M.D., "The Hippocratic Oath: Text, Translation and Interpretation," *Supplements to the Bulletin of the History of Medicine*, Vol. I, ed. Sigerist (Baltimore, 1943).

7. I borrow here from my article "Robert Loveday: Commonwealth Man of Letters," *The Review of English Studies*, II (1951), 262-67. The *DNB* article on Loveday is so sketchy as not even to contain his birth and death dates.

8. *Page's Supplement to the Suffolk Traveler* (Ipswich, 1844), pp. 583-84.

9. *Bysshe's Visitation of the County of Suffolk*, ed. for the Harleian Society (London, 1910), p. 52. Cf. B. M. Add. Mss. 19, 140, fol. 192.

10. Cf. L. J. Moorman, *Tuberculosis and Genius* (Chicago, 1940), especially the case of Marie Bashkirtseff, pp. 86 ff., and Katharine Mansfield's dying words as reported by her husband J. Middleton Murray: "I feel happy—deep down *all is well*" (pp. 122-23).

11. *Religio Medici and Other Essays of Sir Thomas Browne* (London, 1892), Introd., p. xxvi. Reissued in 1898, this item is No. 40 in Keynes' *Bibliography* (p. 32). Dr. Roberts concludes (p. xxvii): "It is, of course, open to dispute that the Dr. B. of Norwich may not be Dr. Browne of Norwich, but the use of the epithet 'great' removes, we think, all reasonable doubt on the subject."

12. *A Bibliography of Sir Thomas Browne* (Cambridge, 1924), No. 229 (p. 153). Both Roberts and Keynes refer to three passages in the 1662 edition on pp. 40, 108, and 190-92. Though I have not seen the 1662 edition, I have compared the first or 1659 edition with the "seventh impression" of 1684 and find no important differences.

13. *Loveday's Letters, Domestic and Forrein, To Several Persons, Occasionally Distributed in Subjects Philosophical, Historical & Morall.* By Robert Loveday Gent. the late Translator of

the three first Parts of *Cleopatra*. London. Printed by J. G. for Nath. Brook, at the Angel in Corn-hill, 1659. References to Loveday's letters will be to this edition, by number and page, and will be incorporated in the text.

14. *University of Cambridge, Matriculation and Degrees, 1544-1659* (Cambridge, 1924), Part I, Vol. III, p. 107. Venn's death-date for Loveday, 1662, is patently wrong.

15. Thomas Alfred Walker, *Admissions to Peterhouse, 1615-1911* (Cambridge, 1912), p. 58.

16. Page 283, lines 17-20.

17. Tradition has it that this was thirty years, which was supposed to be Adam's age at creation.

18. My italics.

19. *Annals of Nottinghamshire* (London, n.d.), II, 838.

20. *Lives of the English Poets*, ed. G. B. Hill (Oxford, 1905), III, 159.

21. On the famous air of Suffolk, cf. Lord Francis Harvey, ed., *Suffolk in the xviith Century: The Breviary of Suffolk by Robert Reyce*, 1618 (London, 1902), pp. 23-24: ". . . the aire is as sweet and healthfull generally, as in any other country whatsoever . . . deemed very apt and fitt for recovery of health in decayed bodies, for what cause it is well observed that the physitians from the universities have prescribed unto their sick patients to live in this aire. . . ."

22. Browne had referred to the Plutarch story in *Vulgar Errors*, VII, xii (ed. Keynes, III, 294), so this cannot be an error.

23. J. Jacobs, ed., James Howell's *Epistolae Ho-Elianae* (1890-92), II, 685, includes this letter as one written to Howell, who had edited Cotgrave's *Dictionary*.

24. Charles Sorel, *Histoire Comique de Françion* [1623, 1626, 1633, etc.], ed. Emile Roy, Societé des Textes Français Moderns (Paris, 1924).

25. "The 1664 Visitation of Norfolk, II, M-Z," *Norfolk Record Soc.*, V (1934), 164-65. He was the son of Sir Augustin Pettus and Abigail, his second wife, daughter of Arthur Haveningham.

26. Francis Blomefield, *An Essay towards a Topographical History of the County of Norfolk*, 11 vols. (2d ed.; London, 1805), V, 427. Cf. pedigree, *ibid.*, X, 448.

27. *Supplement to the Suffolk Traveler*, p. 215.

28. *DNB*.

29. The Reverend J. Granger, *Biographical History of England*, 6 vols. (London, 1824), V, 289. The portrait forms the frontispiece of Sir John Pettus' best-known metallurgical work, *Fleta Minor*, 1683, folio.

30. Sig. A 6 v.

31. Sig. A 3 r.
32. Sig. A 4 v.
33. *Letters,* ed. *Keynes,* VI, 339.
34. *Ibid.,* pp. 157, 214, and 220.
35. *Ibid.,* p. 220. I am aware that there was another Sir John Pettus, the son of Sir Augustin Pettus and the first wife, half-brother to our Sir John. He died in 1698 and apparently gave people less to talk about than our Sir John Pettus.
36. *Fleta Minor,* ed. 1683, Part II of "Spagyrick Laws," "Metals."
37. In the 1670 pref. of *Fodinae Regales* (Sig. B 1 r), Pettus thanks both the Society for the Mines Royal and the Society for Mineral Works for admitting him into their fellowship "about twelve years ago"—i.e., 1657-58. His account of the mines in Wales during the Civil War occurs in ch. xix, p. 25.
38. *Notes and Queries,* Series 7, Vol. IV (1887), 386.
39. Ed. 1621, pp. 248-49. The seventeenth century was fond of anecdotes which illustrate the extrasensory perception on the part of someone of the death of another at some distance away; the exact time was computed and told as a wonder. In this story retold by George Sandys, an English merchant named Gresham set sail from Palermo where there lived a wealthy man called Antonio the Rich. Becalmed near Mount Etna, Gresham's party decided to climb the volcano. At the summit amid rumblings from within the inferno, they heard a voice saying, "Dispatch, dispatch, the rich Antonio is coming." They got down from the mountain just before it erupted, and on their return to Palermo discovered that Antonio had died at that very moment. Wondering whether his recipient had had any premonition of the death of his intimate friend, Browne significantly uses the Sandys story about Antonio.
40. Cf. Greenhill's note on rickets, p. 297, and references to Whistler's *De Morbo Puerili* (Lugd. Bat., 1645) and Glisson's *De Rachitide* (London, 1650). According to *Isis,* X (1928), 160, the earliest description of rickets is chapter xii of Arnoldus Boot (1616-53), *Observationes Medicae de Affectibus Omissis* (London, 1649), which precedes Glisson's work by one year.
41. *Letters,* ed. Keynes, VI, 287.
42. It thus belongs to that type of didactic literature called isagogic, in the form of a letter rather than an oration, such as Horace's *Epistola ad Pisones* and Lipsius' *Epistolica Institutio.* Cf. E. Catherine Dunn, "Lipsius and the Art of Letter Writing," *Studies in the Renaissance,* III (1956), 145-56.

1. This chapter started during a long evening session with Austin Warren when he asked me the question of its initial sentence. It is rewritten from my article "Sir Thomas Browne: The Relationship of *Urn Burial* and *The Garden of Cyrus*," *Studies in Philology*, LIII (April, 1956), 204-19.
2. "The Life of Sir Thomas Browne," *Christian Morals* (London, 1756).
3. "Supplementary Memoir," *Sir Thomas Browne's Works* (London, 1836), Vol. I. Wilkin even reversed the order of the two essays in printing them.
4. *Sir Thomas Browne's Hydriotaphia and the Garden of Cyrus*, ed. W. A. Greenhill (London, 1896).
5. *Sir Thomas Browne*, English Men of Letters Series (London, 1905), p. 121.
6. *Le Chevalier Thomas Browne* (Paris, 1931), p. 31.
7. James M. Cline, "Hydriotaphia," *University of California Publications in English*, VIII (1940), 73-100.
8. Keynes calls them "twin stars in the firmament of literature" [*The Works* (London, 1929), IV, viii]; cf. William P. Dunn, *Sir Thomas Browne: A Study in Religious Philosophy* (Minneapolis, 1950), p. 176; cf. especially Margaret A. Heideman, "*Hydriotaphia* and *The Garden of Cyrus*: A Paradox and a Cosmic Vision," *University of Toronto Quarterly*, XIX (1950), 235-46. Austin Warren notes their generic unity in "The Style of Sir Thomas Browne," *Kenyon Review*, XIII (1951).
9. Browne kept the two essays together and in this order in the four editions published during his life: two in 1658, one in 1659, and one in 1669.
10. Propertius, IV, xi, 14. At the end of her oration (as in Chapter V of *Urn Burial*) Cornelia enters the gates of glory, but at the beginning she bids her husband Paulus not to weep: "What death takes it holds fast; I am now a handful of ashes," she says, "a small burden that can be lifted with the *five* fingers of one hand."
11. *Vulgar Errors*, IV, xii (ed. Keynes, III, 55). Cf. Joseph L. Blau, "Browne's Interest in Cabalism," *PMLA*, XLIX (1934), 963-64; also Mentor Williams, "Why 'Nature Loves the Number Five': Emerson Toys with the Occult," *Papers of the Michigan Academy of Science, Art, and Letters*, XXX (1944), 639-49, which suggests *The Garden of Cyrus* as the source of Emerson's mystic fondness for the number five. Jeremiah S. Finch found the source of Browne's "quincunx" in two sixteenth-century treatises on agriculture which Browne owned, one by Benoit Court and the other

by J. D. Della Porta ["Sir Thomas Browne and the Quincunx," *Studies in Philology*, XXXVII (1947), 274-82].

12. The incorporated references are to Keynes' edition, *The Works*, Vol. IV. The new scholarly text by Mr. John Carter (Cambridge University Press, 1958) does not vary significantly enough to warrant my changing the quoted passages.

13. *Timaeus*, 34c-39a. The edition Browne used was probably the one left in his library, *Sales Catalogue* (London, 1710), p. 11, No. 106, the 1617 edition with notes by Meursius.

14. Hence Dr. Henry Power's correspondence with Browne about the 1658 publication entailed, not a polite appreciation of the "organ tones" of the first essay and the quaintness of the second, but a serious conversation between two scientists on the reproductive principle in plants (*Letters, Works*, ed. Keynes, VI, 288-95).

15. *Christian Morals by Sir Thomas Browne* . . . (London, 1756), p. xxi.

16. Ed. *Hydriotaphia* (London, 1893).

17. Dr. Johnson was struck by the epistemological "vanity of human wishes" in *Urn Burial*: "Of the uselessness of all these enquiries Browne seems not to have been ignorant. . ." (1756 ed., p. xxi).

18. Most recently by J. S. Finch, *Sir Thomas Browne* (New York, 1951), p. 182. Cf. W. H. Barnes, "Sir Thomas Browne's *Hydriotaphia*, with Reference to Adipocere," *Isis*, XX (1934), 337-43.

19. *Religio Medici*, I, xxviii, pp. 45-46.

20. Cf. *Miscellaneous Writings, Works*, ed. Keynes, V, 236.

21. Cf. The Song of Solomon 2:9: ". . . he looketh forth at the windows, shewing himself through the lattice."

22. *The Breaking of the Circle* (Evanston, Ill., 1950), p. 66.

23. St. Augustine, *De Trinitate*, XI, i, i, ed. Migne, XIII, tr. Schaff.

24. *Coleridge on the Seventeenth Century*, ed. Roberta F. Brinkley (Durham, N.C., 1955), p. 449.

25. Browne laughingly dismissed a gross plagiarism of his *Urn Burial* ' (ed. Keynes, V, 247): i.e., John Philipot, *Villare Cantianum: or Kent Surveyed and Illustrated* (London, 1659), pp. 249-51, on urns found at Newington Lucies.

26. *Religio Medici*, I, xi, p. 17.

NOTES TO CHAPTER XIV

1. *The European Magazine*, XL (1801), 89 (cf. ch. I, note 2).

2. Preface, by John Jeffery, Archdeacon of Norwich, to *Christian Morals*, 1716.

3. *European Magazine, loc. cit.*
4. Preface, 1716.
5. B. M. Mss. Sloane 1847, 1848, 1874, 1885, and Bodleian Ms. Rawlinson cix.
6. "Some Minutes for the Life of Sir Thomas Browne, by John Whitefoot, M.A., Late Rector of Heigham, in Norfolk," in Simon Wilkin, *Sir Thomas Browne's Works* (London, 1836), Vol. I, "Supplementary Memoir."
7. *Sir Thomas Browne*, English Men of Letters Series (London, 1905), p. 177.
8. References to *Christian Morals* will be to the edition by Keynes, *The Works of Sir Thomas Browne*, Vol. I (London, 1928), by part, section, and page.
9. The Latin quotation is Browne's marginal note.
10. *The Sale Catalogue of Browne's Library* (London, 1710), p. 42, No. 4. Unfortunately, none of the copies of Browne's books can be identified, but I have sometimes wondered whether these "Three Centuries of Covarrubias his Emblemes in Spanish" were the "3 old Spanish books" which in November 1658 Henry Power took from his dead father's library in Halifax to give to his father's old friend Dr. Thomas Browne of Norwich (*Letters*, ed. Keynes, VI, 289).
11. "The Style of Sir Thomas Browne," *The Kenyon Review*, XIII (Autumn, 1951), 678.
12. *Ibid.*, p. 683.
13. This three-way stylistic distinction is common, but it is referred tellingly to Browne's style by Austin Warren (1951) and by E. L. Parker, PMLA, LIII (1938), 1052.
14. Douglas Bush, *English Literature in the Earlier Seventeenth Century* (Oxford, 1946), p. 308.
15. *Christian Morals: by Sir Thomas Browne . . . 2nd edit. with a life of the author, by Samuel Johnson; and explanatory notes* (London, 1756), pp. i-lxi.
16. Those who know the works of Professor Louis I. Bredvold will recognize the extent here of the debt to my friend and colleague.

NOTES TO CHAPTER XV

1. Jeremiah S. Finch, *Sir Thomas Browne* (New York, 1950), pp. 214-19, has the most trustworthy account of these events.
2. Sir Edmund Gosse, *Sir Thomas Browne*, English Men of Letters Series (London, 1905), pp. 147 and 150.
3. "Observations on *Religio Medici*," in Simon Wilkin, *Sir Thomas Browne's Works* (London, 1836), II, 129.
4. *Works*, ed. Keynes, V, 252 and 254.
5. Admirers of Browne are grateful to two writers for placing the 1664 witch trial in its proper perspective: Malcolm Letts,

N & Q, Series 11, Vol. V (1912), pp. 221-23; and Dorothy Tyler, "Sir Thomas Browne's Part in a Witch Trial in 1664," *Anglia*, LIV (1930), 179-95. Wallace Notestein, *A History of Witchcraft in England* from 1558-1718 (Washington, D. C., 1911), pp. 266-67, says: "No doubt Browne's words confirmed the sentiment of the court room and strengthened the case of the prosecution. But it will not be overlooked by the careful reader that he did not by any means commit himself as to the guilt of the parties at the bar."

6. Keynes, *A Bibliography of Sir Thomas Browne* (Cambridge, 1924), Item No. 495.

7. *Ibid.*, Item No. 240.

8. Cf. Miriam L. Tildesley, *Sir Thomas Browne: His Skull, Portraits, and Ancestry* (Cambridge, 1923), reprinted from *Biometrica*, Vol. XV.

9. I follow the newspaper account of the service in *The Eastern Daily Press*, July 5, 1922.

10. Basil Willey, *The Seventeenth Century Background* (London, 1934), pp. 42-43.

11. D. K. Ziegler, Jr., *In Divided and Distinguished Worlds* (Cambridge, Mass., 1943), Introd., p. ix.

12. *Religio Medici*, I, xviii, p. 31.

13. Cf. Douglas Bush, "Two Roads to Truth: Science and Religion in the Early Seventeenth Century," *English Literary History*, VIII (1941), 81-102.

INDEX

Abraham, 112, 126
Academicks, 174, 178
Achilles, 213, 215
Acquapendente, Fabrizio d', 61,
   66, 70, 80
Adam, 121, 150-51, 229
Adamites, 25
Adams, Robert P., 258
adipocère, 217, 270
Aesop's Fables, 10
Africa, 118
Aguecheek, Sir Andrew, 26
Ahab, 229
Aldrovandus, 78
Allen, Don Cameron, 118, 264
Allen, Phyllis, 251, 253
Allen, Thomas, 3
Alverny, Marie-Thérèse d', 262
Alvey, Richard, 20
Amyot, Jacques, 84, 173
Anabaptists, 25-26
Anderson, C. K., 261
Anderton, Basil, 122
Andrewes, Bishop Launcelot, 19
Anglicans, 14, 17-23, 113, 119
Anglicus, Bartolomaeus, 109
Antinomians, 25
Antisabbatarians, 25
Antiscriptarians, 25
Antitrinitarians, 25
Antonio the Rich, 268
Apollo, 84

Apollonarists, 25
Apostolics, 25
Aquinas, St. Thomas, 109
Arcesilaus, 174
Argan, Dr. (in Molière), 78
Arians, 25
Ariosto, 194, 196
Aristarchus, 74
Aristotle, 40, 43, 73, 76-81, 83-
   84, 128, 160, 166, 173-74,
   181, 229
Arminians, 25
Arminius, Jacobus, 15, 68
Arnold, Thomas, 7
Arundel, Earl of, 63
Ascham, Roger, 10
Ashmole, Elias, 77
Ashmolean Museum, 35
Ashworth, Henry, 90, 258
Astruc, Jean, 68, 255
Atomists, 24-25
Aubrey, John, 94, 136, 263
Auden, W. H., 169
Aurelius, Marcus, Emperor, 79,
   175, 228-29
Averroës, 84, 174

Bacon, Sir Francis, 77, 86-87,
   101, 130, 149, 154, 173, 215,
   258
Bacon, Nicholas, 205
Bacon, Roger, 162

Buxtorf, Jean, 9
Bysshe, Sir Edward, 2, 247

Cabalism, 269
Caesar, Julius, 229
Cain, 112, 126
Calvin, John, 14-15, 18, 28, 88, 173, 177
Cambridge University, 57, 90, 189, 253, 267
Camden, William, 9
Capricornus, 2
Cardan, Jerome, 160, 229, 232
Carmelite, 51
Carneades, 174
Carter, John, 270
Carter, S. B., 248
Cary, Lucius, Viscount Falkland (the elder), 48-50, 135
Casaubon, Isaac, 175
Castiglione, Arturo, 79, 256
Cato, 10, 231
Cato the Younger, 229
Cavendish, Thomas, 39
Cawley, R. R., 265
Celsus, 76
Cerdonians, 25
Cesario, Giulio, 63
Chalmers, Gordon K., 255, 264
Chamberlain, Robert, 99
Chaplin, Arnold, 251, 253
Chapman's *Homer*, 39
Chapperlin, John, 194
Charles I, King, 49, 51, 82, 101, 135-36, 200
Charles II, King, 88, 242
Charron, Pierre, 175-76
Chaucer, 18, 83
Cheapside, 1, 52, 164, 250
Chediston, 188
Cheke, Sir Hatton, 52
Chemiatrist, 76-77
"Cheston," *see* Chediston
Cheyney, Lady Jane, 194
Chilmead, John, 251
Christ Church College, 36, 40, 135

Cicero, 10-12, 118-19, 175, 229, 235, 240
Clapham, Henoch, 85
Clare, Earl of, 189, 194
Clarendon, Edward Hyde, **Earl** of, 44
Clark, Donald L., 11, 249
Clayton, Thomas, 32-33, 37-38, 40-42
Cline, James M., 204, 269
Clinton, Lady, 189
Clotworthy, Sir John, 52
Coke, Sir Edward, 240
Coleridge, Samuel Taylor, 133-34, 223, 263, 270
Coles, John, 194-95
Colie, Rosalie M., 255
Columbus, Christopher, 257
Colvin, Sir Sidney, 101
Commodus, 229
Congregationalists, 26
Cook, Elizabeth, 260
Copernicus, 72-75, 79, 82, 87, 109, 173
Corbett, Bishop Richard, 30, 32, 36
Corpus Christi College, 251
Correggio, 63
Coryat, Thomas, 61, 254
Cotgrave's *Dictionary*, 196, 267
Court, Benoit, 269
Coush, Elisha, 32
Covarrubias, Sebastian de, 183, 232, 271
Coverdale, Miles, 119
Craig, Hardin, 105, 261
Cranmer, Archbishop, 18-19, 119
Croll, Morris W., 118
Crollius, Henricus, 70
Crombie, A. C., 257
Cromwell, Oliver, 199, 201, 240
Crooke, Andrew, 98-100, 136, 143
Crosfield, Thomas, 34-36, 250
Crossley, James, 94, 259
Crow, William, 188

SELECTED ANN ARBOR PAPERBACKS

works of enduring merit

For a complete list of Ann Arbor Paperback titles write:
THE UNIVERSITY OF MICHIGAN PRESS / ANN ARBOR